WANDERINGS IN INDIA

PREFACE.

THE greater part of the Papers which form this Volume have appeared in "HOUSEHOLD WORDS;" and the Author has to acknowledge his thanks to Mr. DICKENS for sanctioning a reprint of them.

LONDON, *July* 15*th*, 1859.

CONTENTS.

NENA SAHIB'S TURN-OUT.--P 115

WANDERINGS IN INDIA:

And other Sketches

OF

LIFE IN HINDOSTAN.

By JOHN LANG.

LONDON:
ROUTLEDGE, WARNE, AND ROUTLEDGE,
FARRINGDON STREET.
NEW YORK: 56, WALKER STREET.
1859.

WANDERINGS IN INDIA

AND OTHER SKETCHES

OF

LIFE IN HINDOSTAN

JOHN LANG

GYAN

Published by

GYAN

Gyan Publishing House
5, Ansari Road
Daryaganj, New Delhi-110002
Phone: 011-47034999, 9811692060
E-mail: books@gyanbooks.com

Distribution Network
gyanbooks.com
India, USA, Canada, UK, Australia, France

ISBN: 978-81-212-9112-5 (PB)
First Published, 1859

2nd Impression 2023

Printed at: Gyan Press, Delhi.

WANDERINGS IN INDIA
AUTHOR: JOHN LANG

WANDERINGS IN INDIA.

WANDERINGS IN INDIA.

THE HIMALAYA CLUB.

It is some eighteen years since this institution was founded, at Mussoorie, one of the chief sanataria in the Himalaya mountains. Here all those who can obtain leave, and who can afford the additional expense, repair to escape the hot weather of the plains. The season begins about the end of April, and ends about the first week in October. The club is open to the members of the civil and military services, to the members of the bar, the clergy, and to such other private gentlemen as are on the Government House list, which signifies, "in society." The club-house is neither an expensive nor an elegant edifice, but it answers the purposes required of it. It has two large rooms, one on the ground-floor, and the other on the upper story. The lower room, which is some sixty feet long by twenty-five wide, is the dining-room, breakfast-room, and reception-room. The upper room is the reading and the ball-room. The club has also its billiard-room, which is built on the ledge of a precipice; and its stables, which would astonish most persons in Europe. No horses, except those educated in India, would crawl into these holes cut out of the earth and rock.

Facing the side-door is a platform about forty yards long by fifteen feet wide; and from it, on a clear day, the eye commands one of the grandest scenes in the known world. In the distance are plainly visible the eternal snows; at your feet are a number of hills, covered with trees of luxuriant foliage. Amongst them is the rhododendron, which grows to an immense height and size, and is, when in bloom, literally covered with flowers. On every hill, on a level with the club, and within a mile of it, a house is to be seen, to which access would seem impossible. These houses are, for the most part, whitened without as well as within; and nothing can exceed in prettiness their aspect as they shine in the sun.

From the back of the club-house, from your bedroom windows (there are twenty-three sets of apartments) you have a view of Deyrah Dhoon. It appears about a mile off. It is seven miles distant. The plains that lie outstretched below the Simplon bear, in point of extent and beauty, to the Indian scene, nothing like the proportion which the comparatively pigmy Mont Blanc bears to the Dewalgiri. From an elevation of about seven thousand feet the eye embraces a plain containing millions of acres, intersected by broad streams to the left, and inclosed by a low belt of hills, called the Pass. The Dhoon, in various parts, is dotted with clumps of jungle, abounding with tigers, pheasants, and every species of game. In the broad tributaries to the Ganges and the Jumna, may be caught (with a fly) the mâhseer, the leviathan salmon. Beyond the Pass of which I have spoken, you see the plains of Hindoostan. While you are wrapped in a great coat, and are shivering with the cold, you may *see* the heat, and the steam it occasions. With us on the hills, the thermometer is at forty-five ; with those poor fellows over there, it is at ninety-two degrees. We can scarcely keep ourselves warm, for the wind comes from the snowy range ; they cannot breathe, except beneath a punkah. That steam is, as the crow flies, not more than forty miles from us.

We are all idlers at Mussoorie. We are all sick, or supposed to be so ; or we have leave on private affairs. Some of us are up here for a month between musters. We are in the good graces of our colonel and our general—the general of our division, a very good old gentleman.

Let us go into the public room, and have breakfast ; for it is half-past nine o'clock, and the bell has rung. There are not more than half a dozen at the table. These are the early risers who walk or ride round the Camel's Back every morning : the Camel's Back being a huge mountain, encircled about its middle by a good road. The majority of the club's members are asleep, and will defer breakfast until tiffin time—half-past two. At that hour the gathering will be great. How these early risers eat, to be sure! There is the major, who, if you believe him, has every complaint mentioned in "Graham's Domestic Medicine," has just devoured two thighs (grilled) of a turkey, and is now asking Captain Blossom's opinion of the Irish stew, while he is cutting into a pigeon-pie.

Let us now while away the morning. Let us call on some of the grass widows. There are lots of them here, civil and military. Let us go first to Mrs. Merrydale, the wife of our old friend Charley, of the two hundredth and tenth regiment. Poor fellow! He could not get leave, and the doctors said another hot summer in the plains would be the death of his wife. They are seven hundred pounds in debt to the Agra bank, and are hard put to it to live and pay the monthly instalments of interest. Charley is only a lieutenant. What terrible infants are these little Merrydales! There is Lieutenant Maxwell's pony under the trees, and if these children had not shouted out, "Mamma! Mamma! here is Captain Wall, Sahib!" I should have been informed that Mrs. Merrydale was not at home, or was poorly, which I should have believed implicitly. (Maxwell, when a young ensign, was once engaged to be married to Julia Dacey, now Mrs. Merrydale, but her parents would not hear of it, for some reason or other.) As it is, we must be admitted. We will not stay long. Mrs. Merrydale is writing to her husband. Grass widows in the hills are always writing to their husbands, when you drop in upon them, and your presence is not actually delighted in. How beautiful she looks! now that the mountain breezes have chased from her cheeks the pallor which lately clung to them in the plains; and the fresh air has imparted to her spirits an elasticity, in lieu of that languor by which she was oppressed a fortnight ago.

Let us now go to Mrs. Hastings. She is the wife of a civilian, who has a salary of fifteen hundred rupees (one hundred and fifty pounds) per mensem, and who is a man of fortune independent of his pay. Mrs. Hastings has the best house in Mussoorie. She is surrounded by servants. She has no less than three Arab horses to ride. She is a great prude, is Mrs. Hastings, She has no patience with married women who flirt. She thinks that the dogma—

> When lovely women go astray,
> Their stars are more in fault than they—

is all nonsense. Mrs. Hastings has been a remarkably fine woman; she is now five-and-thirty, and still good looking, though disposed to *embonpoint*. She wearies one with her discourses on the duties of a wife. That simpering cornet, Stammersleigh, is announced, and we may bid her good morning.

The average rent for a furnished house is about five hundred rupees (fifty pounds) for the six months Every house has its name. Yonder are Cocky Hall, Belvidere, Phœnix Lodge, the Cliffs, the Crags, the

Vale, the Eagle's Nest, &c. The value of these properties ranges from five hundred to fifteen hundred pounds. The furniture is of the very plainest description, with one or two exceptions, and is manufactured chiefly at Bareilly, and carried here on men's shoulders the entire distance—ninety miles.

Where shall we go now, for it wants an hour to tiffin time? Oh! here comes a janpan! (a sort of sedan-chair carried by four hill men, dressed in loose black clothes, turned up with red, yellow, blue, green, or whatever colour the proprietor likes best.) And in the janpan sits a lady—Mrs. Apsley, a very pretty, good-tempered, and well-bred little woman. She is the grand-daughter of an English peer, and is very fond of quoting her aunts and her uncles. "My aunt Lady Mary Culnerson," "my aunt the Countess of Tweedleford," "my uncle, Lord Charles Banbury Cross," &c. But that is her only weakness, I believe; and, perhaps, it is ungenerous to allude to it. Her husband is in the Dragoons.

"Well, Mrs. Apsley, whither art thou going? To pay visits?"

"No. I am going to Mrs. Ludlam's to buy a new bonnet, and not before I want one, you will say."

"May I accompany you?"

"Yes, and assist me in making a choice."

There is not a cloud to be seen. The air is soft and balmy. The wild flowers are in full bloom, and the butterfly is on the wing. The grasshopper is singing his ceaseless song, and the bees are humming a chorus thereto.

We are now at Mrs. Ludlam's. The janpan is placed upon the ground, and I assist Mrs. Apsley to step from it.

Mrs. Ludlam is the milliner and dressmaker of Upper India, and imports all her wares direct from London and Paris. Everybody in this part of the world knows Mrs. Ludlam, and everybody likes her. She has by industry, honesty of purpose, and economy, amassed a little fortune; and has brought up a large family in the most respectable and unpretending style. Some people say that she sometimes can afford to sell a poor ensign's wife a bonnet, or a silk dress, at a price which hardly pays. What I have always admired in Mrs. Ludlam is that she never importunes her customers to buy her goods; nor does she puff their quality.

The bonnet is bought; likewise a neck-scarf for Jack. And we are now returning: Mrs. Apsley to her home, and I to the club. Mrs. Apsley invites me to dine with them; but that is impossible. It is public night, and I have two guests. One of them is Jack, who does not belong to the club, because Mary does not wish it.

Mrs. Apsley says she wants some pickles, and we must go into Ford's shop to purchase them. Ford sells everything; and he is a wine, beer, and spirit merchant. You may get anything at Ford's—guns, pistols, swords, whips, hats, clothes, tea, sugar, tobacco. What is this which Ford puts into my hand? A raffle paper! "To be raffled for, a single-barrelled rifle, by Purdey The property of a gentleman hard-up for money, and in great difficulties. Twenty-five chances at one gold mohur (one pound twelve shillings) each."

"Yes, put my name down for a chance, Ford."

"And Captain Apsley's, please," says the lady.

After promising Mrs. Apsley most faithfully that I will not keep Jack later than half-past twelve, and taking another look into those sweet eyes of hers, I gallop away as fast as the pony can carry me. I am late; there is scarcely a vacant place at the long table. We have no private tables. The same board shelters the nether limbs of all of us. We are all intimate friends, and know exactly each other's circumstances. What a clatter of knives and forks! And what a lively conversation! It alludes chiefly to the doings of the past night. Almost every other man has a nickname. To account for many of them would indeed be a difficult, if not a hopeless task.

"Dickey Brown! Glass of beer?"

"I am your man," responds Major George, N. I. Fencibles.

At the other end of the table you hear the word "Shiney" shouted out, and responded to by Lieutenant Fenwick of the Horse Artillery.

"Billy! Sherry?"

Adolphus Bruce of the Lancers lifts his glass with immense alacrity.

It is a curious characteristic of Indian society that very little outward respect is in private shown to seniority. I once heard an ensign of twenty years of age address a civilian of sixty in the following terms: "Now then, old moonsiff, pass that claret, please."

The tiffin over, a gool, or lighted ball of charcoal, is passed round the table in a silver augdan (fire-holder). Every man present lights a cigar, and in a few minutes there is a general move. Some retire to the billiard-room, others cluster round the fireplace; others pace the platform; and two sets go up-stairs into the reading-room to have a quiet rubber—from three till five. Those four men seated at the table near the window have the reputation of being the best players in India. The four at the other table know very little of the game of whist. Mark the difference! The one set never speak, except when the cards are being dealt. The other set are finding fault with one another during the progress of the hand. The good players are playing high. Gold mohur points—five gold mohurs on the rub—give and take five to two after the first game. And sometimes, at game and game, they bet an extra five. Tellwell and Long, who are playing against Bean and Fickle, have just lost a bumper—twenty-seven gold mohurs—a matter of forty-three pounds four shillings.

In the billiard-room, there is a match going on

between four officers who are famed for their skill, judgment, and execution. Heavy bets are pending. How cautiously and how well they play! No wonder, when we consider the number of hours they practise, and that they play every day of their lives. That tall man, now about to strike, makes a revenue out of billiards. I shall be greatly mistaken if that man does not come to grief some day. He preys upon every youngster in every station he goes to with his regiment. He is a captain in the Native Infantry. His name is Tom Locke. He has scored forty-seven off the red ball. His confederate, Bunyan, knows full well that luck has little to do with his success. He, too, will come to grief before long. Your clever villains are invariably tripped up sooner or later, and ignominiously stripped of their commissions and positions in society.

It is five o'clock. Some thirty horses and as many ponies are saddled and bridled, and led up and down in the vicinity of the club. Everybody will be on the mall presently. The mall is a part of the road round the Camel's Back. It is a level of about half a mile long and twelve feet broad. A slight fence stands between the riders and a deep khud (precipice). To gallop along this road is nothing when you are accustomed to it; but at first it makes one very nervous even to witness it. Serious and fatal accidents have happened; but, considering all things, they have been far fewer than might have been expected.

The mall is crowded. Ladies and gentlemen on horseback, and ladies in janpans—the janpanees dressed in every variety of livery. Men in the French grey coats, trimmed with white serge, are carrying Mrs. Hastings. Men in the brown clothes, trimmed with yellow serge, are carrying Mrs. Merrydale. Jack Apsley's wife is mounted on her husband's second charger. "Come along, Captain Wall," she calls out to me, and goes off at a canter, which soon becomes a hand gallop. I follow her of course. Jack remains behind, to have a quiet chat with Mrs. Flower, of his regiment; who thinks—and Jack agrees with her—that hard riding on the mall is a nuisance, and ought to be put a stop to. But, as we come back, we meet the hypocrite galloping with a Miss Pinkerton, a new importation, with whom—much to the amusement of his wife—he affects to be desperately in love. The mall, by the way, is a great place for flirtations.

Most steady-going people, like Mrs. Flower, not only think hard riding on the mall a nuisance, but make it the theme of letters to the editors of the papers; and sometimes the editors will take the matter up, and write leading articles thereon, and pointedly allude to the fact—as did the late Sir C. J. Napier in a general order—that beggars on horseback usually ride in the opposite direction to heaven. But these letters and leaders rarely have the desired effect; for what can a man do when a pretty woman like Mrs. Apsley says, "Come along; let us have a gallop."

Why are there so very many people on the mall this evening? A few evenings ago it was proposed at the club that a band should play twice a week. A paper was sent round at once, and every one subscribed a sum in accordance with his means. Next morning the required number of musicians was hunted up and engaged. Two cornets, two flutes, two violins, a clarionet, a fife, and several drums. It is the twenty-ninth of May—a day always celebrated in "this great military camp," as Lord Ellenborough described British India. At a given signal, the band strikes up "God save the Queen." We all flock round the band, which has taken up a position on a rock beetling over the road. The male portion of us raise our hats, and remain uncovered while the anthem is played. We are thousands of miles distant from our fatherland and our Queen, but our hearts are as true and as loyal as though she were in the midst of us.

This is the first time that the Himalaya mountains have listened to the joyous sound of music. We have danced to music within doors; but never, until this day, have we heard a band in the open air in the Himalaya mountains. How wonderful is the effect! From valley to valley echo carries the sound, until at last it seems as though

Every mountain now had found a band.

Long after the strain has ceased with us, we can hear

it penetrating into and reverberating amidst regions which the foot of man has never yet trodden, and probably will never tread. The sun has gone down, but his light is still with us.

Back to the club! Dinner is served. We sit down, seventy-five of us. The fare is excellent, and the champagne has been iced in the hail which fell the other night, during a storm. Jack Apsley is on my right, and I have thrice begged of him to remember that he must not stay later than half-past twelve; and he has thrice responded that Mary has given him an extension of leave until daylight. Jack and I were midshipmen together, some years ago, in a line-of-battle ship that went by the name of the House of Correction. And there is Wywell sitting opposite to us—Wywell who was in the frigate which belonged to our squadron—the squadron that went round the world, and buried the commodore, poor old Sir James! in Sydney churchyard. Fancy we three meeting again in the Himalaya mountains!

The cloth is removed, for the dinner is over. The president of the club—the gentleman who founded it—rises. He is a very little man of seventy years of age—fifty-three of which have been spent in India. He is far from feeble, and is in full possession of all his faculties. His voice is not loud, but it is very distinct, and pierces the ear.

They do not sit long after dinner at the club. It is only nine, and the members are already diminishing. Some are off to the billiard-room, to smoke, drink brandy-and-water, and look on at the play. The whist parties are now at work, and seven men are engaged at brag. A few remain; and, drawing their chairs to the fireplace, form a ring and chat cosily.

Halloa! what is this? The club-house is heaving and pitching like a ship at anchor in a gale of wind. Some of us feel qualmish. It is a shock of an earthquake; and a very violent shock. It is now midnight. A thunderstorm is about to sweep over Mussoorie. Only look at that lurid forked lightning striking yonder hill, and listen to that thunder! While the storm lasts, the thunder will never for a second cease roaring; for, long before the sound of one peal has died away, it will be succeeded by another more awful. And now, look at the Dhoon! Those millions of acres are illuminated by incessant sheet lightning. How plainly we discern the trees and the streams in the Dhoon, and the outline of the pass which divides the Dhoon from the plains. What a glorious panorama! We can see the black clouds descending rapidly towards the Dhoon, and it is not until they near that level land that they discharge the heavy showers with which they are laden. What a luxury would this storm be to the inhabitants of the plains; but it does not extend beyond the Dhoon. We shall hear the day after to-morrow that not a single drop of rain has fallen at Umballah, Meerut, or Saharunpore.

The party from the billiard-room has come up to have supper, now that the storm is over. They are rather noisy; but the card-players take no heed of them. They are too intent upon their play to be disturbed. Two or three of the brag party call for oyster-toast to be taken to the table, and they devour it savagely while the cards are dealt round, placing their lighted cheroots meanwhile on the edge of the table.

And now there is singing—comic and sentimental. "Isle of Beauty" is followed by the "Steam Leg," the "Steam Leg" by the "Queen of the May," the "Queen of the May" by the facetious version of "George Barnwell," and so on. Jack Apsley—who has ascertained that dear Mary is quite safe, and not at all alarmed—is still here, and is now singing "Rule, Britannia," with an energy and enthusiasm which are at once both pleasing and ridiculous to behold. He has been a soldier for upwards of sixteen years; but the sailor still predominates in his nature; while his similes have invariably reference to matters connected with ships and the sea. He told me just now, that when he first joined his regiment, he felt as much out of his element as a live dolphin in a sentry-box, and he has just described his present colonel as a man who is as touchy as a boatswain's kitten. Apsley's Christian name is Francis, but he has always been called Jack, and always will be.

It is now broad daylight, and high time for a man on sick-leave to be in bed. How seedy and disreputable we all look, in our evening dresses and patent-leather boots. And observe this carnation in my button-hole—the gift of Mrs. Apsley; she gave it to me on the mall. The glare of the lights, and the atmosphere of smoke in which I have been sitting part of the night, have robbed it of its freshness, its bloom, and perfume. I am sorry to say it is an emblem of most of us.

Go home, Apsley! Go home, reeking of tobacco-smoke and brandy-and-water—with your eyes like boiled gooseberries, your hair in frightful disorder—go home! You will probably meet upon the mall your three beautiful children, with their rosy faces all bloom, and their breath, when they press their glowing lips to those feverish cheeks of yours, will smell as incense, and make you ashamed of yourself. Go home, Jack. I will tiff with you to-day at half-past two.

Two young gentlemen were victimized last night at the brag party. The one, a lieutenant of the N. I. Buffs, lost six thousand rupees; the other, a lieutenant of the Foot Artillery, four thousand. The day after to-morrow, the first of the month, will be settling day. How are they to meet these debts of honour? They have nothing but their pay, and must borrow from the banks. That is easily managed. The money will be advanced to them on their own personal security, and that of two other officers in the service. They must also insure their lives. The premium and the interest together will make them forfeit fourteen per cent. per annum on the sum advanced. The loan will be paid off in three years, by monthly instalments. The paymaster will receive an order from the bank secretary to deduct for the bank so much per mensem from their pay. For the next three years they will have to live very mildly indeed.

There were also two victims (both youngsters) to billiards. One lost three thousand rupees in bets, another two thousand five hundred by bad play. They, too, will have to fly for assistance to the banks. Captains Locke and Bunyan won, between them, last night, one thousand four hundred pounds. There was but little execution done at whist. Not more than one hundred and fifty pounds changed hands. Those four men who play regularly together, and who never exceed their usual bets, have very little difference between them at the end of each month—not thirty pounds either way. This will not hurt them; for they have all good appointments, and have private property besides.

I find, on going to tiffin at Jack Apsley's, that Mrs. Jack has heard all about the winnings and losings at the club. Some man went home and told his wife, and she has told everybody whom she has seen. In a short time the news will travel to head-quarters at Simlah, and out will come a general order on gambling, which general order will be read aloud at the Himalaya Club, with comments by the whole company—comments which will be received with shouts of laughter. Some youngsters will put the general order into verse, and send it to a newspaper. This done, the general order will be converted into pipe-lights. This is no doubt very sad; but I have no time to moralize. My duty is simply to paint the picture.

Mrs. Apsley is not angry with her husband for staying up till daylight. She thinks a little dissipation does him good; and it is but a very little that Jack indulges in, for he is a good husband and a good father. Jack has a severe headache, but he wont confess it. He says he never touched the champagne, and only drank two glasses of brandy and water. But who ever did touch the champagne, and who ever did drink any more than two glasses of brandy and water? Jack came home with his pockets filled with almonds, raisins, prunes, nutcrackers, and two liqueur glasses; but how they got there he has not the slightest idea—but I have. Wywell, from a sideboard, was filling his pockets all the while he was singing "Rule, Britannia."

"Mrs. Apsley, I have some news for you."

"What is it, Captain Wall?"

"The club gives a ball on the 7th of June."

"You don't say so."

"And what is more, a fancy ball."

The tiffin is brought in. Mulligatawny soup and rice, cold lamb and mint sauce, sherry and beer. The Apsleys are very hospitable people; but Mary, who rules the household, never exceeds her means for the sake of making a display.

The soup and a glass of wine set Jack up; and he becomes quite chirpy. He proposes that he and I and Wywell shall go to the fancy ball as middies, and that Mary shall appear as Black-eyed Susan. Then, darting off at a tangent, he asks me if I remember when we were lying off Mount Edgecombe, just before sailing for South America? But he requires a little more stimulant, for the tears are glistening in his soft blue eyes when he alludes to the death of poor Noel, a middy whom we buried in the ocean a few days before we got to Rio. In a very maudlin way he narrates to his wife the many excellent qualities of poor Noel. She listens with great attention; but, observing that his spontaneous emotion is the result of the two over-night glasses of brandy—plus what he cannot remember drinking over-night—she suggests that Jack shall make some sherry cobbler. What a jewel of a woman art thou, Mrs. Apsley! Several of the men who returned home, as Jack did, none the better for their potations, have been driven by their wives' reproaches to the club, where they are now drinking brandy and soda-water to excess; while here is your spouse as comfortable as a cricket on a hearth; and now that he confesses he was slightly screwed, you, with quiet tact, contradict his assertion.

For the next week the forthcoming fancy ball to be given by the club will be the chief topic of conversation amongst the visitors at Mussoorie. Mrs. Ludlam is in immense demand. She knows the character that each lady will appear in; but it is useless to attempt to extract from her the slightest particle of information on that head. This ball will be worth seven hundred and fifty rupees to Mrs. Ludlam.

Let us keep away from the club for a few days; for, after several officers have been victimized at play, their friends are apt to talk about the matter in an unpleasant manner. This frequently leads to a quarrel, which I dislike to witness.

Where shall we go? To the Dhoon. It is very hot there; but never mind. No great-coat, no fires, an hour hence; but the very lightest of garments and a punkah. The thermometer is at eighty-five degrees there. The Dhoon is not a healthy place in the summer. It must have been the bed of an enormous lake, or small inland sea. Its soil being alluvial, will produce anything: every kind of fruit, European and tropical. You may gather a peach and a plantain out of the same garden. Some of the hedges in this part of the world are singularly beautiful, composed of white and red cluster roses and sweetbriers. There is an excellent hotel in the

Dhoon, where we are sure to meet people whom we know.

Sure enough, I find a party of five at the hotel; all club men, and intimate friends of mine. They, too, have come down to avoid being present on the first settling day; for if there should be any duelling, it is just possible that some of us might be asked to act as second.

We must dine off sucking-pig in the Dhoon. The residents at Mussoorie used to form their pig-parties in the Dhoon, just as the residents of London form their whitebait banquets at Greenwich. I once took a French gentleman, who was travelling in India, to one of these pig-parties, and he made a very humorous note of it in his book of travel, which he showed to me. Unlike most foreigners who travel in English dominions, he did not pick out and note down all the bad traits in our character; but gave us credit for all those excellent points which his experience of mankind in general enabled him to observe.

The Governor-General's body-guard is quartered just now in the Dhoon, and there is a Goorka regiment here. The Dhoon will send some twenty couples to the fancy ball on the 7th. Every lady in the place has at this moment a Durzee (man tailor) employed in her back verandah dress-making. We are admitted to the confidence of Mrs. Plowville, who is going as Norma. And a very handsome

Norma she will make ; she being rather like Madame Grisi—and she knows it.

We return to the club on the 2nd of June. There has been a serious dispute, and a duel has been fought; but happily, no blood shed. The intelligence of the gambling at the club has reached the Commander-in-Chief at Simlah ; and he has ordered that the remainder of the leave granted to Captains Locke and Bunyan be cancelled, and that those officers forthwith join their respective regiments. The victims also have been similarly treated ; yet every one of these remanded officers came up here on medical certificate.

It is the morning of the 7th of June. The stewards of the ball are here, there, and everywhere, making arrangements. Several old hands, who hate and detest balls, and who voted against this ball, are walking about the public room, protesting that it is the greatest folly they ever heard of. And in their disgust they blackball two candidates for admission who are to be balloted for on the 10th instant. They complain that they can get no tiffin, no dinner, no anything. But the stewards only laugh at them.

The supper has been supplied by Monsieur Emille, the French restaurateur, and a very splendid supper it is. It is laid out in the dining-room. Emille is a great artist. He is not perhaps equal to Brazier—that great man whom Louis Philippe gave to his friend, Lord William Bentinck, when Lord William was going out to govern India—but Emille, nevertheless, would rank high even amongst the most skilful of cuisiniers in Europe.

It is a quarter past nine, and we of the club are ready to receive our guests. The ladies come in janpans; their husbands following them on horseback or on foot. It is a beautiful moonlight night. We are always obliged to wait upon the moon when we give a ball in Mussoorie. Before ten o'clock the room is crowded. There are present one hundred and thirty-six gentlemen, and seventy-five ladies. Of the former nine-tenths are soldiers, the remainder are civilians. Of the latter, seventy are married; the remaining five are spinsters.

Here we all are in every variety of costume—Turks, Greeks, Romans, Bavarian broom-girls, Medoras, Corsairs, Hamlets, Othellos, Tells, Charles the Seconds, and Quakers. Many have not come in fancy costume, but in their respective uniforms; and where do you see such a variety of uniforms as in an Indian ball-room? Where will you meet with so great a number of distinguished men? There is the old general: that empty sleeve tells a tale of the battle of Waterloo. Beside him is a general in the Company's service, one who has recently received the thanks of his country. He has seen seventy, but there is no man in the room who could at this very time endure so great an amount of mental or bodily fatigue. That youngster to the right of the general is to be made a brevet-major and a C.B. as soon as he gets his company. He is a hero, though a mere boy. That pale-faced civilian is a man of great ability, and possesses administrative talents of the very highest order. Seated on an ottoman, talking to Mrs. Hastings, is the famous Hawkins, of the Third Dragoons. Laughing in the side doorway is the renowned William Mumble. He is the *beau ideal* of a dashing soldier. Yonder is Major Starcross, whose gallantry in Affghanistan was the theme of admiration in Europe. And there is Colonel Bolt, of the Duke's Own. All of these men have been under very hot fire—the hottest that even Lord Hardinge could remember. All of them are decorated with medals and ribbons. Where will you see handsomer women than you frequently meet in a ball-room at Mussoorie or Simlah? Amongst those now assembled there are three who, at any court in Europe, would be conspicuous for their personal attractions—Mrs. Merrydale, Mrs. Plowville, and Mrs. Banks. Mrs. Apsley is a pretty little woman; but the three to whom I have alluded are beautiful.

The dancing has commenced, and will continue until four o'clock, with an interval of half-an-hour at supper-time. The second supper—the ladies being gone—will then commence, and a very noisy party it will be. Unrestrained by the presence of the fair sex, the majority of those who remain will drink and smoke in earnest, and the chances are, there will be several rows. Ensign Jenks, when the brandy and water inflames him, will ask young Blackstone, of the Civil Service, what he meant by coming up and talking to his partner during the last set of quadrilles. Blackstone will say, the lady beckoned to him. Jenks will say, "It is a lie!" Blackstone will rise to assault Jenks. Two men will hold Blackstone down on his chair. The general will hear of this, for Captain Lovelass (who is himself almost inarticulate) has said to Jenks, "Cossider self unarrest!" Jenks will have to join his regiment at Meerut, after receiving from the general a very severe reprimand.

While talking over the past ball, an archery meeting or a pic-nic is sure to be suggested. It must originate at the club; without the countenance of the club, which is very jealous of its prerogative, no amusement can possibly be successful. A lady, the wife of a civilian, who prided herself on her husband's lofty position, had once the temerity to try the experiment, and actually sent round a proposal-paper in her own handwriting, and by one of her own servants. She failed of course. All the club people wrote the word "seen" opposite to their names; but withheld the important word "approved." Even the tradespeople at Mussoorie acknowledge the supremacy of the Himalaya Club.

The season is over. The cold weather has commenced in the plains. It is the 5th of October, and everybody at Mussoorie is on the move—going down the hill, as it is called. Every house which was lately full is now empty, and will remain so till the coming April. The only exceptions will be the schools for young ladies and for little boys; the convent, the branch of the North-West Bank, and the Post-Office. Invalided officers who reside at the sanatarium during the summer will go down the hill, and winter in Deyrah-Dhoon. In another month the mountains will be covered with snow, and it would be dangerous to walk out on these narrow roads, few of which are railed in.

Let us sum up the events of the season. Four young men were victimized—two at cards and two at billiards. Two duels were fought on the day after the ball. In one of these duels an officer fell dead. In another the offending party grievously wounded his antagonist. Four commissions were sacrificed in consequence of these encounters. There were two elopements. Mrs. Merrydale went off with Lieutenant Maxwell, leaving her children under the care of the servants, until her husband came to take them away. Mrs. Hastings, who used to bore us about the duties of a wife, carried off that silly boy Stammersleigh. These elopements led to two actions in H.M. Supreme Court of Calcutta, and seven of us (four in one case and three in the other) had to leave our regiments or appointments, and repair to the Supreme Court to give evidence. Some of us had to travel fourteen hundred miles in the month of May, the hottest month in India.

There was another very awkward circumstance connected with that season at Mussoorie. The reader knows that Captains Locke and Bunyan were ordered to join their regiments, the unexpired portion of their leave having been cancelled by order of his Excellency the Commander-in-Chief. In the hurry of his departure from the hills, Locke had left in the drawer of a table a letter from Bunyan, containing a proposal to victimize a certain officer—then in Mussoorie—in the same manner that they had victimized one Lord George Straw; namely, to get him to their rooms, and play at brag. Lord George Straw had lost to these worthies eighteen hundred pounds on one eventful night. The general opinion was, touching a very extraordinary fact connected with the play, that Lord George had been cheated. This letter from Bunyan to Locke was found by the servant of the officer who now occupied the apartments recently vacated by Locke. The servant handed it to his master, who, fancying that it was one of his own letters, began abstractedly to read it. Very soon, however, he discovered his mistake. But he had read sufficient to warrant his reading the whole, and he did so. A meeting of gentlemen at the club was called; and, before long, Locke and Bunyan left the army by sentence of a general court-martial. I have since heard that Locke lost his ill-gotten gains in

Ireland, and became eventually marker at a billiard-room; and that Bunyan, who also came to poverty, was seen driving a cab for hire in Oxford-street.

It behoves me, however, to inform the reader that, recently, the tone of Anglo-Indian society during the hot seasons is very much improved. Six or seven years ago there never was a season that did not end as unhappily as that which I have attempted to describe; but it is now four years since I heard of a duel in the Upper Provinces—upwards of four years since I heard of a victim to gambling, and nearly three since there was an elopement. It is true that the records of courts-martial still occasionally exhibit painful cases; but, if we compare the past with the present, we must admit that the change is very satisfactory. I do not attribute this altered state of things to the vigilance of commanding officers, or the determination of the commanders-in-chief to punish severely those who offend. It is due chiefly to the improved tone of society in England, from which country we get our habits and manners. The improvement in the tone of Indian society has been very gradual. Twenty years ago India was famous for its infamy. Ten years ago it was very bad. It is now tolerable. In ten years from this date, if not in less time, Indian society will be purged entirely of those evils which now prey upon it, and trials for drunkenness and other improper conduct will happen as rarely as in England. Year by year this communication between our fatherland and the upper part of India will become more speedy and less expensive; and thus will a greater number of officers be enabled to come home on furlough for a year or two. Nothing does an Indian officer so much good as a visit to Europe. When a man has once contracted bad habits in India, he cannot reform in India. To be cured he must be taken away for a while from the country. There have been instances of officers who have had strength of mind to alter their course of life without leaving the East; but those instances are very few.

The East India Company should do all in its power to encourage young officers to spend a certain time every seven years in Europe. Instead of six months' leave to the hills—which six months are spent in utter idleness, and too frequently in dissipation—give them nine months' leave to Europe. This would admit of their spending six months in England, or on the Continent, where they would improve their minds and mend their morals, as well as their constitutions.

The East India Company should also bring the Peninsular and Oriental Company to reasonable terms for the passage of officers to and from India. A lieutenant who wishes to come home, cannot at present get a passage from Calcutta to Southampton under one hundred and twenty pounds. So that he gives up more than four months' pay for being "kept" thirty-six days on board of a steamer. Three pounds ten shillings per diem for food and transit!

THE MAHOMMEDAN MOTHER.

MUSSOORIE and Landour, situated in the lower range of the Himalaya mountains, form the favourite sanitarium of the upper part of India. The scenery is more beautiful than that of Simlah; for Mussoorie and Landour command a view of Dehra Dhoon, which resembles (except that the Dhoon is grander and more extensive) the plains of Italy as seen from the ascent of the Simplon. The mall of Mussoorie is crowded every evening with visitors; some on horseback, some on hill ponies, some on foot, and some in the janpan (something like a sedan-chair carried by four hill men). A gayer scene it would be impossible to conceive. Every one knows his neighbour; and, in passing along the narrow road, stoppages are frequent. Compliments must be exchanged, and the news or scandal of the day gossiped about. Every now and then you hear a cry of "What a shame!" from a terrified lady in a janpan, while a couple of lovers gallop past on spirited Arabs at full speed. Sometimes a shriek from a nervous mamma reverberates through the valleys, when she beholds her children in the way of the heedless pair.

Accidents sometimes occur. A few years ago, a

lady and a gentleman were riding round a place called the Camel's Back; the road gave way, and they fell down a precipice several hundred feet. The horses were killed, but the riders miraculously escaped with only a few severe bruises. On another occasion, a gentleman of the civil service was taking his evening walk, when one of his dogs ran between his legs, and precipitated him. He was killed on the spot.

On the mall every evening was to be seen a native woman standing by the side of the road, near a large rock, watching those who passed by. She was well dressed, and her face was concealed, according to the custom of persons of her apparent station in life. There she stood, attracting general attention. She was a woman of slight, but graceful figure, and rather tall. Many persons were curious to know who she was, and to see her face; but she took care that in this respect none should be gratified. Sometimes she would go away early; at other times she would remain until it was quite dark. Some suspected—and I was amongst the number—that she was the native wife of some European officer who had divorced himself, and visited the "Hills," whither the woman, to annoy, had followed him; and there was no small amount of speculation as to *whose* wife she could be. Some of the guesses, if they were seriously made, were extremely ungenerous, for they included several elderly officials, who could not by any possibility have been married to this mysterious lady. I was determined to know who she was; and one night, when most people were thronged around the band, I approached her, and inquired if I could be of any service to her. She replied (her face closely covered), "Yes; by going away." She had a very sweet voice, and its sorrowful tones inspired me with pity, when she added, "I am a poor woman; my heart is crushed; do not add to my misery by remaining near me." I obeyed her, after apologizing for having intruded. Several other persons had attempted to extract some particulars from the lady, and had received the same sort of reply as that she had given to me.

The rains were about to commence, and storms were not unfrequent. The mall was less frequented; only a few—those who cared little about hearing "heaven's artillery thunder in the skies," or being pelted by hailstones as large as marbles—ventured out; but amongst that few was the native lady, who, punctual as the light of day, visited that huge, dismal-looking rock, and gazed upon the road.

I have seen a storm on the heights of Jura—such a storm as Lord Byron describes. I have seen lightning and heard thunder in Australia; I have, off Terra del Fuego, the Cape of Good Hope, and the coast of Java, kept watch in thunderstorms which have drowned in their roaring the human voice, and made every one deaf and stupified; but these storms are not to be compared with a thunderstorm at Mussoorie or Landour.

In one of these storms of thunder, lightning, wind, and hail, at about five o'clock in the afternoon, I laid a wager with a friend that the native lady would be found as usual standing near the rock. Something secretly assured me that she was there at that moment, looking on unmoved, except by the passions which had prompted her pilgrimage. How were we to decide it? "By going to the spot," I suggested. My friend declined; but declared that, as far as the bet was concerned, he would be perfectly satisfied with my word, either one way or the other; namely, whether I had won or lost.

I set off upon my journey. The rock was at least three-quarters of a mile distant from my abode. My curiosity was so much aroused—albeit I felt certain the woman was there—that I walked through the storm without heeding it. Every now and then I saw the electric fluid descend into a valley; then heard that strange noise which huge pieces of rock make when they bound from one precipice to another, tearing up trees, and carrying large stones and the earth along with them in their headlong career; but still my mind was intent on the woman, and nothing else.

Was she there?

Yes; there she sat, drenched to the skin; but I could not pity her wet and cold condition, for I could see that she cared no more about it than I cared about my own. She drew her garment so closely over her face, that the outline of her features was plainly discernible. It was decidedly handsome; but still I longed to see her eyes, to confirm my impression. I sat beside her. The storm still raged, and presently the lady said, "The heaven is speaking, Sahib." I answered, "Truly; but the lightning, the parent of that sound which I now hear, I cannot see." She understood me, and gave me a glimpse of her eyes. They were not like the eyes of a native; they were of a bluish hue, almost grey. I said to her, in Hindoostanee, "You are not a native; what do you do here in a native dress?"

"I would I were an European," she answered me. "My feelings, perhaps, would be less acute, and I should be sitting over a bright fire. Oh, how loudly the heaven is speaking! Go home, Sahib, you will catch cold!"

"Why do *you* not go home?" I asked. "You will see no one to-day. No—not even your beloved. I am the only being who will venture out in a storm like this; and I do so only for your sake."

"My heart is as hard as this rock," she said, flipping her finger against the granite, "to all except one being—a child. Oh, how the heaven is speaking, Sahib!"

"Do you not fear the lightning and the hail?" I asked her.

"I did once," she replied. "I trembled whenever it came near; but now, what does it signify? *Bidglee* (lightning), come to me," she cried, beckoning to a streak of fluid which entered the ground within a hundred yards of us. "*Bidglee*, come here, and make a turquoise of my heart."

What pretty feet! She had kicked off her shoes, which were saturated and spoiled.

"Go home, Sahib" (such was the refrain of her conversation); "you will catch cold!"

By degrees I had an opportunity of seeing all her features. She was most beautiful, but had evidently passed the meridian of her charms. She could not have been less than twenty-four years of age. On the forefinger of her left hand she wore a ring of English manufacture, in which was set a red cornelian, whereon was engraved a crest—a stag's head.

I took her hand in mine, and said, "Where did you get this?" pointing to the ring.

She smiled and sighed, and then answered, "Jee (sir), it belonged to an Ameer (a great man)."

"Where is he?"

"Never mind."

"Do you expect to see him soon?"

"No; never."

"Is he old?"

"No; not older than yourself. How the heaven is speaking!"

"Let me see you to your home."

"No. I will go alone."

"When do you intend to go?"

"When you have left me."

"You are very unkind thus to repulse my civility."

"It may be so; but my heart's blood is curdled."

I bade her farewell; and through the storm, which still raged, I went home and won my wager.

I could not rest that night. The beautiful face of the native woman haunted me. In vain I tried to sleep, and at last I arose from my bed, and joined a card-party, in the hope that the excitement of gambling would banish her from my brain. But to no purpose. I knew not what I was playing, and ere long I left off in disgust.

Almost every one who visits the Hills keeps a servant called a *tindal.* His duty is to look after the men who carry your janpan, to go errands, to keep up the fire, and to accompany you with a lantern when you go out after dark. These tindals, like the couriers on the Continent, are a peculiar race; and, generally speaking, are a very sharp, active, and courageous people. I summoned my tindal, and interrogated him about the native lady who had caused so much sensation in Mussoorie. The only information he could afford me was, that she had come from a village near Hurdwar; that she was rich, possessed of the most costly jewels, kept a number of servants, moved about in great state on the plains, and, for all he knew, she might be the wife or slave of some Rajah.

Could she, I wondered, be the famous Ranee

Chunda, the mother of Dulleep Singh, and the wife of Runjeet?—the woman who, disguised as a soldier, had escaped from the fort of Chunar, where she had been imprisoned for disturbing, by her plots, the imagination of Sir Frederick Currie, when he was Resident at Lahore? The woman I had seen and spoken to "answered to the description" of the Ranee in every respect, excepting the eyes. Dulleep Singh was living at Mussoorie, and he not unfrequently rode upon the mall. Ranee Chunda had a satirical tongue, and a peculiarly sweet-toned, but shrill voice, and she had remarkably beautiful feet, and so had this woman. Ranee Chunda had courage which was superhuman; so had this woman. Ranee Chunda had a child—an only child; so had this woman.

I asked the tindal where the lady lived. He replied, that she occupied a small house near the bazaar, not very far from my own abode. "She is in great grief," the tindal yawned, "about something or other."

"Endeavour to find out the cause of her misfortunes," said I, "and you shall be rewarded according to your success."

Next day the tindal reported to me that I was not the only Sahib who was deeply interested in the native lady's affairs; that many wished to make her acquaintance, and had sent their tindals to talk to her; but that she had firmly and laconically dismissed them all, just as she had dismissed him—

"Tell your master that the sufferings of an object of pity, such as I am, ought not to be aggravated by the insulting persecution of gay and light-hearted men."

The day after the storm brought forth the loveliest afternoon that can be imagined. The sun shone out brightly, the clouds were lifted from the Dhoon, and the vast panorama resembled what we read of in some fairy tale. All Mussoorie and Landour turned out. The mall was so crowded, that it was difficult to thread one's way through the throng.

Was the lady at the rock? Yes; there she stood, as usual, watching those who passed. The Maharajah with his suite appeared. I was convinced that the woman was the Maharajah's mother; but I did not breathe my suspicions, lest I might cause her to be arrested. When it became dusk, and the visitors were taking their departure, I again approached the lady, and made my "salaam," in that respectful phrase which is always adopted when addressing a native woman of rank. She at once recognised me as the person who had spoken to her during the storm on the previous afternoon, for she alluded to its fury, and said she had taken a wrong road, had lost her way after I had left her, and did not reach home till nearly midnight. She concluded her little speech with a hope that I had been more fortunate.

"You should have allowed me to escort you,"

said I. "I would have helped to carry your load of sorrow."

She looked at me, and suddenly and abruptly said, "Your name is Longford."

"You are right," said I.

"About three or four years ago you stayed for several days with a friend in a tent near Deobund? You were on your way to these mountains?"

"I did."

"You had a little dog with you, and you lost it at Deobund?"

"I did lose my dog, and made a great noise about it. But how do you know all this?"

She smiled and sighed.

I was bewildered. My belief that she was the Ranee Chunda was almost confirmed. It was close to the encampment of the Ranee, when she was on her way to Chunar, that my dog was lost, and my servants and the officers of police declared that it must have been some of the Ranee's people who had stolen the favourite.

"The dog is still alive," said the lady; "and if you will come to-morrow, at twelve o'clock, to my house, you shall see him; but you will promise not to take him from me?"

"Of course I will not take him from you. But let me see him to-night, and tell me how he came into your possession. I will see you to your home."

"No, Sahib; be patient. I will tell you all to-morrow; and, when you have heard my story, you will perhaps do me a kindness. It is in your power to assist me. Tell me where you live, and I will send my brother to you at eleven o'clock. He will conduct you to my house. Salaam, Sahib."

I returned her salaam, and left her.

I did not go to bed till two o'clock the next morning, and when my tindal aroused me at eleven, and informed me that a young man wished to see me, I was disposed to believe that my engagement at twelve had been made in my dreams.

I ordered the young man to be admitted. He came to my bedside, and said in a confidential tone of voice: "The lady has sent me to wait your commands." I got up, made a hasty toilet, drank a cup of very hot tea, and followed the young man, who led me to the little house near the theatre, at the top of the Bazaar. I entered the abode, and found the lady sitting, native fashion, on a carpet on which was strewed marigold and rose leaves. Her silver *kulean* (small hookah) was beside her; and, sure enough, there was my long-lost terrier, Duke, looking as sleek, fat, lazy, and useless as a native lady's dog could be. After expressing my thanks to the lady for her condescension in granting me the interview, I spoke to my former favourite, Duke, but he only stretched himself, and yawned in reply.

"And you have still that ring with the blue stone in it," said the lady, taking my hand, and smiling while she looked at the ring. "I remember observing this when I saw you asleep, one morning, on a couch in the tent at Deobund. Had I noticed it when you addressed me during the storm, I would not have spoken so rudely to you."

"I do not remember having seen you previous to the other evening," said I; "and if I had, I should never have forgotten it. Where have we met?" I repeated.

"Where I had opportunities of seeing you, but where you could not see me."

There was an old serving woman, whom she called mother, attending upon her, and the young man whom she called brother, a soldier-like looking youth, was still standing in the room to which he had conducted me. The lady desired them both to withdraw, and then begged me to bring the *mora* (or stool) upon which I was sitting close to her side. I obeyed her. She placed her finely-formed head in the palms of her hands, and gave vent to a violent flood of tears. I suffered her to weep without interruption. Grief appeared to relieve her rather than to increase her pain. At length she dried her eyes, and said:—

"My father was a *Moolvee* (Mahommedan law officer), attached to the Sudder Court, in Agra. I am his only daughter. He was absent from home all day. Why should he not be? He was paid for it; he ate the Company's salt. Well, when I was about fifteen years of age I was enticed away from my home by the *Kotwall* (native police officer). He sent an old woman, who had silver on her tongue and gold in her hand. She told me long stories about love; and promised me that if I left my home I should marry the *Kotwall's* son, who was young and handsome. I was but a child and very foolish. The servants who had charge of me were all bribed heavily. One received three hundred rupees, another two hundred, a third one hundred. These people encouraged me in the idea that to marry the *Kotwall's* son would be the most prudent thing in the world; and, one day, when my father had gone to the Court at about ten o'clock, I eloped with the old woman whom the *Kotwall* had sent to talk me over.

"We travelled all day in a *bylee* (native carriage), guarded by two sowars. I asked the old woman several times where she was taking me, but her only reply was, 'Set your heart at rest, child, and eat some sweetmeats.' The *pawn* which she gave me must have been drugged, for shortly after eating it I fell asleep. How long I slept I cannot say, but when I awoke I found myself in the house of a Sahib. The old woman was there also. I became alarmed, but my fears were quieted by the old woman's tongue. She told me I was close to Agra, but the truth was, I was one hundred koss (two hundred miles) distant. Nautch girls were sent for, and they danced before me. I had this hookah given to me, and these bangles. A boy very handsomely dressed waited upon me, and brought my food. Parrots, minahs, and doves were purchased for me to play with. Whatever my childish fancy dictated the old woman instantly procured.

"I was so constantly amused, I had no time or inclination to think of my home. My father was a bad-tempered man, and I was only too glad to be out of hearing of the quarrels in which he constantly engaged with his servants and dependents. One evening the old woman said to me, '*Baba* (child), order a Nautch this evening, and let me, in your name, invite the Sahib to witness it.' I had never seen an Englishman—an European—except at a distance. The idea of being in the room with one inspired me with terror. I had been taught to despise the Kafir, whom my father said he was compelled to serve. I objected; but the old woman's eloquence again prevailed.

The night came; I was seated on my *fureesh* (carpet) just as I am now, and dressed in clothes of the gayest description. I was like a little queen, and felt as proud as was Noor Jehan. I was then very handsome. If I had not been, much trouble would have been spared; and my flesh was firm—not as it is now. At about ten o'clock the Sahib made his appearance. When he came into the room I was ready to faint with alarm, and, turning my head away, I clung to the old woman, and trembled from head to foot. '*Dhuro mut*' (do not fear), said the Sahib; and then he reproved, but in a gentle voice, the Nautch girls who were laughing loudly at me. The old woman, too, bade me banish my fears. After a while, I ventured to steal a look at the Sahib; and again averted my face, and clung to the old woman. The Sahib, after remaining a brief while, during which he praised my beauty, retired, and I was once more happy. 'There,' said the old woman, when he was gone; 'you see the Sahib is not a wild beast out of the jungles, but as gentle as one of your own doves.'

"On the following day I heard the Sahib talking in the next room; I peeped through the keyhole of the door, and saw him seated at a table. The *nazir* (head clerk) was standing beside him, reading. There was a man in chains surrounded by *burkandâzes* (guards) at the other end of the room, and a woman was there giving her evidence. The Court-house was undergoing some repairs, and the Sahib was carrying on his magisterial duties in his dining-room. The man in chains began to speak, and deny his guilt. The Sahib called out, '*Choop!*' (Silence!) in a voice so loud, that I involuntarily started back and shuddered. The prisoner again addressed the Sahib, and one of the *burkandâzes* dealt him a severe blow on the head, accompanied by the words, '*Suer! Chor!*' (Pig! Thief!) The case was deferred until the following day, and the court closed at about four o'clock in the afternoon, when the Sahib again paid me a visit.

"I was now afraid to show my fears, lest the Sahib should order me to be killed; and I therefore put on a cheerful countenance, while my heart was quivering in my breast. The Sahib spoke to me very kindly, and I began to dread him less.

"In this way I spent a fortnight; and, at the end of that time, I ventured to talk to the Sahib as though I were his equal. It afforded me great amusement to watch the administration of justice through the keyhole; and, young as I was, I imbibed a desire to have a share in the arbitrary power which was daily exercised.

"One day, when the Sahib came into my room, I began to talk to him about a case of which he had just disposed. He laughed, and listened to my views with great patience. I told him that the evidence upon which the prisoner had been convicted was false from beginning to end. He promised me that he would reverse the sentence of imprisonment; and, in the ecstasy of my joy at finding that I really had some power, I was intoxicated and unconscious of what I was doing. I suffered the Sahib's lips to touch mine. No sooner had I done so than I felt a degraded outcast, and I cried more bitterly than I have words to describe. The Sahib consoled me, and said that his God and his Prophet should be mine; and that in this world and the next our destinies should be the same.

"From that day I was a wife unto him. I ruled his household, and I shared his pleasures and his sorrows. He was in debt; but, by reducing his expenses, I soon freed him, for his pay was fifteen hundred rupees a month. I suffered no one to rob him, and caused the old woman, who was a great thief and cheat, to be turned away. I loved him with all my soul. I would rather have begged with him than have shared the throne of Ackbar Shah. When he was tired, I lulled him to sleep; when he was ill, I nursed him; when he was angry, I soon restored him to good-humour; and, when I saw him about to be deceived by subordinates, I put him on his guard. That he loved me I never had any reason to doubt. He gave me his confidence, and I never abused his trust."

"Who was the man?" I inquired; for I was in doubt, although I suspected.

"Be patient, Sahib," she replied, and then resumed. "At the end of two years I became a mother."

Here she gave vent to another flood of tears.

"The Sahib was pleased. The child seemed to bind us more closely together. I loved the child; I believe it was because it bore such a strong likeness to its father. When the Sahib was away from me on duty in the district, he seemed still by my side, when I looked at the boy, who was as white as you are."

"Is the child dead?" I asked.

"Be patient, Sahib. When you passed through Deobund, and stayed in the tent with your friend, my child was two years old. I was the mistress of that encampment at Deobund, and the wine you drank was given out with this hand."

"How little do men know of each other!" I exclaimed; "even those who are the most intimate! I had not the least idea there was a lady in the camp, I assure you."

"How angry with you was I," said she, "for keeping the Sahib up so late. You talked together the whole night long. Therefore I had no remorse when I took your dog. Well, as you are aware, soon after that the Sahib was seized with fever, from which he recovered; but he was so shattered by the attack that he was compelled to visit Europe, where you know—" She paused.

A native woman will never, if she can avoid it, speak of the death of a person whom she has loved. I was aware of this, and bowed my head, touching my forehead with both hands. The father of her child had died on his passage to England.

"Before he left me," she continued, "he gave me all that he possessed; his house and furniture; his horses, carriage, plate; his shares in the bank; his watch, his dressing-case, his rings;—everything was given to me, and I own all to this hour. When I heard the sad news I was heartbroken. Had it not been for the child I would have starved myself to death; as it was, I took to opium and smoking *bhung* (hemp). While I was in this state, my Sahib's brother—the Captain Sahib—came, and took away the boy; not by violence. I gave it to him. What was the child to me then? I did not care. But the old woman whom you heard me call my mother, who now attends me, gradually weaned me from the desperation in which I was indulging; and, by degrees, my senses returned to me. I then began to ask about my child, and a longing to see him came over me. At first they told me he was dead; but when they found I was resolved to destroy myself by intemperance, they told me the truth; that the child was living, and at school in these hills. I have come hither to be near my child. I see him almost every day, but it is at a distance. Sometimes he passes close to where I stand, and I long to spring upon him and to hug him to my breast, whereon in infancy his head reposed. I pray that I could speak to him, give him a kiss, and bless him; but he is never alone. He is always playing with, or talking to, the other little boys at the same school. It seems hard that he should be so joyous while his own mother is so wretched. Of what use to me is the property I have, when I cannot touch or be recognised by my own flesh and blood. You know the master of the school?"

"Yes."

"Could you not ask him to allow my child to visit

you? I could then see him once more, and speak to him. You were a friend of his father, and the request would not seem strange."

I felt myself placed in a very awkward position, and would make no promise; but I told the woman I would consider the matter, and let her know on the following day, provided she would stay at home, and not visit that rock upon the road any more. She strove hard to extract from me a pledge that I would yield to her request; but, difficult as it was to deny her anything—she was still so beautiful and so interesting—I would not commit myself, and held to what I had in the first instance stated.

I paid a visit to the school at which my friend's child had been placed by his uncle, a captain in the East India Company's service. I saw some thirty scholars, of all colours, on the play-ground; but I soon recognised the boy whom I was so curious to see. He was indeed very like his father, not only in face and figure, but in manner, gait, and bearing. I called to the little fellow, and he came and took my hand with a frankness which charmed me. The schoolmaster told me that the boy was very clever, and that, although only six years old, there were but few of his playmates whom he did not excel. "His father was an old friend of mine," I said. "Indeed our acquaintance began when we were not older than this child. Would you have any objection to allow the boy to spend a day with me?"

"I promised his uncle," was the schoolmaster's reply, "that he should not go out, and that I would watch him closely; but of course he will be quite safe with you. Any day that you please to send for him he shall be ready."

"Does he know anything of his mother?" I inquired.

"Nothing," said the schoolmaster. "He was very young when he came to me. I have no idea who, or what, or where the mother is, for his uncle did not enter into the particulars of his parentage. The mother must have been very fair, if she were a native, the boy is so very slightly touched with the tar-brush."

I went home, and sent for the mother. She came; and I entreated her to forego her request, for the child's sake. I represented to her that it might unsettle him, and cause him to be discontented. I assured her that he was now as happy and as well taken care of as any mother could desire her offspring to be. On hearing this the poor woman became frantic. She knelt at my feet and supplicated me to listen to her entreaty—a sight of her child, a few words with him, and a kiss from his lips. She said she did not wish him to know that she was his mother; that if I would have him brought into my house, she would dress in the garb of a servant woman, or *syce's* (groom's) wife, and talk to the boy without his being aware that she was the person who had brought him into the world.

"And you will not play me false?" said I, moved by her tears. "You will not, when you have once got hold of the boy, decline to relinquish that hold, and defy his friends—as mothers *have* done—to take him from you, except by an order of Court? Remember, Dooneea (that was her name) that I am running a great risk; and am, moreover, deceiving the schoolmaster, and behaving badly to the boy's uncle, by allowing myself to be swayed by your tears and my own feelings. Consider what disgrace you will bring upon me, if you fail to keep your word in this matter." She bound herself by an oath that she would do all I required, if I would only give her the longed-for interview.

"To-morrow, at twelve," said I, "you may come here. At that hour, in this room, the child shall be with me. Come in the dress of a poor woman, and bring an infant with you. Let your excuse be that you have come to complain of the ill-treatment you have received from your husband, who is in my service. This will give me an opportunity of bidding you remain until justice be done, and meanwhile you will see the boy; and when I go out of the room, which will be only for a short time, you can talk to him. Do you know your part Dooneea?"

"Yes, Sahib."

"To-morrow, at twelve. Salaam, Dooneea!"

"Salaam, Sahib." She went away with a cheerful countenance.

There are no such actors in the world as the people of Hindostan. The boy came to me a little before twelve, and was reading to me, when Dooneea, with a child in her arms, and dressed in the shabbiest apparel, rushed into the room, and commenced an harangue. She said she had been beaten unmercifully by her husband, for no cause whatever; that he had broken one of her fingers, and had attempted to stab her; but she had saved her life by flight. All this she accompanied with gesticulations and tears, according to the custom of complainants in the East. I feigned to be very angry with the husband, and hastily left the room, as if to make inquiry and to send for him.

I ran round to an outer door, and peeped in upon Dooneea and her boy. She was repeating the same tale to the child, and the child was imploring her not to cry. It was a strange scene. The tears she was now shedding were not mock tears. The boy asked her how her husband came to beat her? She began thus:—"I was sitting near the fire talking to my eldest boy, and had my arm round his waist—there, just as I put my arm round your waist—and I said to the boy, 'It is getting very late and you must go to sleep,' and I pulled him to my breast—like this—and gave him a kiss on his forehead, then on his eyes — there — just as gently as that, yes, just like that. Well, the boy began to cry—"

"Why did he cry? Because you told him to go to bed?"

"Yes," said Dooneea; "but his father came in, and thought I was teasing the child. He abused me and then he beat me."

The woman gazed at her child; and, having a good excuse for weeping in her alleged wrongs, she did not scruple to avail herself of it. From behind the screen which concealed me from her sight, and that of the boy, I, too, shed tears of pity.

I returned to the room, and said, "Dooneea, since you are afraid of your life, do not leave this house until I tell you to do so; but give your infant to the sweeper's wife to take care of. I do not like your children in my house."

How thankful she was! She placed her head upon my feet, and cracked her knuckles over my knees.

Charles Lamb says that the children of the poor are adults from infancy. The same may be said of the children of the rich in India. Dooneea's little boy discussed the conduct of the cruel husband, and sympathised with the ill-used wife, as though he had been called upon to adjudicate the affair in a court of justice. He even went so far as to say, "What a wicked man to beat such a dear looking woman!" and he gave Dooneea the rupee which I had given to him on the day previous when I saw him at the school. With what delight did Dooneea tie up that piece of coin, from the child's hand, in the corner of her garment. It seemed far more precious to her than all the jewels which his dead father had presented to her in days gone by. It was a gift from her own child, who was living, but to her, dead. Dooneea spoke Persian—a language the boy did not understand. His father had taught Dooneea that language in order that their servants might not know the tenor of their discourse. In that language Dooneea now spoke to me, in the boy's presence.

"Is he not very like his father?" she said.

"Very," I replied.

"Will he be as clever?"

"He is too young for any one to judge of that."

"But he will be as generous" (she pointed to the coin), "and he will be as tall, as good-looking, as passionate, as gentle, and as kind."

The boy's boots were muddy. Dooneea observed this, and with her own little hands cleaned them; and smiling, she asked him for a present, in that tone and manner which the poorest menial in Hindostan adopts when addressing the most haughty superior.

The boy blushed, and looked at me.

"Have you nothing to give her?" said I.

"Nothing," said he; "I gave her my rupee."

"Give her that pretty blue ribbon which is round your neck, and I will give you one like it," said I.

He took the ribbon from his neck and gave it to Dooneea.

Dooneea twisted the ribbon in her hair, and began to weep afresh.

"Do not cry, you silly woman," said I; "I will see that your husband does not beat you again."

She understood me, and dried her tears.

Dooneea again spoke to me in Persian. "Sahib," said she, "they do not wash the children properly at that school. Order me to do this."

"Charley, why did you come to me in this state, with your neck unwashed?" I asked the boy.

"We only wash in warm water once a week; on Saturdays," he replied. "This is Thursday."

"But I cannot allow you to dine with me in this state," said I, in Hindostanee. "You must be well washed, my boy. Dooneea, give the child a bath."

"With reluctant steps, the child followed his mother to my bathing-room. I peeped through the purdah; for I began to fear that I should have some trouble in parting the mother from her child, and half repented that I had ever brought them together. While Dooneea was brushing the child's hair, she said, "*Toomara mama kahan hai?*—Where is your mother?"

The boy answered, "I do not know."

I began to cough, to inform Dooneea that I was within hearing, and that I objected to that strain of examination. She ceased immediately.

I had an engagement to ride with a lady on the Mall. My horse was brought to the door; but I was afraid to leave Dooneea alone with the boy, notwithstanding her solemn promise that she would not run off with him. Yet I did not like to hurry that eternal separation on earth which, for the boy's sake, I was determined their separation should be.

I walked up and down my verandah for some time, meditating how I could part them. At last it occurred to me that I would send the boy away to his school by stratagem, and trust to chance how I might best explain to Dooneea that he would not return. I ordered a *syce* (groom) to saddle a little pony that I possessed, and told Dooneea that I wished the boy to take a ride with me, and that while we were absent, she ought to take some food. It stung me to the soul to witness how innocent she was of my intentions; for she seemed pleased that I should show her child so much attention as to be seen in public with him.

As soon as we were out of sight of my house, I took the road for Landour, delivered the boy over to his schoolmaster, told my groom to keep the pony out till after dark, cantered to the Mall, kept my engagement, and returned to my home at about half-past seven o'clock. There was Dooneea waiting for us in the verandah.

"Where is the boy?" she inquired, on finding me return alone.

I gave her no reply; but dismounted and approached her. Taking hold of her wrists, I said, in the gentlest voice, "Dooneea, I have fulfilled my promise. You have seen your child, you have spoken to him, you have kissed him. Enough. He has now gone back to school. You must not see him again, if you really love him."

She trembled in my grasp, looked piteously in my face, gasped several times for breath, as though she longed to speak, and swooned at my feet. I lifted her, carried her into the house, and laid her upon my bed; then sent for servants, and for a doctor, who lived near my bungalow. The doctor came. While he felt her pulse, and placed his hand over her heart, I briefly explained to him what had taken place. He still kept his finger on the vein, and gazed on Dooneea's beautiful face. Blood began to trickle from her nostrils, and from her ears, staining the bed linen and the squalid garments in which she had attired herself. In a few minutes the doctor released his hold of her wrist. "Poor thing!" he ejaculated. "Her troubles are over! She is at rest!"

———Never more on her
Shall sorrow light, or shame.

She was dead.

* * * *

The old woman whom Dooneea called "mother," and the soldier-like looking youth whom she called "brother," decamped with her jewels and moveables, including my dog, "Duke;" but the house near Hurdwar, and the bank shares—property to the value of about four thousand pounds—remain invested in the names of trustees for the benefit of the boy; who will, I trust, make good use of his little fortune, when he becomes of age.

BLACK AND BLUE.

FORTY years ago there went out to India, in the good ship *Globe*, Ensign the Honourable Francis Gay, a younger son of the Right Honourable the Earl of Millflower. The ensign was in his nineteenth year, and was proceeding to join his regiment, which was stationed at Chinsurah.

Lord Millflower, in his heart, hoped that his son would never return: he was so great a disgrace to his family. There was no vice with which this youth was unfamiliar. He had been expelled from no fewer than seven schools. In two instances his offence was theft. His conduct had so preyed upon the mind of Lady Millflower that she lost her reason. At seventeen, he committed several forgeries of his eldest brother's, Lord Larkspeare's name; and he took a similar liberty with the name of his father's steward. But these offences were hushed up. He was also guilty of a deed of violence, for which his life would have been forfeited had the case been tried, instead of compromised; for in those days such a deed of violence was a capital offence. His family were in constant fear lest he should be transported as a felon, or hanged at Newgate. It was, therefore, some satisfaction to them when the Honourable Francis consented to hold a commission and join his regiment in India. Lord Millflower's other sons, four in number, were all steady, well-conducted, and rather dull beings, while Francis was remarkably gifted, as well as remarkably vicious. He had both talent and genius, humour and wit; and, much as he had neglected his education, he was well read and well informed for his time of life. In personal appearance, also, the reprobate had the advantage over his brethren. None of them were even good-looking except Francis, who was really very handsome, well proportioned, and tall. His manners also, always frank, were, when he pleased, dignified and courteous, and his bearing peculiarly graceful. What he wanted was feeling, to regulate his passions. Of feeling, he was in his youth, wholly destitute.

Lord Millflower had taken the precaution of writing to the colonel of the regiment his son was about to join, and of at the same time enclosing a sum of money for the purpose of freeing Francis from any pecuniary difficulty. Colonel Role himself had the misfortune to have a very bad boy, and he, therefore, sympathized deeply with the worthy nobleman, and resolved to do all in his power to reform the Honourable Francis.

After a passage of four months, the *Globe* arrived at Calcutta, and the Honourable Francis Gay proceeded to Chinsurah and joined. For several weeks he conducted himself with (for him) wonderful propriety. It is true, that he drank and played at billiards and cards, and sometimes an oath would escape his lips, but he indulged in no excesses. The officers of the regiment, indeed, thought the ensign a great acquisition, for he was not only a very pleasant but an entertaining companion.

But, by degrees, the Honourable Francis fell off; and ere long, so far from having a friend in the regiment, there was no one who would speak to him. Even the colonel was compelled to forbid him his house. Many, very many acts, unbecoming the character of an officer and a gentleman, had been looked over by his seniors; but it was resolved that, on the very next occasion of his transgressing, the Honourable Ensign should be brought to a court-martial and dismissed the service. This resolve was communicated to the ensign by the colonel, who had become tired of lecturing him.

"The next time you are intoxicated on the parade ground, or the next time you use bad language in the mess-room, or the next time you publicly insult a brother officer, provoking him to quarrel with you, you will forfeit your commission." Being the son of an earl, he was entitled—many colonels think—to every possible chance of redemption. Had he been the son of a commoner, he would, most probably, have been court-martialled and cashiered for the very first offence.

"Thank you, sir," replied the ensign, with a low bow; "I will be more cautious in future."

He kept his word. From this time he did his duty extremely well; and, to all outward appearance, was a reformed character. The officers observing this, generously made advances with a view to resuming their former relations with him. But the Honourable Francis repulsed their advances. The whole regiment had thought proper to cut him; and he now thought proper to cut the whole regiment.

Several months passed, and during that period the ensign applied himself to Hindostanee and Persian. He encouraged the natives to come to his bungalow, to talk with him, and by night and by day pursued his studies. The result was, that he soon conversed with perfect ease and accuracy. He now began to live like a native—a Mahommedan; and, except when he had to attend to his regimental duties, he wore the native costume, and abstained from drink entirely. With truth, he might have said with Conrad,—

> The grape's gay juice my bosom never cheers;
> I'm more than Moslem when the cup appears.

His food was rice, milk, vegetables, and fruit; the bed upon which he slept was hard and mean; such as the natives use. The whole of his European furniture he sold by auction.

His desire—the desire of a doubtfully reformed reprobate—to convert to Christianity a young Mahommedan girl, astonished all those who became acquainted with this desire. The girl was the daughter of a water-carrier (Bheestie). She was not like the natives of India, but more like those of Africa. She was coal black, and had thick lips and wavy hair. She was short for her age—fourteen years—but thickset, with powerful limbs. The girl's father told the servants belonging to other officers of the regiment, and the curious whim of Gay's became a topic of conversation.

Jehan, the bheestie's daughter, was a virtuous girl, and Francis Gay had never approached her with a view to undermining her virtue. It was no easy matter to persuade her to change her religion; but, strange to say, he at length succeeded, and Noor Jehan was baptized as Ellen by a missionary who journeyed to Chinsurah for the purpose of performing the ceremony. The sanity or otherwise of the ensign was now very generally discussed in the regiment, and the prevalent opinion was that he was a lunatic. But the good colonel was a little angry at the surmise. "Surely," he said, "you do not accuse a man of being a maniac because he has converted an infidel."

The regiment was ordered to march to Cawnpore, whither Ellen and her father also proceeded. Cawnpore was then the chief station in the upper provinces of India. Five thousand troops were quartered there. A regiment of dragoons, a regiment of native cavalry, a regiment of British infantry, and two of native infantry. Besides horse and foot there were companies of artillery, and sappers and miners.

Very shortly after the regiment was settled in Cawnpore, the Honourable Francis Gay paid a visit to the chaplain, and intimated a desire to be married. The chaplain of course replied that he should be most happy, and there and then a day and hour was appointed for the performance of the rite ; but, when the reverend gentleman came to hear who was to be the Honourable Ensign's bride—the black daughter of a native water-carrier—he could not help remarking :

"I am sorry, Mr. Gay, that I cannot with sincerity offer you my congratulations."

To which the ensign responded :

"My good sir, I did not ask them." And retired with a bow.

The chaplain drove to the house of Colonel Role, and told him of the interview which had just taken place between himself and ensign the Honourable Francis Gay. The colonel called upon the young man, and entreated him to reflect. "I *have* reflected, sir," was the ensign's reply. The colonel then went to the general, and the general sent for Mr. Gay to attend at his bungalow. Mr. Gay obeyed the summons, and listened with attention and much calmness to a long and violent speech. When it was ended, however, Mr. Gay, with extreme courtesy, and in the quietest of tones, spoke thus :

"General, you had a right to command my attendance here upon any military matter, but not upon any civil matter. However, I waive that, because I believe your intention to be a good one. You, general, have arrived at the years of discretion—perhaps at something beyond those years. You have, at all events, arrived at a time of life when the tumultuous passion of youth can no longer be pleaded in extenuation of certain follies. Now tell me, general, which of us, think you, sins the most, and sets the worst example to the men, European and native, in this station?—I, who wish to marry this good Christian girl; or you, who have in your house——" Mr. Gay then made mention of two very discreditable members of the general's establishment. "This is a question which I shall put to the commander-in-chief, if you abide by your threat to report me to his excellency."

That night the general and Colonel Role held a consultation. The colonel still doubted the ensign's insanity. It had become a fixed idea in the regiment that Gay was insane. The general caught at this, and a committee of doctors was appointed to examine the ensign. They reported that Ensign the Honourable Francis Gay was not only of sound mind, but one of the most intellectual young men in the station; and that he had explained to their entire satisfaction certain conversations which he had frequently held with himself in Chinsurah, at the mess-table.

The wedding-day had been put off in consequence of these proceedings; but the parties now met in the church, which was crowded with officers, including nearly the entire medical staff, who were curious to witness the spectacle. There stood the tall and handsome English aristocrat, and beside him his coal-black bride, dressed in garments of red silk, trimmed with yellow and gold tinsel. The ensign acted as the interpreter, and explained to Ellen in Hindoostanee the vows she was required to take. This made the ceremony a very long one. When it was concluded, the bride got into her palanquin and was carried home. The bridegroom mounted his pony, and rode by her side.

Ellen—now the Honourable Mrs. Gay—was a girl of great natural ability, of an excellent disposition, and was blessed with an excellent temper. She had, moreover, a very sweet voice. After her marriage she was never seen by any European in Cawnpore, except her husband. It was believed that the ensign saved more than two-thirds of his pay, which Ellen, who had an excellent idea of business, used to lend out in small sums to people in the bazaar at the rate of fifty per cent. per mensem. If she lent a rupee (two shillings), she would get back at the end of the month a rupee and eight annas (three shillings) by way of interest.

A year passed away, and a son and heir was born to the Honourable Francis Gay. The child had light blue eyes, exactly like those of his father; but his complexion was quite as black as his mother's. When the child was three months old, it was brought to the church, and publicly christened, Mr. Gay and the pay-sergeant of the company he belonged to being the godfathers, and Ellen the godmother. The names given to the infant were Ernest Augustus George Francis Frederick—such being the names respectively of Lord Millflower's sons. Ernest was the eldest, Augustus the second, George the third, Francis the fourth, and Frederick the fifth and youngest. Not long after the birth of his son, Ensign Gay obtained his promotion to the rank of lieutenant, and received, of course, an increase of pay.

Fever became prevalent, and cholera. Several of the captains and senior lieutenants fell victims; and, in less than three years, Lieutenant Gay got his company (the regiment was now at Meerut), and retired from the army by the sale of his captain's commission. It was supposed that he was worth a great deal of money—a lac of rupees (ten thousand pounds) at the very least. Whither he went no one knew, and no one cared. One of the servants, whom he discharged previous to leaving the station of Meerut, said he believed that his master had gone either to Affghanistan or to Lahore.

Let us now return to Europe. A few years after Captain Gay had sold out of the army, his eldest brother, Lord Larkspeare, was killed while grouse-shooting, by the accidental discharge of his gun; his second brother, Augustus, a captain in the army, was lost in a vessel which was bringing him home from

Canada; his third brother, George, died of small-pox three days after he had taken his father's second title. Of his son Francis's marriage, Lord Millflower had been informed, and also of the birth of the black child, the Honourable Ernest Augustus George Francis Frederick Gay. Colonel Role had deemed it his duty not to withhold these facts, albeit they were disagreeable to communicate to the noble earl. Lord Millflower begged of Colonel Role to institute an inquiry into the fate of his Francis, and the Colonel did so, but without success. No clue to his whereabout could be discovered, nor could any one say what had become of him. Under these circumstances it was taken for granted that he was dead. Another five years passed away, and the Earl of Millflower departed this life. He was, of course, succeeded in his titles and estates by his son Frederick.

Now let us return to Francis. He became a dealer in precious stones, and travelled over the whole of India, under the name of Mustapha Khan, visiting the various native courts. Every tour that he made occupied him three years. Constantly moving about in the sun had tanned his once fair face; and neither from his appearance—for he was dressed as a native—nor from his speech, could the natives themselves detect that he was an European. He gave out that his birthplace was Nepaul, where the natives are sometimes born with blue eyes. He bought and sold, and was apparently very happy in his occupation

His wife and son invariably accompanied him in his travels. He had never written to his family since his arrival in India, and had not received letters from any member thereof. India he loved, England he detested, and would not have taken up his father's title if it had been a dukedom. He never approached the abode of an European, and never saw a newspaper. He was not likely, therefore, to hear of the changes that had taken place at home. In the bazaar at Delhi Captain Gay had a small house, in which were deposited his effects, a few boxes filled with clothes, books, &c., his sword, and the uniform he used formerly to wear. These were under the care of a man-servant, a sweeper. The bulk of his worldly wealth he invariably carried about his person, as many natives of India do.

Ernest Gay was now twelve years of age. He was usually called by his parents Chandee, a word signifying silver. Chandee was clever and cunning, and had a wonderful talent for calculating numbers. In less than a minute, by counting on his fingers, he would tell you the interest due on such sums as three rupees, five annas, and seven pic, for twenty-one days, at forty-one three-fourth per cent. English he had never heard spoken; and as he had never been taught that language, he did not understand a single word of it. Nor could he read or write Hindoostanee, although he spoke it in all its purity and elegance.

There was about to take place a marriage in the

family of the Rajah of Pulbecala. Mustapha Khan (Francis Gay) journeyed from Delhi to the Rajah's court, to exhibit his jewels. He had diamonds, rubies, and emeralds of great price, and some of these he hoped to dispose of to advantage. The Rajah, however, had already provided himself with these matters, and therefore confined his purchases to a large cat's-eye ring, for which he paid Mustapha fifty gold mohurs (eighty pounds). On his way back to Delhi, at a place called Kunda Ka Serai, a band of robbers attacked the jewel-merchant. They hacked him to pieces with their swords, but they spared his wife and the boy. The whole of their treasures were stolen; even the rings from Ellen's ears and fingers, and the gold bangles which Chandee wore upon his arms.

When her senses were restored to her, Ellen, with the assistance of her son, dug a grave in the sand, and buried her butchered husband. The bearers who carried the palanquins ran away as soon as the robbers attacked the party, and were no more seen. Most probably they had some small share of the booty, the value of which the Sirdar estimated at four lacs of rupees (forty thousand pounds). Whatever had been Francis Gay's vices when a youth—and they were great enough in all conscience—he had been a kind and affectionate husband to Ellen, and she most bitterly deplored his loss; violent was the grief of Chandee, who was devotedly fond of his father.

They heaped stones over the grave of the dead

man, to mark the spot where he was laid, and, after their own fashion, offered up prayers for the repose of his soul.

The murder having been committed within the dominions of an independent prince, Ellen knew that her wrongs were not likely to be redressed if she complained; and that the British Government would not interfere, unless she made known that her husband was an Englishman. This she felt would be contrary to the wishes of the dead. Hopeless and helpless, she and her son made the best of their way to Delhi, where, having collected a few debts that were due to them, they established a small shop for the sale of native sweetmeats. They carried on this business for three or four years, when Chandee grew weary of it, and set up in the world as a box-waller, or pedler. His box contained pens, ink, and paper, needles, pins, knives, scissors, soap, eau de Cologne, tooth-brushes, matches, and so forth. His customers were the European officers, who gave him the name of Black and Blue, from the colour of his eyes and skin. A box-waller is always a great cheat—as great a rascal as was Autolycus himself; Black and Blue, if the truth must be told, was not an exception to the rule or race. But no one could grudge him his profits when the cuffs and kicks which were playfully administered to him by the young lieutenants and ensigns are taken into consideration. Black and Blue always took the rough usage of his customers in excellent part; and would generally make some such appeal as this (he had picked up a little English by this time): "Ah, well! I know! You rich white gentlemans—I poor black devil. I pray all day all night that ensign be made leeft'nunt; leeft'nunt, capitaine; capitaine, capitain-meejor; meejor, kunnull; kunnull, meejor-jinneral; and then God bless your father and mother, and brother and sister; and then, for all that pray, I get so much kick and so many bad words. God make us all—black and white; all equal right up above. You want blacking? Here you are. Very good blacking—quite genuine; only one rupee a bottle. I suppose you not got ready money! Very well, I wait till pay-day come. I very poor man. You my master. Khuda Lord Kuren." The meaning of this expression, with which most natives wind up a speech to an European, signifies, May God make you a lord!

When Black and Blue was no more than five years old, he way playing one morning in his father's compound (enclosure—the land around the bungalow), when a pariah dog rushed in and mangled him very severely. The dog was rabid. Captain Gay called in the doctor of a native cavalry regiment, who lived in the next bungalow, who cauterized the wounds. The child was bitten on the arms, legs, and chest, and was under the doctor's treatment for upwards of five weeks. On several occasions when he visited his patient, the doctor saw and conversed with Ellen, who was naturally very anxious touching the child's safety. This doctor was one of the number who witnessed the marriage of Ensign Gay at Cawnpore, and was also present when his offspring was christened.

Shortly after the recovery of the little boy, the doctor had been appointed a presidency surgeon, and had charge of one of the hospitals in Calcutta, where he remained for upwards of twenty years. He was then appointed superintending surgeon of the Meerut division. He had a son at Delhi, a lieutenant in the foot artillery, and occasionally went over (the distance is only forty miles from Meerut) to pay him a visit. On one of these occasions, Black and Blue, who had been sent for, made his appearance with his box, sat down on the carpet cross-legged, and opened out his treasures. There were several young officers in the bungalow, chums of the lieutenant; and, while the bargaining was going on, they began to tease Black and Blue. One removed his turban with the point of a stick; another sprinkled him with his eau de Cologne; a third touched the tip of his great toe (he had left his shoes, out of respect, in the verandah) with the lighted end of a cheroot. Black and Blue howled with pain, whereupon the two roared with laughter. The doctor, who was reading a paper, begged the young men to desist, and, somewhat angrily, expostulated with his son for treating a native so cruelly; for he was touched with poor Black and

Blue's appeal—"God make us all. When fire burns black man, black man feels as much pain as white man. In hell, you rich gentlemans sing out just as much as poor box-waller."

"Black and Blue is used to it, governor," said the lieutenant.

"Stuff, Robert!" said the doctor; "I address myself to you, and not to these gentlemen, when I say that I have no patience with such flippant cruelty."

"Sahib," said Black and Blue, looking up at the doctor, "you are very good gentlemans—very kind man, and very handsome. May God make you a lord; may your throne be perpetual, and may your end be peace; but do not be angry with these gentlemen. They play tricks with Black and Blue; but they are no enemies. If enemies, what for send to buy Black and Blue's property? Sir, you greatly oblige Black and Blue if you smile once more on these gentlemans. Sir, do you want any violent (violet) powder, or one small patent corkiscrew (corkscrew). All men born equal; God's rain wet black man and white man all the same. Devil's fire burn, too, both the same." Here he laughed at the lieutenant. "Take one packet of violent-powder. Every one rupee a packet. Well, then, take two for one, twelve. That can't hurt anybody. Less than prime cost, I give you my solemn word. Handsome sir, don't be angry."

The doctor, his attention attracted by those light

blue eyes, set in that very black skin, stared at Black and Blue for several minutes after he had finished the speech above quoted. He had never before seen such a peculiar expression as that on the face of the box-waller. Suddenly he recollected an instance of black skin and light blue eyes; but in that case the boy was half-European, the child of the Honourable Francis Gay.

Black and Blue had occasion to change his position; and, in doing so, exposed the calves of his legs. On one of them was a scar, quite round, and about the size of a shilling.

"Good God!" exclaimed the doctor, who became both surprised and agitated, and allowed the newspaper to fall from his hand.

"What is the matter, governor?" asked the lieutenant.

"Nothing—nothing!" said the doctor, still staring at Black and Blue, whose countenance was no longer strange to him. "How did you come by that mark?" he at length asked, pointing to the scar.

"I don't know, Sahib."

"But did not your parents ever tell you?"

"No, Sahib. Parents used to say that it come of itself."

This was no doubt true.

"Have you another mark like that on your right arm—just here?"

The doctor placed his finger on the sleeve of the man's dress.

"Yes. But bigger mark that one. How you know that, Sahib?" He pulled up his sleeve and exhibited a scar the size of half-a-crown.

"And another here—on your hip—and another here, on your ribs?"

"Yes. All them marks got, sir. How you know that, Sahib?"

The doctor was quite satisfied that Black and Blue was no other than his little patient of former years, and consequently the heir to the Earldom of Millflower. Could it be possible, he thought, that Captain Gay eventually abandoned his black wife and child! If not, how came it that the boy (now a man of two or three and twenty) should be a miserable pedler, living in the Bazaar at Delhi? When Black and Blue had sold all that the young officers wanted to buy—when no amount of coaxing and flattering would induce them to take anything more—he was about to take his departure; but the doctor desired him to stay, and intimated to his son that he wished to have some conversation in private with Black and Blue.

"Where is your father?" the doctor asked.

"He dead, Sahib."

"When did he die?"

"Long time ago—ten or twelve year ago."

"Where did he die?"

"Mans—robber mans—kill him with sword."

"And your mother?"

Black and Blue told the doctor the whole of their history since the death of Captain Gay, and his statements were substantially true. Black and Blue, however, declared most positively that his father was a native, and no European.

"Do you think," the doctor inquired, "that your mother would see me, if I went down to her home?"

"O yes—why not? Come along, Sahib. I will show where she live. You call for palanquin and get on. I run alongside."

The doctor's curiosity was very strong, and he could not resist the desire to satisfy it at once. He accepted Black and Blue's invitation, and went to the house occupied by Ellen. Habited as a native, she was sitting on a coarse mat, smoking, and at the same time mending an old garment of her son's.

The doctor recognised Ellen immediately, albeit she was now aged. But at first she did not recognise him. He was altered very much in appearance. His hair and whiskers had become very grey, and he no longer wore a moustache.

Ellen parried all the questions that were put to her, and affected to be as much surprised by them as by the doctor's visit. The statement of her son she supported, that her husband was a native of India.

"O, but surely," said the doctor, "this was the boy whom I attended at Meerut, many years ago, when you and your Sahib were living near the Begum's bridge?"

The poor woman looked at him for a moment, then repeated his name, and burst into tears. Her recollections crowded before her too thickly to admit of her dissembling any further with her visitor; and she admitted that she was the widow of Captain Gay, of her Majesty's — Regiment of Foot.

The doctor was under no promise to Ellen to keep his discovery secret; and feeling at liberty to speak of it, did so publicly as well as in private. The peerages were looked into, and Black and Blue's pedigree examined. There were the names of all the late lord's sons, and sure enough there was Francis's name above that of Frederick's, the present earl; opposite to the name of Francis were the letters signifying, "died unmarried." Black and Blue of course became an object of great curiosity. His right to a title did not induce him to alter his prices in any way, and hence he was kicked and cuffed, and abused as much as ever, by the young lieutenants and ensigns, who, by-the-bye, always addressed him as "my lord," and "your lordship."

"Pomatum, my lord! Pomatum, did you say? Yes! But let me smell it. O! your lordship calls this pomatum! I call it hog's lard washed in sandal-wood water. How much? One rupee! O, you villanous peer of the realm! are you not ashamed of yourself?"

Another would thus address him:

"Look here, Lord Black and Blue. Why don't you go home and upset your uncle? Turn him out of his title and estates—eh? You would be sure to marry some beautiful girl."

To this Black and Blue would respond:

"What do I want with title and beautiful gal! This is my home, and I got good business, good many friends, and two or three very beautiful gal."

"Where, Black and Blue?"

"Ah! that is my business."

"Well, what will you sell your title for?"

"Well, what you offer?"

"One hundred rupees" (10*l.*)

Say one hundred and twenty-five."

"No."

"Well, take it—there. Give money, and I give receipt. You write it out; I sign it. Sold one title to Ensign Matheson for a hundred rupees."

"But there are two titles, you ass; one an earldom, and the other a viscounty."

"Well, you take the two; give two hundred rupees for both."

"No. The one I have already bought is the biggest and of the best quality; the other is the small one, and of inferior quality."

"Well, I make reduction in price; take one with the other, and give me one hundred and seventy-five rupees. That can't hurt anybody that wants a title."

Would any of these lads, who had nothing in the

world beyond their pay, have consented to an union between Black and Blue and one of their sisters, after he had come into what were his rights? No! Would the poorest and most unprincipled officers—civil and military—in the whole of India? No! Would any European girl of respectability who had lived in India, to say nothing of the daughters of gentlemen and ladies, have wedded the black heir to the title and estates of the Earl of Millflower? No. Not in India could his sable lordship have found a virtuous white woman to accept his hand!

In due course the story of Black and Blue's birth crept into the columns of one of the Calcutta newspapers, and ere long an attorney of the Supreme Court paid a visit to the imperial city, and had an interview with Black and Blue. He proposed to the box-waller to take him to England, and establish his claim to the estates, which he truthfully represented as worth more than half a million sterling—fifty lacs of rupees. He, the attorney, would pay all expenses of the suit, and in the event of success, which was certain, would receive only five per cent. or fifty thousand pounds, leaving Black and Blue a balance of forty-five lacs.

Black and Blue, who loved and adored money, on hearing such a sum spoken of, rolled his blue eyes and red tongue, and almost fainted. But then, to cross the black water!—as the natives call the ocean—that thought made him shudder and shake his head.

The attorney represented to him that he should live in great comfort during the voyage; that the best cabin in the ship should be taken for him; that he should have servants about him; and drawing forth a number of prints of English beauties, he exhibited them to the gaze of Black and Blue.

Black and Blue said he would consult his European friends. He did so, and many of those friends dissuaded him from going to England. Not that they had any doubt as to the issue of his claim, if it should be disputed; but upon the reasonable ground that he was very happy where he was. Others advised him to go by all means, and take up his title and the wealth that pertained to it. His mother entreated him not to leave her. But in the end the voice of the attorney prevailed, and Black and Blue declared himself ready to accompany him.

Ten thousand rupees (one thousand pounds) were given to Ellen for her support during the temporary absence of her son, who was to return as soon as he had realized his forty-five lacs (four hundred and fifty thousand pounds). It was said that a mercantile firm in Calcutta, in which an illustrious native gentleman was a partner, advanced the means required for the purpose of establishing the black man's right to the earldom.

The attorney possessed himself of the proofs. He had the papers of the Honourable Francis Gay, amongst which were letters from the late Lord Millflower to his eldest brother, Lord Larkspeare. He also, in the presence of credible witnesses, received from the hands of Ellen the dead man's uniform; secondly, he had the deposition on oath of the superintending surgeon, and of several other officers who were cognizant of every particular. Many gave these depositions with reluctance, but felt bound to speak the truth when interrogated. In a word, the attorney got his case up remarkably well.

Black and Blue and the attorney left Calcutta in one of the large passenger ships, and in the month of April landed at Gravesend, whence they journeyed to London. Here Black and Blue was prevailed upon to wear Christian clothes. In his snow-white muslin dress, his pink turban, and his red slippers covered with gold embroidery, Black and Blue had looked an aristocratic native, notwithstanding he was so very black. [Colour is no criterion of high caste or rank in India. The late Maharajah Rooder Singh, of Darbungah, whose family—to borrow a phrase from "Burke's Peerage"—is one of stupendous antiquity, had the complexion of an African; while his younger brother, Basdeo, who now sits on the throne, is far fairer than his Highness the Maharajah Duleep Singh.] But in his black trousers, black waistcoat, black surtout coat, white neckcloth, black beaver hat, and Wellington boots, poor Black and Blue looked truly hideous; while his slouching Indian gait would have led most people to conclude that he was intoxicated. Poor Black and Blue had never tasted anything stronger than water in the whole course of his life.

The attorney had an interview with Frederick Earl of Millflower. He wrote to the firm in Calcutta to that effect, and he further stated that the Earl had set him at defiance, and that he was about to institute a suit in the proper court.

This was the last that was ever heard in India of Black and Blue, or of the attorney. Inquiries were instituted, but with no avail. There were many contures; the one most generally entertained was, that poor Black and Blue and his undoubted claim were disposed of by the attorney for a sum which satisfied him, and that Black and Blue was secrctly led into indulgences in some foreign country and died of their effects. But his mother, who is still living, will not believe that he is dead, and feels convinced that some day or other he will turn up and be restored to her.

"What on earth became of that black earl?" is a question very often put by many who were acquainted with his strange history.

THE RANEE OF JHANSI.

ABOUT a month after the order had gone forth for the annexation of the little province of Jhansi (in 1854), and previous to a wing of the 13th Native Infantry occupying the country, I received a letter in Persian, written upon "gold paper," from the Ranee, begging me to pay her a visit. The letter was brought to me by two natives of rank. One had been the financial minister of the late Rajah. The other was the head vakeel (attorney) of the Ranee.

The revenues of Jhansi were some six lacs (60,000*l.*) a year, and after disbursing the expenses of government, and paying the troops in the late Rajah's service, the balance was some two lacs and a half (25,000*l.*) profit. The "troops" were not numerous, under 1000 in all, and they were chiefly horsemen. The arrangement, when the country was annexed, was simply this: that the Ranee should receive a pension of 6000*l.* a year, to be paid monthly.

The Ranee's object in asking me to visit her at Jhansi was to consult me as to the possibility of getting the order for annexation annulled, or reversed. I should mention that the Ranee had applied to me at the instance of a gentleman of the Civil Service, who had once been the Resident, or Governor-General's agent, at a native court in the upper provinces; a gentleman who, in common with many other officials of rank in India, regarded the annexation of Jhansi—"a trumpery state after all"—not only as impolitic, but unjust and without excuse. The facts were briefly these:—The late Rajah had no issue by his only wife (the woman who caused our countrymen and countrywomen and children to be put to death in the fort, and who, according to late advices, has been killed), and some weeks previous to his death, being "sound of mind, though infirm in body," he publicly adopted an heir, and gave notice to the Government of having done so through the proper channel—namely, the Governor-General's representative then stationed at Jhansi. In short, all the forms required by the Government to prevent fraud in such cases, had been complied with. The child was taken into the Rajah's lap, in the presence of his assembled people, and in the presence of the Governor-General's representative, and he, moreover, signed a document, duly attested, reciting his act and deed. The Rajah was a Brahmin; the adopted boy was a near relative of his.

The Jhansi Rajah had been particularly faithful to the British Government, and Lord William Bentinck had presented the brother of the late Rajah with a British ensign, and a letter giving him the title of "Rajah," and assuring him that that title, and the independence attached to it, would be guaranteed by the British Government to him, the Rajah, and his heirs and *successors* (by adoption). That that treaty (for such it purported to be) of Lord William Bentinck was violated, without the slightest shadow of a pretence, there cannot be any sort of doubt. In the time of the Peishwah, the late Rajah of Jhansi was simply a large zemindar (landholder), and had he remained untitled, there can be no question that his last wishes, so far as the disposition of his property was concerned, would have been attended to. It was the acceptance of the "Rajahship" which led to the confiscation of his estates, and the exchange of 6000*l*. a year for 25,000*l*. a year. Strange as that assertion may seem to the reader, it is nevertheless true.

I was at Agra when I received the Ranee's letter, and Agra is two days' journey. Even as I travelled from Jhansi, I sympathized with the woman. The boy whom the Rajah had adopted was only six years old, and during his minority, that is to say, until he had attained his eighteenth year, the Ranee—so the Rajah willed—was to have been the Regent, and the boy's guardian; and it is no small matter for a woman—a native woman of rank, too—to give up such a position and become a pensioner, even on 6000*l*. a year. Let me detail the particulars of my journey to the residence of the Ranee of Jhansi. I got into my palanquin at dusk, and on the following morning, at daylight, arrived at Gwalior. The Rajah of Jhansi had a small house about a mile and a half from the cantonment, which was used as a halting-place, and thither I was taken by the minister and the vakeel who accompanied me. At ten o'clock, after I had breakfasted and smoked my hookah, it was proposed that we "go on at once." The day was very warm, but the Ranee had sent a large and comfortable palanquin carriage; in short, it was more like a small room than a carriage, fitted up as it was with every convenience, including even a punkah, which was pulled from the outside by a servant, who sat upon a foot-board. In the carriage, beside myself and the minister and vakeel, was a khansamah, or butler, who, with the apparatus between his knees, kept on cooling water, and wine, and beer, in order that, whenever I felt thirsty, I might be supplied at a moment's notice. This enormous carriage was drawn by a pair of horses of immense strength and swiftness. Each stood about seventeen hands high. The late Rajah had imported them from France at a cost of 1500*l.* The road was rather rough in many places, but, on the average, we got over it at the rate of about nine miles an hour. At about two o'clock in the day we entered the Jhansi territory, having changed horses twice, and we had now some nine miles to drive. Hitherto we had been escorted only by four sowars (horsemen), but now our escort amounted to about fifty, each horseman carrying an immense spear, and dressed much in the same way as the Irregular Cavalry in the pay of the East India Company. And along the road, at intervals of a few hundred yards, were horsemen drawn up, and as we passed, they joined the cavalcade; so that by the time we came in sight of the fortress—if those old weak walls, surmounted by some nine pieces of old ordnance of inferior calibre, deserved the name—the whole strength of the Jhansi cavalry was in attendance. The carriage was driven to a place called "the Rajah's garden," where I alighted, and was conducted by the financial minister and the vakeel and other servants of state, to a large tent, which was pitched beneath a clump of gigantic mango trees. The tent, which was that in which the late Rajah used to receive the civil and military officers of the British Government, was elegantly fitted up, and carpeted; and at least a dozen domestic servants were ready to do my bidding. I must not omit to mention that the companions of my journey—the minister and the vakeel—were both men of good ability and pleasing manners. They were, moreover, men of learning, so that my time upon the road had been beguiled very agreeably.

The Ranee had consulted one of the many Brahmins who were supported by her as to the most propitious hour for me to come to the purdah behind which she sat; and the Brahmins had told her that it must be between the setting of the sun and the rising of the moon, which was then near her full; in other words, between half-past five and half-past six o'clock.

This important matter having been communicated to me, I expressed myself perfectly satisfied with the time of the appointment, and ordered dinner accordingly. This done, the financial minister, after betraying some embarrassment, intimated that he wished to speak to me on a rather delicate subject, and that, with my permission, he would order all the menial servants in attendance on me, including my own sirdar-bearer (valet), to leave the tent and stand at a distance. I complied, of course, and presently found myself alone with only the "officials" (eight or nine in number) of the little native state of Jhansi. What the finance minister wished to ask me was this—Would I consent to leave my shoes at the door when I entered the Ranee's apartment? I inquired if the Governor-General's agent did so. He replied that the Governor-General's agent had never had an interview with the Ranee; and that the late Rajah had never received any European gentleman in the private apartments of the palace, but in a room set apart for the purpose, or in the tent in which we were conversing. I was in some difficulty, and scarcely knew what to say, for I had a few years previously declined to be presented to the King of Delhi, who insisted on Europeans taking off their shoes when they entered his presence. The idea was repugnant to my mind, and I said as much to the minister of the late Rajah of Jhansi; and I asked him whether he would attend a levée at the palace of the Queen of England, if informed that he must enter her Majesty's presence with his head uncovered, as did all her subjects, from the lowest to the highest. To this question he would not give me a direct answer, but remarked, " You may wear your hat, Sahib ; the Ranee will not mind that. On the contrary, she will regard it as an additional mark of respect towards her." Now this was what I did not want. My desire was, that she should consider the wearing of my hat, supposing I consented to take off my shoes, as a species of compromise on her part as well as on my part. But I was so amused with this bargaining, as it were, that I consented ; giving them distinctly to understand, however, that it was to be considered not as a compliment to her rank and dignity, but to her sex, and her sex alone. That great point settled, I partook of a very sumptuous repast that was prepared for me, and awaited patiently the setting of the sun or the rising of the moon, determined, however, that I would wear my hat—a black "wide-awake," covered with a white turban.

The hour came, and the white elephant (an Albino, one of the very few in all India), bearing on his immense back a silver houdah, trimmed with red velvet, was brought to the tent. I ascended the steps, which were also covered with red velvet, and took my place. The mahoot, or elephant-driver, was attired in the most gorgeous manner. The ministers of state, mounted on white Arabs, rode on either side of the elephant ; the Jhansi cavalry lining the road to the palace, and thus forming an avenue. The palace was about half a mile distant from my encampment ground.

Ere long we arrived at the gates, at which the attendants on foot began to knock violently. A wicket was opened, and closed hastily. Information was then sent to the Ranee; and, after a delay of about ten minutes, the "hookum" (order) came to open the gates. I entered on the elephant, and alighted in a court-yard. The evening was very warm, and I fancied that I should be suffocated by the crowd of natives (retainers) who flocked around me. Observing my discomfiture, the minister imperiously commanded them to "stand back!" After another brief delay, I was asked to ascend a very narrow stone staircase, and on the landing was met by a native gentleman, who was some relative to the Ranee. He showed me first into one room and then into another. These rooms (six or seven), like all rooms of the kind, were unfurnished, save and except that the floors were carpeted; but from the ceiling punkahs and chandeliers were suspended, and on the walls were native pictures of Hindoo gods and goddesses, with here and there a large mirror. At length I was led to the door of a room, at which the native gentleman knocked. A female voice from within inquired, "Who is there?"

"Sahib," was the reply. After another brief delay, the door was opened by some unseen hand, and the native gentleman asked me to enter, informing me, at the same time, that he was about to leave me. A brief delay now occurred upon my part. It was with great difficulty that I could bring myself to take off my shoes. At length, however, I accomplished it, and entered the apartment in "stocking feet." In the centre of the room, which was richly carpeted, was an arm-chair of European manufacture, and around it were strewn garlands of flowers (Jhansi is famous for its beautiful and sweet-smelling flowers). At the end of the room was a purdah or curtain, and behind it people were talking. I sat myself down in the arm-chair, and instinctively took off my hat; but recollecting my resolve, I replaced it, and rather firmly—pulling it well down, so as completely to conceal my forehead. It was a foolish resolve, perhaps, on my part, for the hat kept the breeze of the punkah from cooling my temples.

I could hear female voices prevailing upon a child to "go to the Sahib," and could hear the child objecting to do so. Eventually, he was "launched" into the room; and upon my speaking kindly to the child, he approached me—but very timidly. His dress and the jewels on his person, satisfied me that the child was the adopted son of the late Rajah, and the rejected heir to the little throne of Jhansi. He was rather a pretty child, but very short for his years, and broad-shouldered—like most of the Mahratta children that I have seen.

Whilst I was speaking to the child, a shrill and discordant voice issued from behind the purdah, and I was informed that the boy was the Maharajah, who had just been despoiled of his rights by the Governor-General of India. I fancied that the voice was that of some very old woman—some slave or enthusiastic retainer, perhaps; but the child having imagined that he was spoken to, replied, "Maharanee!" and thus I was told the error of my conclusion.

And now the Ranee, having invited me to come closer to the purdah, began to pour forth her grievances; and, whenever she paused, the women by whom she was surrounded, set up a sort of chorus—a series of melancholy ejaculations—such as "Woe is me!" "What oppression!" It reminded me somewhat of a scene in a Greek tragedy—comical as was the situation.

I had heard from the vakeel that the Ranee was a very handsome woman, of about six or seven and twenty years of age, and I was very curious indeed to get a glimpse of her; and whether it was by accident, or by design on the Ranee's part, I know not, my curiosity was gratified. The curtain was drawn aside by the little boy, and I had a good view of the lady. It was only for a moment, it is true; still I saw her sufficiently to be able to describe her. She was a woman of about the middle size—rather stout, but not too stout. Her face must have been very handsome when she was younger, and even now it had many charms—though, according to my idea of beauty, it was too round. The expression also was very good, and very intelligent. The eyes were particularly fine, and the nose very delicately shaped. She was not very fair, though she was far from black. She had no ornaments, strange to say, upon her person, except a pair of gold ear-rings. Her dress was a plain white muslin, so fine in texture, and drawn about her in such a way, and so tightly, that the outline of her figure was plainly discernible—and a remarkably fine figure she had. What spoilt her was her voice, which was something between a whine and a croak. When the purdah was drawn aside, she was, or affected to be, very much annoyed; but presently she laughed, and good-humouredly expressed a hope that a sight of her had not lessened my sympathy with her sufferings nor prejudiced her cause.

"On the contrary," I replied, "if the Governor-General could only be as fortunate as I have been, and for even so brief a while, I feel quite sure that he would at once give Jhansi back again to be ruled over by its beautiful Queen."

She repaid this compliment, and the next ten minutes were devoted to an interchange of such matters. I told her that the whole world resounded with the praises of her beauty and the greatness of her intellect; and she told me that there was not a corner of the earth in which prayers for my welfare remained unsaid.

We then returned to the point—her "case." I informed her that the Governor-General had no power to restore the country, and recognise the claim of the adopted son, without a reference to England, and that the most prudent course for her to adopt would be to petition the throne, and meanwhile draw the pension of 6000*l.* a year, under protest that it was not to prejudice the right of the adopted son. At first she refused to do this, and rather energetically exclaimed: "Mera Jhansi nahin dengee" (I will not give up my Jhansi). I then pointed out to her, as delicately as possible, how futile would be any opposition; and told her, what was the truth, that a wing of a native regiment and some artillery were within three marches of the palace; and I further impressed upon her that the slightest opposition to its advance would destroy her every hope, and, in short, jeopardize her liberty. I did this because she gave me to understand—and so did her attorney (and my impression is that they spoke the truth)—that the *people* of Jhansi did not wish to be handed over to the East India Company's rule.

It was past two o'clock that night before I left the palace; and ere I took my departure, I had talked the lady into my way of thinking, except that she would not consent to draw any pension from the British Government.

On the following day I returned to Gwalior, *en route* to Agra. The Ranee presented me with an elephant, a camel, an Arab, a pair of greyhounds of great swiftness, a quantity of silks and stuffs (the production of Jhansi), and a pair of Indian shawls. I accepted these things with great reluctance, but the financial minister entreated me to take them, insomuch as it would wound the Ranee's feelings if I refused. The Ranee also presented me with a portrait of herself, taken by a native, a Hindoo.

The state of Jhansi was not restored to the rule of the Ranee, and we know that she afterwards rivalled that fiend Nena Sahib, whose "grievance" was identical with her own. The Government would not recognise Nena Sahib as the adopted son and heir of the Peishwah; the Ranee of Jhansi sought to be recognised as the Regent during the minority of the late Rajah's adopted son and heir.

TIRHOOT, LUCKNOW, BHITOOR, ETC.

It is some years since I first landed in Calcutta. I was in no way connected with the Government, and was consequently an "interloper" or "adventurer." These were the terms applied by certain officials to European merchants, indigo-planters, shopkeepers, artisans, barristers, attorneys, and others.

It was not long before I made up my mind to become a wanderer in the East. I had no occupation, was my own master, and had a large tract of country to roam about in. My first step was to acquire a knowledge of Hindostanee and of Persian. By dint of hard study, at the end of six months I found myself capable, not only of holding a conversation, but of arguing a point in either of these languages: and with a light heart I took my departure from the City of Palaces, and proceeded to Monghyr, on the Ganges.

The chief civilian of that district had invited me to spend a month with him. Every day I accompanied my friend to his court, and thereby got some insight into the administration of justice in India, both civil and criminal. Here, too, I first made acquaintance with Thugs. Several most notorious characters of that tribe were at Monghyr—not imprisoned, but permitted to move about. They had been pardoned on condition that they would become informers, and, to a certain extent, detectives, in the suppression of Thuggee in the British dominions. It was a curious feeling to be in conversation with men who had each committed his ninety or a hundred murders—to see the fingers that had strangled so many victims—to watch the process, for they were good-natured enough to act it. There was the unsuspecting traveller with his bundle; the decoy Thug, who engaged him in conversation; the two men, who, at the given signal, were to seize; the executioner, standing behind with the handkerchief, ready to strangle the victim. They even went through the operation of searching the "deceased," upon whom they found nothing in this case; but they assured me this frequently happened in reality. The reader is of course aware that it is a part of the Thug's religion not to rob a live body. The crime of murder must precede that of theft. The play—the tragedy—over (to these domesticated demons it was a mere farce), they laughed at the solemn expression which, I doubt not, was stamped upon my features.

These Thugs were permitted to have their families at Monghyr; and one morning when I strolled down to their camp, an old man made five children, the eldest boy not more than eight years old, go through the business of strangling and robbing a victim. In one respect these urchins outdid their progenitors in the acting. They not only went through the ceremony of searching the dead body, but, that done, they dragged it by the legs to a well, and, in dumb show, threw it down, and then uttered a prayer to Heaven.

"Was that good?" said one of the children, running up to me for applause and a reward. I scarcely knew what to reply. Before I had time to give any answer, the child's father said, "No; it was not good. You used the handkerchief before the signal was given. Go through it again, and remember, this time, that you must have patience." The boys began again, much in the same spirit that an actor and actress would go through the strangling scene in "Othello," to please a fastidious manager.

Approaching a very interesting-looking woman, of about two-and-twenty years of age, I said to her, "What do you think of this?"

She replied in a proverb: "The mango always falls beneath the shade of the parent tree."

"But the crime?" said I. "What think you of that?"

She looked up with as lovely a pair of eyes as ever saw the light, smiled, and responded:

"Heaven will hold us all, Sahib!"

I was about to reason with her, but her husband, with an expression of pride, interfered, and informed me that she had taken eighteen lives.

"Twenty-one!" she exclaimed.

"Eighteen only!" said he.

"Twenty-one!" she persisted, and ran them over, counting on her fingers the places and the dates when the murders were committed. Her husband then admitted that she was in the right, and, turning to me, remarked:

"She is a very clever woman, Sahib."

"Were your victims men or women?" I said to her.

"All women," she answered me. "Some old and some young."

I was tempted to ask her to show me how it was done; and after considerable coaxing she complied with my wishes. To my surprise she was the only actor in the scene, except the victim, with whom she went through the process of strangling with a piece of cord. The victim, another Thuggess, was supposed to be sleeping when the operation was performed, and I could not help admiring—horrible as the sight was—the accuracy with which she performed the throes and agony of death. To borrow an idea from Junius, "None but those who had frequently witnessed such awful moments could describe them so well."

At the house of my Monghyr friend I met a French gentleman, an indigo-planter of Tirhoot, in Behar. He invited me to pay him a visit, and to accompany him in his boat. He was about to sail on the following day. I say "sail," for at that time (the month of August), the country was inundated, and it would have been impossible to travel by land. I accepted the invitation, and we sailed from Monghyr to Hajeepore without going near the Ganges for several days.

Monsieur Bardon, the French planter, was one of the most accomplished and agreeable men I had ever met, and in truth one of the greatest characters. The hospitality of the Tirhoot planters is proverbial in India, and I believe I might have lived in that Garden of the East, as it is called, from that day to this, as a welcome guest of the various planters, if I had chosen still to be their guest. As it was, I was eight months in the district, and then had very great difficulty in getting away. A now celebrated officer, at that time commanding the Irregular Cavalry at Segowlie, induced me to visit him; and after leaving his abode, I went to the Bettiah Rajah, who initiated me into the mysteries of tiger-shooting. It was in the dominions of this small chief that my hands and face were so browned that I became far less fair than many natives of the country. Before leaving Tirhoot, however, I paid a visit to Rooder Singh, the Rajah of Durbungah, the richest native perhaps in all India. He has two hundred thousand pounds a year net revenue; and in a tank in his palace there is lying, in gold and silver, upwards of a million and a half sterling. Chutter Singh, the father of the Rajah of Durbungah, was a firm friend of the British Government during the Nepal war. He raised a regiment of horse and provisioned it. . When asked by the authorities for his bill, he replied that the Government owed him nothing.

After leaving the Bettiah Rajah, I proceeded to Lucknow, where I improved myself greatly in Hindostanee. In this city, and in Delhi, the purest is spoken. At Lucknow I made the acquaintance of Ally Nucky Khan (the prime minister of the King of Oude, who is now imprisoned in Fort William), of Wuzy Ally Khan (a celebrity of Oude, who is since dead), and of Rugburdiall, the eldest son of the late Shah Beharee Lall, one of the richest bankers in India. Shah Beharee Lall is said to have died worth seven millions in cash; but I have reason to believe that three millions sterling was the utmost that he died possessed of. Rugburdiall held the office of treasurer to the King of Oude. Ally Nucky Khan gave me the idea of a man of small mental capacity, but of immense cunning and inordinate vanity. The late Mr. Beechy, the King of Oude's portrait-painter, must have taken at least a score of likenesses of Ally Nucky, who, to say the truth, is a remarkably good-looking personage. Wuzy Ally Khan was a tall and handsome man of about five-and-forty. His manners were refined, his address charming, and his bearing altogether that of a well-bred gentleman. Of his talents there could be no question; and he was, moreover, a learned and well-informed man. There could be no doubt that Wuzy Ally Khan, in point of fact, ruled the kingdom. The conversational powers of this man were immense, and he was both witty and humorous. A more agreeable companion it would be difficult to meet with in any country. When I first made his acquaintance, he was in great favour with the then resident at the court of Oude; but, on the appointment of Colonel Sleeman, he fell into disrepute with the British officials and continued so up to the time of his death, which occurred about two years ago. I was five months in Oude, and, during that period, spoke nothing but Hindostanee or Persian. I made a point of avoiding my own countrymen, and of associating only with the natives of India.

Previous to leaving Lucknow, a letter was despatched to Nena Sahib, informing him that a gentleman of distinction, a most intimate friend of the Governor-General, and related by birth or marriage to every member of the council in Calcutta, as well as a constant guest of the Queen of England, was travelling through Hindostan in disguise, and would most probably, by his presence, illumine the abode of Maharajah Bahadoor, and it was hoped that every respect would be paid to the dignity of the Sahib's exalted position, &c. &c. When the draft of this epistle was read aloud by the moonshee, who had written it from dictation, I expostulated, on the ground that the contents were not in accordance with the truth. My scruples, however, were eventually overcome, and I took leave of my Lucknow friends, after being provided with all that I should require on my journey (of about forty-five miles), and an escort of fifteen sowars (horsemen); for the road, at that time, between Lucknow and Cawnpore, was infested by robbers. About a mile from Bhitoor my palkee was placed upon the ground. I was asleep, but awoke, and inquired, "Kia hua?" (What is the matter?)

I was informed by the bearers of my palkee that the Maharajah Peishwa Bahadoor had sent out an escort in honour of my approach, and presently there appeared at the door of my palkee a soldier-like looking Hindoo, who made me a very respectful salaam. The escort consisted of eight foot-soldiers with drawn swords, and four sowars. The former, running by the side of my palkee, encouraged the bearers to make haste; while the latter caused their horses to curvet and prance, and thus kick up a frightful dust. At the abode of the Maharajah Bahadoor, I was met by several of his musahibs (courtiers), who were exceedingly polite, and conducted me to a suite of apartments which had apparently been made ready for my reception; and so far as servants were concerned, I was literally surrounded. A sirdar bearer (personal attendant, or Indian valet) took charge of my two boxes which contained my wearing apparel. A khansamah (butler), followed by three khidmutghars (table servants), asked me if I would take some iced water, and in the same breath informed me that every kind of European drink was at hand. Brandy, gin, champagne, claret, sherry, port, beer cherry-brandy, and soda-water. And what would I take for dinner? Whatever the Sahib's heart might desire, was in readiness. Turkey? goose? duck? fowl? beefsteak? mutton-chop? ham and eggs? And here the khansamah (a venerable Mussulman) informed me, sotto voce, that the Maharajah was constantly in the habit of entertaining European gentlemen; and that, although his highness was himself a strict Hindoo, he had no kind of prejudice, so that if I preferred beef to any other kind of meat, I had only to give the order. I assured the khansamah that since my arrival in India, I had never tasted beef, or hog's flesh, and that if he would have prepared for me, as speedily as possible, some rice and vegetables, I should be quite satisfied. With a profound salaam the khansamah took his departure, followed by the khidmutghars. The sirdar bearers, and four other men, then approached me reverentially, and begged to conduct me to my sleeping apartment and the bathing-rooms.

There is something peculiarly quaint about the arrangement of European furniture in the house of a native gentleman. In the house of an European, the servants are, of course, taught how to arrange tables, chairs, and beds, according to European ideas; but it is otherwise with the servants of a rajah, or native gentleman. The consequence is that in the dining, or drawing-room, you will find a wash-hand stand, and a chest of drawers, and a toilet-table, while in the bed-room you will, perhaps, discover an old piano, an organ, a card-table, or cheffonier. The furniture has, for the most part, been purchased at various sales, and has belonged to officers of all grades, civil and military. There are the tent-table and the camp-stool of the dead ensign, in the same room with the marble-topped table and crimson damask covered easy chair of some luxurious judge. On the mantel-piece you will find a costly clock of the most elegant design and workmanship, and on each side of it, a pair of japan candlesticks, not worth half-a-crown. In this way are arranged the pictures on the walls. Immediately underneath a proof print of Landseer's "Bolton Abbey," or "Hawking," you will observe a sixpenny coloured print of the Duke of Wellington or Napoleon Bonaparte. The pictures, also, have been bought indiscriminately at various sales, and have been as indiscriminately suspended on the walls. There are the print-shop ballet girls intermingled with engravings of the most serious character. Fores's sporting collection with the most classical subjects. Footstools, musical-boxes, and elegantly bound books, writing-desks, work-boxes, plated dishes, sugar-basins, and teapots, are arranged in the most grotesque fashion imaginable. Upon an elegant mahogany sideboard you will find decanters and glasses of every description and quality. Upon another sideboard, in the drawing-room, you will find a variety of dinner-services, and earthen fragments thereof, all mixed.

There was but one set of rooms at Bhitoor for the reception of "Sahib logue," and this was the set that I then occupied.

I had scarcely made myself comfortable, when the khansamah informed me that dinner was on table. This was welcome intelligence, for I had not tasted food since morning, and it was half-past five P.M. I sat down to a table twenty feet long (it had originally been the mess table of a cavalry regiment), which was covered with a damask table-cloth of European manufacture, but instead of a dinner-napkin there was a bed-room towel. The soup—for he had everything ready—was served up in a trifle-dish which had formed part of a dessert service belonging to the 9th Lancers—at all events, the arms of that regiment were upon it; but the plate into which I ladled it with a broken tea-cup, was of the old willow pattern. The pilao which followed the soup, was served upon a huge plated dish, but the plate from which I ate it, was of the very commonest description. The knife was a bone-handled affair; the spoon and the fork were of silver, and of Calcutta make. The plated side-dishes, containing vegetables, were odd ones; one was round, the other oval. The pudding was brought in upon a soup-plate of blue and gold pattern, and the cheese was placed before me on a glass dish belonging to a dessert service. The cool claret I drank out of a richly cut champagne glass, and the beer out of an American tumbler, of the very worst quality.

I had not yet seen "the Maharajah." It was not until past eight that a moonshee came and inquired if I would have an interview with his highness. I replied that it would give me great joy, and was forthwith conducted through numerous narrow and gloomy passages to an apartment at the corner of the building. Here sat the Maharajah on a Turkey carpet, and reclining slightly on a huge bolster. In front of him were his hookah, a sword, and several nosegays. His highness rose, came forward, took my hand, led me to the carpet, and begged of me to be seated on a cane-bottomed arm-chair, which had evidently been placed ready for my especial ease and occupation. After the usual compliments had passed, the Maharajah inquired if I had eaten well. But, perhaps, the general reader would like to know what are "the usual compliments."

Native Rajah. "The whole world is ringing with the praise of your illustrious name."

Humble Sahib. "Maharaj. You are very good."

Native Rajah. "From Calcutta to Cabul—throughout the whole of Hindoostan—every tongue declares that you have no equal. Is it true?"

Humble Sahib (who, if he knows anything of Asiatic manners and customs, knows that he must not contradict his host, but eat his compliments with a good appetite). "Maharaj."

Native Rajah. "The acuteness of your perceptions, and the soundness of your understanding, have, by universal report, became as manifest as even the light of the sun itself." Then, turning to his attendants of every degree, who, by this time, had formed a circle round me and the Rajah, he put the question, "Is it true, or not?"

The attendants, one and all, declare that it was true; and inquire whether it could be possible for a great man like the Maharajah to say that which was false.

Native Rajah. "The Sahib's father is living?"

Humble Sahib. "No; he is dead, Maharaj."

Native Rajah. "He was a great man?"

Humble Sahib. "Maharaj. You have honoured the memory of my father, and exalted it in my esteem, by expressing such an opinion."

Native Rajah, "And your mother? She lives?"

Humble Sahib. "By the goodness of God, such is the case."

Native Rajah. "She is a very handsome woman?"

Humble Sahib. "On that point, Maharaj, I cannot offer an opinion."

Native Rajah. "You need not do so. To look in your face is quite sufficient. I would give a crore of rupees (one million sterling) to see her only for one moment, and say how much I admired the intelligeut countenance of her son. I am going to England next year. Will the Sahib favour me with her address?"

Humble Sahib. "Maharaj."

Here the Native Rajah calls to the moonshee to bring pen, ink, and paper. The moonshee comes, sits before me, pen in hand, looks inquiringly into my eyes, and I dictate as follows, laughing inwardly all the while: "Lady Bombazine, Munnymunt, ka uper, Peccadilleemee, Bilgrave Isqueere, Sunjons wood-Cumberwill;" which signifies this: "Lady Bombazine, on the top of the Monument, in Piccadilly, Belgrave Square, St. John's Wood, Camberwell." This mystification must be excused by the plea that the Rajah's assertions of his going to Europe are as truthful as Lady Bombazine's address.

The Maharajah then gives instructions that that document shall be preserved amongst his most important papers, and resumes the conversation.

Native Rajah. "The Sahib has eaten well?"

Humble Sahib. "Maharaj."

Native Rajah. "And drunk?"

Humble Sahib. "Maharaj."

Native Rajah. "The Sahib will smoke hookah?"

Humble Sahib. "The Maharajah is very good."

A hookah is called for by the Rajah; and then at least a dozen voices repeat the order: "Hookah lao, Sahib ke waste." (Bring a hookah for the Sahib.) Presently the hookah is brought in. It is rather a grand affair, but old, and has evidently belonged to some European of extravagant habits. Of course, no native would smoke out of it (on the ground of caste), and it is evidently kept for the use of the Sahib logue.*

While I am pulling away at the hookah, the musahibs, or favourites of the Rajah, flatter me, in very audible whispers. "How well he smokes!" "What a fine forehead he has!" "And his eyes! how they sparkle!" "No wonder he is so clever!" "He will be Governor-General some day." "Khuda-kuren!" (God will have it so.)

Native Rajah. "Sahib, when you become Governor-General, you will be a friend to the poor?"

Humble Sahib (speaking from the bottom of his heart). "Most assuredly, Maharaj."

Native Rajah. "And you will listen to the petition of every man, rich and poor alike."

Humble Sahib. "It will be my duty so to do."

Native Rajah (in a loud voice). "Moonshee!"

Moonshee (who is close at hand). "Maharaj, Protector of the Poor."

Native Rajah. "Bring the petition that I have laid before the Governor-General."

The moonshee produces the petition, and at the instance of the Rajah, reads, or rather sings it aloud. The Rajah listens with pleasure to its recital of his own wrongs, and I affect to be astounded that so much injustice can possibly exist. During my rambles

* The word "logue" simply signifies people; but, when applied as above, it is nothing more than a plural. "Sahib logue" (sahibs) "mem logue" (ladies), "baba logue" (children).

in India I have been the guest of some scores of rajahs, great and small, and I never knew one who had not a grievance. He had either been wronged by the government, or by some judge, whose decision had been against him. In the matter of the government, it was a sheer love of oppression that led to the evil of which he complained; in the matter of the judge, that functionary had been bribed by the other party.

It was with great difficulty that I kept my eyes open while the petition—a very long one—was read aloud. Shortly after it was finished, I craved permission to retire, and was conducted by a bearer to the sleeping-room, in the centre of which was a huge bedstead, a four-poster, but devoid of curtains. On either side were large looking-glasses in gilt frames, not suspended on the walls, but placed against them. Over the bed was a punkah, which was immediately set in motion. The movement of the punkah served a double purpose; it cooled the room, and drove away the musquitoes. Having thrown myself on the bed, the bearer, who was in attendance, inquired if I would be shampooed. This was a luxury to which I was always partial, and, having signified that I desired it, four men were shouted for. Each took an arm or a leg, and began to press it, and crack the knuckle-joints of my fingers and toes. This continued until I had fallen asleep. I did not wake until eight o'clock on the following morning, when I was waited upon by the khansamah, who wished to know my pleasure with respect to breakfast. He informed me that he had "Futnum and Meesum's," Yorkshire pie, game pie, anchovy toast, mutton-chop, steak, sardines—in short, all that the Sahib logue were accustomed to take.

My breakfast over, and my hookah smoked, I lighted a cheroot, and walked out into a verandah, where I was soon joined by some of the Maharajah's favourites and dependents, who poured into my ear a repetition of the flattery to which I had listened on the previous night. It is not very tedious when you become used to it, and know that it is a matter of course, and is applied to every European guest of any real or supposed importance. Whilst thus engaged, smoking and listening, I was joined by the Maharajah, who held in his hand the Delhi Gazette, the Mofussilite, and the Calcutta Englishman. Of their entire contents he had been made acquainted by a half-caste, whom he kept (so he informed me) for the sole purpose of translating, orally, into Hindostanee, the Indian journals and the government gazettes, published in the English language. There was no occasion for me to read these papers, for the Maharajah gave me a very accurate resumé of them; having done this, he asked me to play a game of billiards. I am not a bad billiard-player; on the contrary, I have the vanity to think that I play remarkably well; but it was quite evident to me that the Maharajah did not play his best, and that he suffered me to beat him as easily as I did, simply out of what he considered to be politeness. All the while we were playing the favourites or courtiers of the Maharajah were praising us both. Neither of us made a stroke, good or bad, that did not bring down a shower of compliments. My impression is, that if I had run a cue, and cut the cloth at the same time, the bystanders would have shouted in praise of my skill and execution. I had already seen enough of native character to know exactly how I was to act. I feigned to be charmed with my success—childishly charmed. Whilst I was thus (to the delight of my host) ostensibly revelling in my triumph, the marker—a native, a Hindoo—took up a cue, and began to knock the balls about. He cannoned all over the table, went in off the red and white, screwed back under the cushion, and, in short, did whatever he pleased, and with perfect ease.

I could not help expressing to the Rajah my astonishment at the Hindoo marker's skill; whereupon, he informed me that, when he was a mere boy, he had been taught by the best player (an officer in the Light Cavalry) that ever came to India, and that for several years past he had been marker at various mess-rooms where billiards were played. The name of this Hindoo Jonathan was Runjeet. He was six-and-twenty years of age, about five feet five in height, remarkably slim, had a very handsome face, and eyes full of fire and spirit. He was for a long time marker to the Horse Artillery mess at Meerut, where I once saw him play a game with an officer celebrated for his skill. Runjeet gave his adversary sixty points out of a hundred, and won easily. What with his pay, or salary, the presents he received from gentlemen to whom he taught the game, and the gold mohurs that he occasionally had given to him when he won bets for his backers, Runjeet was in possession of some six hundred pounds a-year; but he was so extravagant in his habits, that he spent every anna, and died, I was told, "not worth money enough to buy the wood to burn him."

The Maharajah, on leaving the billiard-room, invited me to accompany him to Cawnpore. I acquiesced, and the carriage was ordered. The carriage was English-built—a very handsome landau—and the horses were English horses; but the harness! It was country-made, of the very commonest kind, and worn out, for one of the traces was a piece of rope. The coachman was filthy in his dress, and the whip that he carried in his hand was an old broken buggy-whip, which some European gentleman must have thrown away. On the box, on either side of the coachman, sat a warlike retainer, armed with a sword and a dagger. In the rumble were two other retainers, armed in the same manner. Besides the Rajah and myself there were three others (natives and relatives of the Rajah) in the vehicle. On the road the Rajah talked incessantly, and amongst other things that he told me was this, in reference to the praises that I bestowed on his equipage.

"Not long ago I had a carriage and horses very superior to these. They cost me twenty-five thousand rupees; but I had to burn the carriage and kill the horses."

"Why so?"

"The child of a certain Sahib in Cawnpore was very sick, and the Sahib and the Memsahib were bringing the child to Bhitoor for a change of air. I sent my big carriage for them. On the road the child died; and, of course, as a dead body had been in the carriage, and as the horses had drawn that dead body in that carriage, I could never use them again." The reader must understand that a native of any rank considers it a disgrace to sell property.

"But could you not have given the horses to some friend—a Christian or a Mussulman?"

"No; had I done so, it might have come to the knowledge of the Sahib, and his feelings would have been hurt at having occasioned me such a loss."

Such was the Maharajah, commonly known as Nena Sahib. He appeared to me not a man of ability, nor a fool. He was selfish; but what native is not? He seemed to be far from a bigot in matters of religion; and, although he was compelled to be so very particular about the destruction of his carriage and horses, I am quite satisfied that he drank brandy, and that he smoked hemp in the chillum of his hookah.

It was half-past five o'clock when we arrived at Cawnpore. The officers, civil and military, and their wives, were just coming out for their evening drive on the mall. Some were in carriages, some in buggies, some on horseback. Every soul saluted the Maharajah; who returned the salute according to Eastern fashion—raising the hands to the forehead. Several gentlemen approached the carriage when it was drawn up near the band-stand, and inquired after the Maharajah's health. He replied that it was good; and then introduced me to them in the following manner, and in strict accordance with the letter he had received from Lucknow: "This Sahib who sits near me is a great friend of the Governor-General, and is a relation of all the members of Council—a constant guest of the Queen of England" (then came this addition of his own) "and of both Houses of Parliament." I need scarcely say that I wished my Lucknow friends had not covered me with such recommendations; for, wherever we went, and to whomsoever we spoke—no matter whether it was an European shopkeeper or an official magnate of Cawnpore—I was doomed to hear, "This Sahib who sits (or stands) near me is a great friend," &c., &c. Having exhibited me sufficiently in Cawnpore, the heads of the horses were turned towards Bhitoor, and we were dragged along the road at a slow pace, for the animals were extremely fatigued. The natives of India have no mercy on their cattle, especially their horses. During the ride back, I was again bored with the Rajah's grievance; and, to quiet him—for he became very much excited—I was induced to promise that I would talk to the Governor-General and the Council on the subject; and that if I did not succeed in that quarter, I would, on my return to England, take the earliest opportunity "some day, quietly, after dinner" (this was his suggestion), of representing to her Majesty the exact state of the case, and that an adopted son of a Hindoo was entitled to all the rights and privileges of an heir born of the body. I furthermore promised him most solemnly that I would not speak to the Board of Control, or to the Privy Council on the subject; for the Maharajah assured me that he had the most positive proof that both these institutions had eaten bribes from the hand of the East India Company in respect of his claim. On probing him, however, I discovered that this positive proof was a letter from a villanous agent in England, who had written to him to say that "the Company had bribed the Board of Control and the Privy Council, and that if his Highness expected to succeed, he must bribe over the head of the Company. Three lacs (thirty thousand pounds) would do it all."

The Maharajah gave a nautch (native dance by women) that night.

On the following morning I awoke with a very bad headache, and in a philosophic mood. The various perfumes which had been sprinkled over my dress had somewhat overpowered me, and it may have been that the story told me in whispers by one of the three slaves who came to sing me to sleep had disordered my imagination. I was told that two women of rank were kept in a den not far from my apartments, and treated like wild beasts; and a third—a beautiful young creature—had recently been "bricked up in a wall," for no other fault than attempting to escape.

After breakfast, the Rajah showed me his elephants, his camels, his horses, his dogs, his pigeons, his falcons, his wild asses, his apes, his aviary full of birds, and all the rest of his curiosities. Then he exhibited his guns and pistols—by Purdey, Egg, and other celebrated makers—his swords, and his daggers, of every country and age, and when he had observed that he was very happy, under the influence of some stimulant recently imbibed, I took an opportunity of discoursing on the vanity of human wishes, and especially with reference to his Highness's grievance. I translated many sentiments of Juvenal and Horace into Hindoostanee; but, I regret to say, they had no effect on Nena Sahib.

THE UPPER PROVINCES.

It is impossible for an English gentleman to take his departure from the house of a native of India without giving a number of testimonials, in the shape of "letters of recommendation," addressed to no one in particular. Nena Sahib had a book containing the autographs of at least a hundred and fifty gentlemen and ladies, who had testified in writing to the attention and kindness they had received at the hands of the Maharajah during their stay at Bhitoor. Having expressed my satisfaction as emphatically as possible in this book, the khansamah (house steward) demanded a certificate, which I gave him. Then came the bearer, the men who guarded my door, the coachman, the grooms, the sweeper. For each and all of these I had to write characters, and recommend them to such of my friends as they might encounter by accident or otherwise. It is a fearful infliction, this character writing; but every one is compelled to go through it.

I was now on my road to Agra, to pay a visit to a schoolfellow, who was then in the civil service, and filling an appointment in the station. It was in the month of September that I made the journey—the most unhealthy season of the year. Opposite to the first dâk bungalow, some twelve miles from the station of Cawnpore, I was stopped by a set of twelve palkee bearers, who informed me that a Sahib whom they were taking to Allyghur had been seized with cholera, and was dying in the bungalow. I hastened to the room and there found, stretched upon the couch, a young officer of about nineteen years of age.

His face was ashy pale, and a profuse cold perspiration stood upon his forehead. His hands and feet were like ice, and he was in very great pain. The only person near him was the sweeper, who kept on assuring me that the youth would die. As for the youth himself he was past speech, and I was disposed to think with the sweeper, that he was beyond cure. I administered, however, nearly a teaspoonful of laudanum in a wine-glass half-full of raw brandy, and then took a seat near the patient, in order to witness the effect. Ere long the severe pain was allayed, and the youth fell into a profound sleep, from which, I began to fear, he would never awake. To have administered a smaller dose at that stage of the disease would have been useless, for the body was on the very verge of collapse. Nevertheless, I began to feel the awkwardness of the responsibility which I had taken upon myself. Presently a palanquin carriage, propelled by bearers, came to the bungalow. An elderly lady and gentleman alighted, and were shown into a little room which happened to be vacant. [A dâk bungalow has only two little rooms.] To my great joy I discovered that the new arrival was a doctor of a regiment, who, with his wife, was journeying to Calcutta. I was not long in "calling in" the doctor; and I had the satisfaction of hearing him pronounce an opinion that the young ensign was "all right," and that the dose I had administered had been the means of saving his life. How readily, to be sure, do people in India accommodate each other. Although the doctor and his wife were hurrying down the country, and albeit the youth was pronounced out of danger, they remained with me until the following afternoon; when, having dined, we all took our departure together—the youth and I travelling northward, the doctor and his wife in the opposite direction.

The night was pitchy dark; but the glare from the torches rendered every object near to us distinctly visible. The light, shining on the black faces of the palkee bearers, they appeared like so many demons—but very merry demons; for they chatted and laughed incessantly, until I commanded them to be silent, in order that, while we moved along the road, I might listen to the ensign's story, which he told me in the most artless manner imaginable.

"I have only been six weeks in India," he began, "and at present only know a few words of the language. How I came into the Bengal army was this. My father was in the civil service of the Company, in the

Madras Presidency; and, after twenty-one years' service, retired on his pension of one thousand pounds a year, and his savings, which amounted to twenty thousand pounds, and which were invested in five per cent. government securities, so that his income was two thousand year. We lived during the winter near Grosvenor-square: a house of which my father bought the lease for twenty years, and the summer we used to spend at a little place in Berkshire which he had bought. It was only a good sized cottage, and the land about it did not exceed three acres. But it was a perfect gem of a residence, and quite large enough for our family, which consisted of my father and mother, myself, and a sister who is a year and a half older than I am. I was at Harrow. My father intended that I should go to Oxford, and eventually be called to the bar. My sister had a governess, a very clever and accomplished girl, and the most amiable creature that ever lived. We were not an extravagant family, and saw very little company; but we had every comfort that a reasonable heart could desire, and I fancy that we lived up to the two thousand pounds a year. You see the education of myself and my sister was a heavy item. The governess had a hundred pounds a year, and then there was a singing-master and a drawing master. About two years ago my father died, and my mother became almost imbecile from the excess of her grief. She lost her memory; and, for days together, knew not what she was doing.

Under my father's will she was entitled to all that he died possessed of, and was appointed his sole executrix. The house in South-street was given up, the unexpired portion of the lease disposed of, and the little place in Berkshire became our only home. My father's pension of course expired when he died, and we, the family, had now to live on the interest of the government securities. My mother, who was as ignorant as a child on all matters of business, was recommended to sell her government securities, and invest the proceeds in a joint-stock bank which was paying, and for more than a year did pay, eight per cent. But, alas, one wretched day the bank failed, and we were reduced suddenly from comparative affluence to poverty. The cottage, furniture, and all that my mother possessed, was seized, and sold. This happened only two years ago. Fortunately for me, my school education was pretty well completed; but of course the idea of my going to Oxford, and subsequently to the bar, was at once abandoned. My sister was obliged to take a situation as governess, in the family of a director of the East India Company: and through that gentleman's influence I obtained an ensigncy in the Native Infantry. The loss of her fortune, the parting with my sister (who is now on the Continent with the director's family) and myself, had such an effect upon my mother, that it was deemed necessary to place her in an asylum; where at all events she will be taken care of and treated with kindness. But I have my plans!" exclaimed the young man, who had just escaped the jaws of death. "In ten years I will save enough to take me home to them; for, if I study hard —and I will do so—I may get a staff appointment, and——"

Here the bearers of my palkee informed me that two other travellers were coming down the road. They saw the light in the distance, more than a mile off, and they—the bearers—began to talk loudly and argue, that it was impossible for me to hear what the ensign was saying, and all attempts to silence them were vain. They were discussing, as they carried us along, whether they would exchange burdens with the down-coming bearers, insomuch as they were nearly midway between the stages. This is very often done by arrangement between them, and thus, in such cases, they get back more speedily to their homes. It was decided that the exchange should take place, if the other party were agreeable; for, on the down-coming travellers nearing us, the bearers of us—the up-going travellers—called a halt. Forthwith the four palkees were gently lowered till they rested on the ground. And now the chattering of the bearers became something awful. A native of Hindostan can settle nothing without a noise; and, as each palkee had twelve men attached to it besides the torch-bearers and those who carried our boxes, the number of voices, whooping, shouting, asserting, contradicting, scolding, and soothing, exceeded sixty. I and my companion, the ensign, shout to them to "go on!" At length I got out of my palkee in a rage, and not only screamed at, but shook several of the black disputants. Whilst thus engaged, the doors of one of the downward palkees were opened, and a voice—that of a lady—thus greeted me, very good humouredly.

"My good sir, depend upon it that you are retarding your own progress, and ours, by attempting, so violently, to accelerate it. Pray let them settle their little affair amongst themselves."

"I believe you are quite right," I replied.

"Have you any idea of the hour?" she asked.

"Yes. It is about a quarter to twelve," said I.

"I have lost the key of my watch; perhaps the key of yours would fit it."

I hastened to my palkee, brought forth from beneath the pillow my watch and chain; and, taking them to the door of the lady's palkee, presented them through the opening.

"Thanks," said the lady, after winding up her watch, "thanks. It does very well," and she returned the watch and chain. I saw, by the light of the torch, not only her hand—which was very small and pretty—but her face, which was more bewitching still, being lovely and young.

"Is there anything else you require?" I asked.

"Nothing. Unless you happen to have with you some fresh bread. My children, who are asleep in the other palkee, are tired of biscuits, and I imagine we shall not reach Cawnpore before midday to-morrow."

It happened that I had a loaf in my palkee, and, with all the pleasure of which the heart of man is capable, placed it in the hands of the fair traveller. On this occasion she opened the doors of her palkee sufficiently wide to admit of my having a really good gaze at her beautiful features. She was enveloped in a white dressing-gown, and wore a hood made of black silk, and lined with pink. Her hair was brushed back off the forehead; but the long dark tresses came from behind the ears, and rested on her covered shoulders.

"Are you going to Agra?" she inquired.

"Yes," I replied.

"Perhaps you would be good enough to return two books for me to the wife of the assistant magistrate. They will, no doubt, afford you as much amusement on your journey as they have afforded me. I finished them this afternoon, and they are now an encumbrance." With these words she handed me the volumes, which I faithfully promised to return. By this time the bearers had settled their affair, and were ready to lift the palkees. I bade the fair traveller "good night, and a safe journey." We shook hands.

The reader may ask, "Who was your friend?" I did not know at the time. It was not until I had arrived at Agra that I was informed on this head. The books which she entrusted to my care I had not read; and, after parting with the ensign at the dâk bungalow at Bewah, they were, indeed, most agreeable companions. I have mentioned this little episode in my journey, not because there is anything in it worth recording, or because there is anything romantic therewith connected; but simply to show how readily we (Christians) in India obliged one another, albeit utter strangers, and how gladly we assist each other, whenever and wherever we meet. Such an episode in the journey of a traveller in India is one of its most commonplace incidents.

Since the news of the recent deplorable disasters has reached this country, many persons have expressed their surprise that a lady should be suffered to travel alone with her children, or be accompanied by no more than one female servant. The fact is, or rather was, that, on any dangerous road, a lady utterly unprotected was safer than a gentleman. The sex was actually its own protection. During my stay in India, I knew of at least a score of instances in which officers and civilians were stopped upon the roads, plundered, assaulted, and in one or two cases murdered, in the Upper Provinces; but I can only bring to mind two instances of European ladies having been molested. This is not to be attributed to any ideas of gallantry or chivalry on the part of marauders in the East; but simply to the fact that they knew the perpetrators of an offence committed against a lady would be hunted down to the death, while the sympathies entertained for the sufferings of a Sahib would be only those of an ordinary character, and soon "blow over." Even the palkee-bearers knew the amount of responsibility that attached to them, when they bore away, from station to station, a female burden; and, had tne lady traveller been annoyed or interrupted by an European traveller, they would have attacked and beaten him, even to the breaking of his bones and the danger of his life, had he not desisted when commanded by the lady to do so. This has happened more than once in the Upper Provinces of India.

In December, eighteen hundred and forty-nine, the road between Saharumpore and Umballah was infested by a gang of thieves. Several officers had been stopped, robbed, and plundered of their money and valuables. I had been invited to Lahore, to witness the installation of Sir Walter Gilbert and Sir Henry Elliot as Knights Commanders of the Bath. The danger, near a place called Juggadree, was pointed out to me by a mail contractor, who, finding me determined to proceed, recommended me to dress as a lady for a couple of stages. I did so. I borrowed a gown, a shawl, and a nightcap; and, when I came near the dangerous locality, I put them on, and commanded the bearers to say I was a "mem-Sahib," in the event of the palkee being stopped. Sure enough, the palkee was stopped, near Juggadree, by a gang of ten or twelve armed men, one of whom opened the door to satisfy himself of the truth of the statement made by the bearers. The moment the ruffian saw my nightcap—a very prettily-frilled one it was, lent to me by a very pretty woman—likewise a small bolster, which, beneath my shawl, represented a sleeping baby, he closed the door, and requested the bearers to take up the palkee, and proceed ; ay, and what was more, he enjoined them to be "careful of the mem-Sahib!"

I have incidentally spoken of the installation of Sir Walter Gilbert and Sir Henry Elliot, in December, eighteen hundred and forty-nine. Eight years have not yet elapsed, and how many of the principal characters in that magnificent spectacle have departed hence! Sir Walter is dead; Sir Henry is dead. Sir Charles Napier and Sir Dudley Hill, who led them up to Lord Dalhousie, are dead. Colonel Mountain, who carried the cushion on which was placed the insignia of the order is dead. And Sir Henry Lawrence is dead; and poor Stuart Beatson. Alas! how many of that gay throng, men and women, husbands, fathers, wives, and daughters, who had assembled to withess the ceremony, have perished during the recent revolt in the Upper Provinces of India! Those who were present on that sixth of December, eighteen hundred and forty-nine, and who, in eighteen hundred and fifty-seven, quietly reflect on what has occurred since, will scarcely believe in their own existence. It must appear to them —as it often appears to me—as a dream; a dream in which we saw Sir Charles Napier, with his spare form, his eagle eyes, his aquiline nose, and long grey beard, joking Sir Dudley Hill on his corpulence and baldness, and asking him what sort of figure he would cut now, in leading a forlorn hope? and Sir Dudley, proudly and loudly replying, that he felt a better man than ever. Presently, a meek civilian, in a white neckcloth, and ignorant of Sir Dudley's early deeds, was so unfortunate as to put the question :—

"*Did* you ever lead a forlorn hope, Sir Dudley?" a query which induced Sir Dudley Hill to groan, previously to exclaiming—

"Such is fame! A forlorn hope, my dear sir! I have led fifty!"

This was, of course, an exaggeration; but I believe that Sir Dudley Hill had, in the Peninsular War, led more forlorn hopes than any other officer in the British army.

I have wandered away from the high road to Agra, and must return to it. I parted with the ensign at Bewah, and commenced reading the books which the then unknown lady had entrusted to my care. The day, towards noon, became hot, damp, and extremely oppressive; and there was no dâk bungalow, or other abode, within nine miles of me. Before long, I heard thunder in the distance, and presently the bearers communicated to me that a heavy storm was approaching, and that, in order to escape its fury, they wished to halt at a village just a-head of us. I consented, and was now hurried along the road at the rate of five miles an hour. My palkee was placed beneath a shed, and the bearers congregated around it. One of the number lighted his pipe (hubble-bubble), and passed it to his neighbour; who, after three whiffs, passed it to the next; who, after three whiffs, sent it on, until each had partaken of the smoke.

The little village, which was a short distance from the road, contained about sixty or seventy inhabitants, and about double that number of children of various ages. My presence excited no small degree of curiosity, and the whole of the villagers approached the shed, to have a look at me. The men and women, of course, were not alarmed, and looked on simply with that stupidity which is characteristic of the cultivators of the soil in the Upper Provinces of India. But it was otherwise with the more youthful, the children. They held aloof, and peeped from behind their parents, as if I had been some dangerous wild animal. My bearers wished to drive them all away; but I forbade this, partly because I had no desire to deprive the villagers of whatever pleasure a long inspection of me might afford them, and partly because I wished to sketch the group and listen to their remarks, which were chiefly of a personal character, and for the most part complimentary, or intended so to be.

A vivid flash of lightning, and an awfully loud clap of thunder, accompanied by a few large drops of rain, speedily dispersed the crowd, and I was left to myself and my bearers, who now huddled themselves together for warmth's sake. The air had become chilly, and even I was compelled to wrap my cloak and my blanket about my thinly-clad limbs. Another vivid flash of lightning, and another awful clap of thunder; then down came such hailstones as I had never seen before, and have never seen since in the plains of Hindostan. In size and weight they equalled those which sometimes fall in the Himalaya mountains in June and July. With these storms the rains usually "break up," and then the cold weather sets in, and with this season of the year, what climate in the world is superior to that of the Upper Provinces of India? When the thunder, lightning, and hail had ceased, and their continuance did not exceed fifteen minutes, the sun came out, and the face of heaven was as fair as possible, but the earth gave evidence of the severity of the storm. Not only was the ground covered with leaves and small branches, intermingled with the hail, but cattle and goats had been killed by the furious pelting of the huge stones; whilst the electric fluid had descended on one of the mud huts of the village in which I had taken refuge, and had stretched out in death an old man and two of his grandchildren, a boy of six years of age, and a girl of four. The parents of these children were absent from the village, and were not expected to return until the evening. On being informed of the accident, I expressed a desire to see the bodies, and was conducted by several of the villagers to the hut in which they were lying. I recognised at once the features of the old man who was a prominent figure in my sketch, and of one of the children, the little girl who held the old man so tightly by the hand while she peeped at me. The face of the boy had not struck me. There they were lying dead, but still warm, and their limbs, as yet, devoid of rigidity. The matter-of-fact way in which the natives of India regard the death of their relations or friends is something wonderful to behold. It is not that their affections are less strong than ours, or their feelings less acute. It is that fatality is the beginning and end of their creed. They are taught from their childhood to regard visitations of this character as direct and special acts of God—as matters which it is not only futile, but improper to bewail. None of the villagers—men, women, or children, exhibited any token of grief while gazing on the lifeless bodies they surrounded. And, on asking my bearers whether the parents of the children would weep when they returned, and found their offspring thus suddenly cut off, they replied, rather abruptly, "Why should they weep at God's will?"

As I was preparing to leave the village, a middle-aged woman came up to me, and said:—

"Sahib, the parents of the dead children are very poor, and the expense of burning their remains will press very hard upon them. The wood for the old man will cost eight annas, and the fuel for each of the children four annas; in all, one rupee."

I placed the coin in the woman's hand, and left, besides, a donation for the bereaved parents who were absent; having previously called several of the villagers to witness the proceeding. This I did at the suggestion of the palkee bearers, who entertained some doubts of the woman's honesty. We had not proceeded far, when I descried a small encampment beneath a clump of mango trees. It consisted of an officer's tent, and two long tents for native soldiers—Sepoys. One of these long tents was for the Hindoos, the other for the Mussulmans. When we came opposite to the encampment, I desired the bearers to stop, and to put some questions to a Sepoy who was standing near the road. I gleaned from him that the encampment was that of "a treasure party," consisting of a Lieutenant, and a company of native infantry, proceeding from Mynpoorie to Agra.

"Won't you go and see the Sahib?" asked the Sepoy.

"I don't know him," said I.

"That does not signify," said the Sepoy. "Our Sahib is glad to see everybody. He is the most light-hearted man in Hindostan. His lips are the home of laughter, and his presence awakens happiness in the breast of the most sorrowful. His body is small, but his mind is great; and, in his eyes, the Hindoo, the Mussulman, and the Christian, are all equal."

This description, I confess, aroused my curiosity to see so philosophical a Lieutenant, and it was not long before my curiosity was gratified; for he made his appearance at the door of his tent; and, observing my palkee, bore down upon it.

The Lieutenant wore a pair of white pyjamahs, which were tucked up to his knees, no shoes or stockings; a blue shirt, no coat, no jacket; a black necktie, and a leather helmet with a white covering, such as one sees labelled in the shop-windows "for India." His person was very small certainly, and the calves of his legs not bigger than those of a boy of twelve years of age. In his mouth he had a huge (number one) cheroot, and in his hand, a walking-stick, with a waist nearly as big as his own. Resting his chest upon this walking-stick, and looking me full in the face, perfectly ignorant, and seemingly indifferent, as to whether I might be a secretary to the government, or a shopkeeper, he thus familiarly accosted me:—

"Well, old boy, how do you feel after the shower?"

"Very well, I thank you."

"Come in and have a cup of tea, and a round of toast, if you are not in a hurry to get on. It will set you up, and make you feel comfortable for the night." This offer was so tempting, and so cordially made, that I was induced to accept it.

"Bring the Sahib into my tent, in the palkee," said Lieutenant Sixtie to my bearers; and then addressing me, he remarked—"Don't get out. You'll wet your slippers."

The bearers followed the Lieutenant, and put down my palkee upon two tiers of small boxes, which were spread over the space of ground covered by the tent.

"I was obliged to resort to this box dodge," said my host, "or I should have been drowned. I wish I owned only a quarter of this rhino we are treading on. If I did, catch me at this work any longer, my masters!" It was the treasure that the boxes contained, in all about twenty-five thousand pounds. "Look here, old boy. Forego, like a good fellow, the tea and the toast. My servants will have such a bother to get a fire and boil water. Have some biscuits and cold brandy-and-water instead. You should never drink tea while travelling. It keeps you awake; and, what is more, it spoils the flavour of your cheroots. By the bye, have one of these weeds."

I thanked my host; and, without any sort of pressing, yielded to his every wish—even unto playing *écarté* with him, while smoking his cheroots and drinking his brandy-and-water. The stakes were not very high. Only a rupee a game. During the deals, my host would frequently exclaim:

"By Jove! what a godsend it is to have some one to talk to for a few hours! I have been out for five days; and, during that time, have not uttered a word in my own language. Haven't had the luck to come across a soul. This escorting treasure is the most awful part of an officer's duty, especially at this season of the year."

"But it must be done," I suggested.

"Yes. But why not by native officers?"

"Would the treasure be safe with them?"

"Safe? Just as safe as it is now, if not safer; for, although I am responsible for the money in these boxes, I don't know that the whole amount is here. I didn't count it; and, if there was any deficiency, I should say so. Now, a native officer would satisfy himself on the subject before he took charge. Don't you see?"

Here our conversation was interrupted by a havildar (native sergeant), who appeared at the door of the tent, saluted the Lieutenant, and uttered in a deep and solemn tone of voice the word Sa-hib!

"Well. What's the matter?" said the Lieutenant.

"Maun Singh Sipahee is very ill."

"What ails him?"

"He has fever."

"Then I will come and see him in one moment." With these words the Lieutenant threw down his cards, and invited me to accompany him to the tent wherein the patient was lying.

Maun Singh Sipahee was a powerful Brahmin, who stood upwards of six feet two. He was a native of Oude, and had a very dark skin. When we entered the tent, he attempted to rise from the charpai (native bedstead) on which he was reclining; but the Lieutenant told him to be still, then felt the sick man's pulse, and placed his small white hand across the broad black forehead of the soldier.

"Carry him into my tent. The ground is too damp for him here," said the Lieutenant; and forthwith the bedstead was raised by half-a-dozen of the man's comrades. In the tent medicine was administered—a small quantity of tartar emetic dissolved in water, and given in very small doses, until nausea was produced, and a gentle perspiration stood upon the skin of the patient.

"You are all right, now, Maun Singh," said the Lieutenant.

"No, Sahib, I am dying. Nothing can save me."

"Then you know better than I do?"

"Forgive me, Sahib."

"Listen. Lie very quiet; and, before we march, I will give you another sort of medicine that will set you up."

The Sepoy covered his head over with his resaiee (counterpane), and lay as still as possible.

"They always fancy they are going to die, if there is anything the matter with them," said the Lieutenant to me. "I have cured hundreds of fever cases by this treatment. The only medicines I ever use in fever, sir, are tartar emetic and quinine. He has taken the one, which has had its effect; the other he shall have by and bye. I wouldn't lose that man on any account. His death would occasion me the greatest grief."

"Is he a great favourite?" I asked.

"Not more than any of the rest of them who were

with the regiment at Affghanistan, where they not only proved themselves as brave as the European soldiers, but where they showed themselves superior to prejudices most intimately connected with their religion—their caste. That man, whom you see lying there, is a Brahmin of the highest caste; yet, I have seen him, and other Brahmins now in my regiment, bearing upon their shoulders the remains of an officer to the grave. Of course, you are aware that to do a thing of that kind—to touch the corpse of an unbeliever—involves a loss of caste?"

"Yes."

"Well, sir, these fellows braved the opinion and the taunts of every Hindoo in the country, in order to pay respect to the memory of those officers whose dangers and privations they had cheerfully shared. You are aware, perhaps, that at last the government found it necessary to issue a general order to the effect that any Sepoy of any other regiment who insulted the men of this regiment, by telling them they had lost their caste, would be severely punished and dismissed the service? Such was the case, sir; and many courts-martial were held in various stations far the trial of offenders against this order; and many Hindoo Sepoys and Mussulman native officers were very severely dealt with. And the thing was put down, sir; and now-a-days there is nothing more common than for the Hindoo Sepoys, in all the regiments, to ask permission to carry the remains of a popular officer to the grave. Indeed, ladies are often thus honoured, and children. They seem to have agreed amongst themselves that this does not involve a loss of caste. So much for caste, if it can be got over by an understanding amongst themselves! Caste! More than four-fifths of what they talk about it is pure nonsense and falsehood, as any straightforward native will confidentially confess to you. I don't mean to say that some Hindoos are not very strict. Many, indeed, are so. But I mean to say that a very small proportion live in accordance with the Shasters, and that when they cry out, "if we do so and so we shall lose our caste," it is nothing more than a rotten pretext for escaping some duty, or for refusing to obey a distasteful order. There are hypocrites in all countries, but India swarms with them more thickly than any country in the world. And the fact is that we foster hypocrisy. Our fellows, and most of them Brahmins, released a good many cats from the bag, when they were taunted with having lost their caste! If you are not in a frightful hurry to get on, stay till we march, and go with us; and I'll tell you and show you something more about caste. You can send on your palkee and bearers to the next encampment ground, and I'll drive you in my old trap of a buggy. It is not a remarkably elegant affair, but it is very strong and roomy. By the bye, we shall have to travel 'three in a gig;' for I must put Maun Singh, my sick Sepoy, between us; and you will find him a very intelligent fellow, I can tell you, and the dose I intend giving him will make him as chirpy as possible."

The conversation and the manners of the Lieutenant — free and easy as were the latter — had fascinated me, and I accepted his invitation.

MARCHING.

THE small but heavy boxes containing the rupees were placed upon the hackeries (native carts), and the treasure party was now ready to march to the next encampment. The night was warm, and the Sepoys in what might strictly be termed half-dress. They wore their red cloth coats and their chacos; but their lower clothing was purely native; a dhotee (narrow strip of thick calico) wound round their loins, and falling in graceful folds about and below the knees. Some sat upon the boxes of treasure: others, not in line or military order, walked by the side thereof. The Lieutenant, Maun Singh, and myself brought up the rear. A syce (native groom) led the horse, and thus saved the Lieutenant the trouble of driving. The buggy was not, certainly, a very elegant affair. It was of very ancient construction, and the lining was entirely worn out; nor had the panels been painted for some years. The Lieutenant told me that he had bought this vehicle at a sale, five years previously, for the sum of five pounds, and that since that time it had travelled (marched, was the word he used) all over Bengal. The harness was of Cawnpore make; and, when new, had cost only two pounds ten shillings. Cawnpore, until recently, was chiefly famous for its harness, boots and shoes, bottle-covers, cheroot-cases, helmets, and other articles made of leather. A nest of Chinese settled in the bazaar many years ago and introduced the manufacture of such matters. The horse which drew the buggy had been a caster; that is to say, a horse considered no longer fit for the cavalry or horse artillery, and sold by public auction, after being branded with the letter R (signifying rejected) on the near shoulder. He was a tall, well-bred animal; and, according to the Lieutenant's account, had won no end of races since the day he had been knocked down to the Lieutenant for sixteen rupees, or one pound twelve shillings. The fault, or rather the misfortune, for which this animal had been dismissed the Company's service, was total blindness of one eye, and an inability to see much out of the other.

"But, he is a ripper, nevertheless," said the Lieutenant, touching the animal very gently with the whip, and making him hold his head up; "and will put some more money in my pocket next cold weather, I hope. He is entered for the Merchant's Plate, gentlemen riders, sir, and I am his jockey." I expressed a hope that he would be successful.

It was a moonlight night, and slow as was the pace at which we proceeded, I never so much enjoyed a ride in my life. The scene altogether was highly picturesque, and, as far as I was concerned, had the wonderful charm of novelty; while it was impossible not to be extremely entertained by the volubility and lightheartedness of my military friend, who, notwithstanding he had extracted from me that I did not belong to the civil service or the army, had refrained from inquiring my name or pursuit, and invariably addressed me as Old Boy, albeit my years were certainly not in excess of his own.

"Well, Maun Singh!" cried the Lieutenant, "how do you feel now?"

"Quite well, but very weak," was the Sepoy's reply.

"Then you must have a little drop of weak brandy-and-water. Hold hard, syce, and give me the suraiee (water-bottle)."

The brandy-and-water was mixed in a silver tumbler, and handed to Maun Singh, who, *as soon as the groom went again to the horse's head,* applied it to his lips, and drank, without any scruple. On the contrary, it struck me that he liked the liquor.

"You have lost your caste," said the Lieutenant, jocularly. "You ought to have drunk it, you know, as medicine, out of your own lota (brass vessel)."

This observation—made with a view to draw the Sepoy out for my edification—had its effect. It was thus Maun Singh discoursed, while the Lieutenant and myself smoked our cheroots on either side of him:—

"The Sahib logue believe everything that the

natives tell them about caste, and the consequence is they believe a great many falsehoods. If I could lose my caste by drinking medicine out of this tumbler, I would lose it by drinking it out of my own cup, because it came out of a bottle which you have handled, and perhaps some drops of it touched your fingers, while you were pouring it from one vessel to the other. Empty a bottle of brandy or gin into your chillumchee (brass wash-hand basin), and tell one of your palkee-bearers to throw it away. He and his companions will drink it, but not in your presence. Ask the same man to drink the liquor from your tumbler. He will put his hands together, and implore you to excuse him, as he would lose his caste."

"But is it not forbidden in the Shasters?" said I.

"There is no mention of brandy in the Shasters, Sahib," returned Maun Singh, with some humour. "The Shasters are silent on the subject. But, supposing that it were forbidden; do not men of every religion frequently and continually depart from the tenets thereof, in minor things, or construe them according to their own inclination or convenience, or make some sort of bundobust (agreement) with their consciences? Indeed, if we did not make this bundobust, what Hindoo or Mussulman would come in contact at all with one another, or with Christians, and certainly we, the natives of India, would not serve as soldiers."

"How so?"

"Because we should be in continual dread of having our bodies contaminated and our souls placed beyond the reach of redemption—and who would submit to that for so many rupees a-month? Who can say what animal supplies the skin which is used for our chacos and accoutrements? The cow, or the pig? The Mussulmans, when we laugh together about it, say the cow. We protest that it is pigskin."

"And how do you usually settle these disputes?" I inquired, with an eagerness which seemed to amuse the Sepoy.

"O, Sahib!" he replied, "it would be a pity to settle any dispute of that kind, since it always affords us some merriment on a long march. When Pertab Singh came down to Barruckpore to corrupt the regiments of native infantry there stationed, in eighteen hundred and forty-eight, he wanted them to protest against wearing the chacos."

"And how was he received?" I inquired.

"They listened to him as long as his money lasted, and then made known to their officers what he was about."

"And who was Pertab Singh?"

"A relation of the Ranee of Lahore."

"And had he money?"

"Yes; and distributed freely."

Here the Lieutenant informed me of the particulars relating to the mission of Pertab Singh, which was simply to excite the native troops to mutiny and to kill their officers; but the plot was happily discovered by the information given by the Sepoys of the 16th Grenadiers. "There was an investigation, but the government deemed it best to treat the whole affair as a farce, and Pertab Singh was looked upon as a fool and a madman, and eventually set at liberty. It was said that the Sepoys who gave the information were to receive an order of merit; they had no reward at all, however, beyond some expressions of praise from the authorities."

Suddenly, the treasure party halted, and all the Sepoys were speedily congregated beneath a mango tree.

"What is the matter?" cried the Lieutenant.

"Adjutant Bargow Sahib's grave," said Maun Singh. "Do you not remember the spot?"

"I did not, in this light," said the Lieutenant, alighting from the buggy, followed by myself and Maun Singh. "Yes; here he rests, poor fellow—one of the best and bravest beings that ever breathed. He died suddenly one morning when we were encamped here. He was a great favourite with the men, as you may judge from the respect paid by those now present to the spot where his ashes repose.

One of the Sepoys suddenly began to call down curses on the head of some sacrilegious thief. He had discovered that the piece of marble which had been let into the head of the chunam (plaster) tomb, and on which was cut the name, age, and regiment of the deceased, had been abstracted.

"Ah! that of course," said the Lieutenant. "It is always the case. They steal the bit of marble to make a currystone—a stone on which they grind the ingredients for a curry. It was not worth more than a shilling, intrinsically; but if it had only been worth one anna, or a quarter of an anna—half a farthing—they would have carried it away all the same, just as they steal pieces of iron and lead from the stone bridges, and thus do immense mischief. All along the Grand Trunk Road you will find the stones used for headstones carried away from the graves."

The march, thirteen miles, occupied us five hours, so slowly did the bullocks crawl along with the treasure. It was about four o'clock when we came to the ground—the hour at which, in strictness, the Lieutenant should have started; but he informed me that when on separate duty, he took a good deal of responsibility on himself, and without detriment to the interests of government, suited his own convenience and that of his men. He therefore preferred making night work of the business, and having the whole day at his own disposal.

"Send your bearers away, and spend the day with me," said the lighthearted Lieutenant. "You can get other bearers at any of the villages in the neighbourhood; or, if you are not in a violent hurry, march the whole distance to Agra with me. I can stick your palkee and boxes on the top of the treasure, you know."

I accepted the invitation with pleasure, and entered the tent, where we found tea and biscuits ready. After partaking of this refreshment we threw ourselves down on charpoys (native bedsteads), and soon fell fast asleep.

We slept till ten, when we arose, had breakfast, consisting of—the old story—grilled fowl, curried fowl, and eggs, with beer instead of tea; and then we went out and sat under the mango trees, which formed a dense shade over the encampment. The Lieutenant had with him a pellet bow, and was shooting at the squirrels, which abound in the Upper Provinces of India. While he was thus employed a Sepoy—a Brahmin—called out: "Sahib, you have no right to do that. It is written in the general orders that you must respect the religious feelings of the Hindoos, and here are you wantonly destroying the life of animals in our presence. I shall report this to the Colonel Sahib, when we return to the regiment."

From the tone in which the Sepoy spoke, I thought he was in earnest. The Lieutenant, however, assured me that he was only ridiculing one of those absurd general orders which frequently appear, but of which bad and discontented Sepoys often take advantage. Ere long this Brahmin, observing that the light of the Lieutenant's cheroot was extinguished, brought him some fire. The Lieutenant gravely shook his head, and said—"No; it is written in general orders that no officer shall employ for his own purposes a Sepoy who is a soldier and not a servant, and that any officer so offending will subject himself to be tried by a court martial." Then, taking the fire from the hand of the Brahmin, he remarked to me—"The consequence of that order, for which there never was the slightest occasion, is simply this: those men who are willing to oblige their officers laugh at it, while the disaffected will insolently quote it if required only to pick up a glove or a walking-stick. Many an officer has been severely reprimanded for asking a Sepoy to carry a letter for him to the post office."

It was a very pretty scene, that encampment. The tents; the arms piled in front of them; the horse under a tree, and his syce seated near him; the old buggy and harness not far off; the Sepoys in groups employed in cooking their food for the mid-day meal; the numbers of brass vessels lying about in all directions; the score of squirrels hopping from branch to branch, or running up and down the trunks of the trees; the crows, the minars, and the sparrows on the look out for crumbs; the bullocks taking their rest after the fatigues of the past night; and then, before as well as after the meal, the men crowding round the well, and washing themselves from head to foot, and washing also their under garments, which are speedily dried in the sun of that climate. It is impossible to witness and not admire this part of the Hindoo and Mussulman religions.

After one o'clock, when every man had enjoyed his smoke, there was scarcely a soul, except myself and the Lieutenant, awake in the encampment. All were fast asleep in the open air. The Asiatic must sleep after his mid-day meal, if it be only for half an hour. The loss of this little sleep is a very severe privation.

At three o'clock the encampment was again all life. Some of the Sepoys wrestled, and exhibited amazing skill and strength in the art. To an European it is a mystery how men who live upon nothing but farinaceous food can be so muscular and powerful. Others smoked their pipes (small hookahs), and played at a native game called puchesee, resembling lotto; while a goodly number congregated around a Mussulman, who was reading aloud the Bagh-o-Bahar, a Hindoostanee work of great celebrity. Two or three of the company were musical, and played alternately on the sitarre (native guitar or violin), accompanied by the tom-tom (native drum), and the voices of those who were disposed and able to sing. As for the Lieutenant and myself we beguiled the time in conversation and with *écarté*. Towards sunset a palkee dâk carriage was reported to be in sight, coming down the road. "Hooray!" cried the Lieutenant; "come along! let us board him. I am in want of a few small matters."

It was not long before the dâk carriage was abreast of the encampment.

"Stop!" shouted the Lieutenant to the driver, who instantly pulled up. "Whom have you got inside?"

Before the driver had time to reply, the door was slided open, and an elderly gentleman, rubbing his eyes with his knuckles, put out his night-capped head, and exclaimed:

"Hulloa!"

"What! have we woke you out of your sleep, old boy?" said the Lieutenant, laughing.

"Yes," replied the old boy, very good-humouredly, "what do you want?"

"Only to ask you how you are."

"I'm pretty well," was the reply, "but half choked with the dust."

"What's taking you down the country?"

"Urgent private affairs."

"Going to be married, I suppose?"

"Well, you have just guessed it."

"Make my most respectful salaam to your intended, will you?"

"By all means."

"When do you expect to reach Cawnpore?"

"To-morrow, at three P.M."

"And how do you stand affected for liquors and weeds? Do you want anything, old boy? Brandy, beer, soda-water? Say the word."

"Nothing; I have more in the well here than I shall be able to consume."

"Then I'll trouble you for the surplus; for I am very short, and cannot get anything till I reach Agra, while you can replenish at every station, you know."

"All right, my child," exclaimed the old boy; and, with the greatest cheerfulness, he alighted and began to unpack his stores. From these, the Lieutenant took six bottles of beer, two bottles of brandy, a dozen of soda-water, and three hundred Manilla cheroots. This done, the old boy expressed a desire to push on; but the Lieutenant detained him for at least ten minutes with a series of questions, several of which (I thought), were somewhat impertinent; for instance, he inquired his intended's name? whether she was tall, short, or of the middle height? what was the colour of her hair and eyes? good-looking, and accomplished? And to all these questions, the old boy responded with as serious an air as if the Lieutenant had a perfect right to put them.

At last the old boy proceeded on his journey.

"Do you know him?" I inquired of the Lieutenant, as the carriage rolled away.

"Oh, yes," was the reply; "he is a Major commanding a native infantry regiment at Banda. He is a very good fellow, and has heaps of property; but a frightful fool, except in the way of money-making, and at that he is awfully clever. I first made his acquaintance in Affghanistan. He was then in the commissariat department, and was only taken out of that department about a year ago, when he attained his majority. He knows nothing whatever of soldiering, having been in staff employ ever since he was an ensign. All the Sepoys, as well as his officers, laugh *at* him as he comes on the parade ground and attempts to handle the regiment; and, after the farce is over, he laughs *with* them. For thirty years he was employed in commissariat duties, in which he is very efficient. At the expiration of that period, he became a Major; and then, according to the rules of the service, he was withdrawn from staff employ, and appointed to command a corps!"

"Surely you are jesting?"

"On my honour, I am serious. That is a part of our military system, sir."

Here our conversation was interrupted by the approach of the soubadhar—native commissioned officer—who pronounced in a deep, sonorous, but feeble and inarticulate voice, that familiar word "Sahib!" or, as more commonly pronounced, "Sarb!"

"Well, old man, what is the matter?" said the Lieutenant to the almost imbecile native veteran, who had served in the time of Lord Lake, and who ought to have been pensioned many years previously, despite any remonstrances against such a measure. The old man forthwith began to detail a string of grievances, which the Lieutenant faithfully (?) promised to see remedied, albeit he could understand but a few words the old man said—so very indistinct was his speech, from sheer old age, and the loss of his teeth.

"A grievance, real or imaginary, is quite necessary for that old man's existence," said the Lieutenant; "and if he can't find one for himself (which is a very rare circumstance), he will concoct one for the Sepoys. To make grievances is the end and object of that old man's life; and, I am sorry to say, that he is a perfect representative of the entire body of native commissioned officers, who are, generally speaking, despised by the men of the regiment, as well as by the European officers. These are the gentlemen who brew or ferment all the mischief that occasionally occurs in native regiments. They suggest to the men to make all sorts of extortionate demands, just as a regiment is on the point of marching. That old man's present grievance, as far as I could collect, is that the water is very bad here, at this encampment ground, and that government ought to have a new well sunk. He happens just now to be suffering severely from one of the very many ailments consequent on his time of life, and he attributes it to the water."

"Which happens to be very good," I remarked.

"Precisely so. These native officers, of every rank and grade, are, in my opinion, the curse of the native service. Many very clear-headed and experienced officers have recommended doing away with them, and appointing in their stead more European officers; but the advice has never been heeded, and never will be, I fear."

It was not until midnight that the little camp was broken up, and we resumed the march towards Agra. During the drive, the Lieutenant entertained me by relating a number of stories connected with the war in Affghanistan. Several of them interested me exceedingly; one, in particular. It was this; which I now give in the Lieutenant's own words, as nearly as I can recollect them.

"About a year ago," said he, "I was passing through Meerut, on my way from the Hills, whither I had been on sick certificate, and was putting up for a few days with my friend Richards, of the Light Cavalry—a man whom I had known during that disastrous campaign to which this narrative has reference. One morning, after breakfast, there came to the bungalow of my friend an Affghan, who was a dealer in dried fruits—such as grapes, apples, and pomegranates,—and inquired if the Sahib or mem Sahib was in want of any of these commodities, which he had just brought from Caubul. My friend's wife, who had also been in Affghanistan, and spoke the mongrel Persian current in that country, replied in the affirmative, and the Affghan was admitted to the verandah to exhibit his specimens and declare his prices. To talk to these dealers is rather amusing at times, especially when you know their habits, and customs, and peculiarities, as well as their language. To people who have been in their country, it is like meeting with an old friend, and one lingers as long as possible over the business of the bargain and sale. And so was it this morning. We had him for at least an hour in the verandah before my friend's wife would decide upon what she would take. This matter concluded, the Affghan inquired if the lady would buy a kitten —a Persian kitten; kittens being also a commodity with these travelling Affghans.

"'Yes; where are the kittens?' said the lady.

"'Here,' said the merchant, putting his hand into a huge pocket at the back of his chogah (a sort of gaberdine), and withdrawing, one by one, no less than sixteen of these little animals (all males). For more than the hour which was consumed in negotiating about the fruit, and talking on other subjects, this living bustle had remained perfectly motionless, and had not uttered a single sound; but now, when they saw the light, and were placed upon all-fours, they ran about and mewed—bushy tails on end—after the most vigorous fashion imaginable. There they were! Kittens as black as the blackest ink, kittens white as the whitest snow, kittens as yellow as the yellowest gold, and kittens piebald, brindled, and grey.

"'There, mem Sahib; take your choice. Twenty rupees (two pounds) each.'

"The lady selected one of the white and one of the black kittens, and for the two he was induced to accept thirty-five rupees (three pounds ten shillings).

This may seem a large sum of money to give for a brace of young cats; but it must be remembered that they came from Bokhara, and were of the purest breed that could possibly be procured.

"The Affghan dealer took his leave, and promised to send the fruits in the course of the day. He fulfilled his promise; at tiffin-time there came a boy of about eleven years of age, bearing the basket containing them upon his head, which was shawled after the fashion of the Affghan people. The boy was admitted to the room. No sooner was he shown in, than his exceedingly beautiful countenance, and its peculiar expression, riveted the attention of all of us, and we put to him a variety of questions which he answered with great intelligence, and in a tone of voice so soft and silvery that even the guttural sounds he uttered came like music on the ear.

"'Look into that boy's face,' said the lady to her husband and myself; 'observe his every feature, and his teeth,—regard especially his smile,—yes, and even the shape of his fingers, and then tell me of whom he is the very image.'

"'I know,' said my friend.

"'So do I,' exclaimed your humble servant.

"'Stay!' said the lady, energetically. 'Do not speak; but let each of us write the name on a slip of paper, and see if we agree;' and tearing up an envelope and taking a tiny pencil-case from her watch-chain, she wrote a name upon one slip, and then handed to me and to her husband, respectively, a slip and the pencil-case. When we had each written a name, we compared them,—and they did not agree exactly. My friend and his wife had written Captain Percy ——, and I had written Mrs. Percy ——. That the boy was the offspring of that unfortunate couple (cousins), who perished in that campaign, and of whose young child no one ever knew what had become, we were all quite satisfied; and our reflections became extremely melancholy.

"We questioned the boy as to his parentage, his relation to the Affghan dealer in cats and fruit, and on a variety of other matters. His replies were simply to the effect that he was an orphan and a slave; that he knew not the place of his birth, but believed it was Affghanistan; that he was a Mahommedan, and that his earliest recollections were associated with Caubul.

"Whilst we were thus interrogating the boy, the Major of my friend's regiment, accompanied by his wife, drove up to the door. They had come to pay a visit. When asked to look at the boy, and say to whom he bore a resemblance, they at once declared, 'Poor Percy ——!' Several officers of the regiment were sent for. They came, and immediately on seeing the boy expressed an opinion that he was the child of the unfortunate officer whose name has been partially recorded. The poor boy, meanwhile, exhibited some anxiety to return to his master. But he was detained and further questioned as to the manner in which he was treated. He confessed that his master was rather severe, but withal a very good man.

"It was resolved to summon the Affghan dealer and make him render an account of the boy, and of how he became possessed of him. For this purpose a messenger was dispatched, and enjoined to make haste.

"The Affghan dealer came, and was cautioned that he must speak the truth; whereupon—as is the custom in India from one end to the other—he declared that he never spoke falsely, and that he would rather have his tongue torn out. This little preliminary over, the examination (which was conducted by the Major of the regiment, a very shrewd and clever man, and who, by the way, was distantly related to the unfortunate couple to whom the boy bore such a strong resemblance) commenced:—

"'Who is this boy?'

"'He belongs to me.'

"'Your son?'

"'No.'

"'Any relation of yours?'

"'No.'

"'Your slave?'

"'Yes.'

"'You bought him?'

"'Yes.'

"'Where?'

"'Caubul.'

"'When?'

"'Four years ago.'

"'From whom did you buy him?'

"'A merchant.'

"'His name?'

"'Usuf Ooddeen.'

"'What did you give for him?'

"'Three camels.'

"'Of what value?'

"'Thirty rupees (3*l.*) each.'

"'The boy was cheap, then?'

"'No.'

"'How so?'

"'He was young and sickly.'

"'Did Usuf say where he got him from?'

"'Yes.'

"'Then tell me.'

"'From a woman.'

"'What woman?'

"'A native of Hindostan.'

"'An ayah?'

"'Yes.'

"'Was she his mother?'

"'No.'

"'Is she living?'

"'No.'

"'When did she die?'

"'Eight years ago.'

"'Where?'

"'In Caubul.'

"'Now tell us all you know about this boy.'

"'I have answered all the Sahib's questions; will the Sahib answer a few of mine?'

"'Yes.'

"'Do you believe this boy to be of European birth?'

"'Yes.'

"'Do you think you know who were his parents?'

"'Yes.'

"'Were they people of a distinguished family?'

"'Yes.' (This question was answered rather proudly.)

"'Of pure blood?'

"'Yes.'

"'But is the Sahib certain that this boy is the child of certain parents?'

"'Yes.'

"'Then will the Sahib take him?'

"'Yes.'

"Here the poor boy placed his hands together and supplicated the Major to let him remain where he then was, in the service of the Affghan dealer. Heedless of this interruption, which was soon silenced, the examination—or rather the conversation, as it now became—was continued:—

"'What will you give for him?'

"'What do you ask?'

"'*You* must speak, Sahib.'

"'One hundred rupees.'

"'He cost me nearly that when he was very young and sickly.'

"'Well, two hundred rupees.'

"'No; Sahib. Half a lac of rupees would not purchase him.'

"'But, my good man, slavery is not permitted in the British dominions, and we will detain the boy.'

"'Against his will?'

"'Yes.'

"'On suspicion that he is born of European parents of distinction?'

"'Yes.'

"'Then I will give the boy his liberty; and if he then wishes to follow me, and you detain him, he is your prisoner instead of my slave.'

"Here the boy again entreated the Major to spare him.

"'Never mind that.'

"'But suppose that I could prove to you that he is the child of a sergeant of the Queen's 13th Regiment of Foot, and of his wife? What then? Would you take the boy?'

"'Yes.'

"'You would?'

"'Yes.'

"'Then you shall have the boy. Many of your questions I answered falsely, on purpose. The true history of the child I will recount to you, and produce such proofs as I have in my possession. I vowed to God and to the Prophet that I would never sell the child, and I have kept my word. It will be a bitter grief to me to part with him; but, for his own sake, I will endure it.

" 'Usuf Ooddeen was my elder brother. He kept a shop in the bazaar at Caubul. This child was brought to him by a woman of Hindostan, who not not only deposited with him the child, but a sum of money in gold mohurs and rupees; likewise a quantity of English jewellery, and her own gold and silver bangles. She represented to my brother that the child's parents had been killed, and that she was afraid every European in Affghanistan would share their fate. My brother knew the woman, that is to say, she had been a customer at his shop, and had purchased from him sundry articles of warm clothing for her employers and herself. After leaving the child, and the money, and the jewellery, in all to the value of about four thousand rupees, she went her way, and never returned. It is most likely that she died suddenly of cold, like very many of the native servants of Hindostan, both male and female. The frost settled about their hearts, and they slept their lives away; or, if they escaped death, they lost their toes, fingers, ears, or noses.

" 'When the British army was victorious, and affairs were in a somewhat settled state, my brother was most anxious to deliver up the child, the money, and the jewels, to the British authorities ; but a number of his friends dissuaded him from so doing, on the ground that the bare possession of the child would place my brother's life in jeopardy, by inducing a conclusion that he was the affrighted accomplice of murderers, assassins, and thieves. I confess that I was one who entertained this opinion, and I shook my head whenever my brother repeated his desire. Four or five years ago, my brother died, and I, a wandering dealer, became the guardian of this boy (for whom I have a great affection), and the holder of his money, for which I care not, and which I have no desire to retain. He has travelled thousands and thousands of miles with me. He has been to Bokhara, to Cashmere, all over the Punjab, to Mooltan, Scinde, all through the north-west provinces down to Calcutta, to Simlah, Mussooree—wherever the English have settled themselves in India ; and I have done all in my power to expose him, in a quiet way, to the gaze of ladies and gentlemen, in the hope that some day he would be recognised and restored to his proper position in life. Never, until now, has any one been struck with his countenance, beyond casually remarking to me that he was a very pretty boy ; certainly, no one ever seemed to have the slightest idea that he was born of European parents, and is a Christian ; for he is not a Mussulman—though he thinks he is a Mussulman, and says his prayers, and is very constant to all the observances of the Mussulman faith. Gentleman, I am a wandering dealer from Affghanistan, but I am not destitute of good feeling and integrity, little as you may credit my assertions in this respect. Give me a proof that you know who were the child's parents, and I am willing to restore him, and all that rightfully belongs to him, to your custody.'

" 'But are you not satisfied with my word? Never mind the money and the jewels—much as I should like to see the latter—all I require is the boy,' said the Major.

" 'Of course, the Sahib would not speak an untruth knowingly,' returned the Affghan. 'But I require some proof that the boy is the child of certain European parents.'

" 'Well, there is the likeness, the unmistakeable likeness, that he bears to his father and his mother.'

" 'That will not do,' said the Affghan, interrupting the Major. 'Can you write in the Persian character, Sahib?'

" 'Yes.'

" 'Then, write the name of this boy's father in the Persian character, and let me see it.'

" The Major did this, and handed it to the Affghan, who looked at the writing, smiled, and said:

" 'What else? What was the Sahib's nishan (crest)?'

" 'This,' said the Major, holding out the little

finger of his right hand, upon which was a signet-ring. 'This was his nishan. We are of the same family, and the nishan is the same.'

"The Affghan, having examined the crest, again smiled, and said :—

"'What else?'

"'What more do you want?' said the Major.

"'Do not be impatient, Sahib,' said the Affghan. 'The identification of a child, who may be an heir to property, is not so light a matter as the purchase of a kitten. Did you know the child's mother?'

"'Yes,' said the Major. 'She was also a relation of mine.'

"'What kind of person was she? Was she handsome?'

"'Very.'

"'The colour of her eyes?'

"'Dark—almost black.'

"'And her hair?'

"'Brown; the colour of this lady's' (pointing to the wife of my friend).

"'If you saw her likeness, in miniature, do you think you could recognise it?'

"'If it were a faithful likeness, I could.'

"The Affghan put his hand into the breast pocket of his chogah, and produced a greasy leathern bag, into the mouth of which he inserted his finger and thumb, and presently produced a small tin box, round and shallow, which he very carefully opened.

Having removed some cotton, he handed the box to the Major. All of us instantly recognised the features of the unfortunate lady who had perished by the side of her husband, in Affghanistan. Who could possibly forget that sweet feminine face of hers, which had been painted for her husband by one of the most distinguished miniature painters of the age? The production of the likeness in the presence of the boy (who appeared to take little interest in what was going on), had a sad effect upon the Major. He sat down upon a chair, covered his manly face with his hands, and wept bitterly.

"'And do you know this, Sahib?' asked the Affghan, when the Major had somewhat recovered his violent emotion: placing in his hand poor Percy's seal.

"We all recognised the seal, the crest of which, of course, corresponded with the crest on the signet-ring of the Major.

"'And this?' asked the Affghan, holding up a bracelet which we had seen Mrs. Percy wear many and many a time.

"'And this?' holding up to our gaze a small brooch she used to wear constantly. And, amongst numerous other things, he exhibited to us a little pocket-book, in which she kept her memoranda, such as:—'November 9th. Cut the ends of my dear little boy's hair. Sent mamma a small portion.—November 12th. Had a long talk to the old ayah, who swore to me that she would . . . . and I believe her, for she has been a good and constant creature to us, in our dangers and our difficulties.'

"'And this? And this? And this? and this?' said the Affghan, withdrawing from the leathern bag its entire contents, every article of which was instantly identified. 'There, Sahib, take them all, and the boy, into your custody. The money, which was left with him, I will restore to you to-night. It is at present in the bazaar, in the charge of my camel, whom no one dare approach, except myself and this boy.'

"Here a very extraordinary and painful, but perhaps natural, scene occurred. The boy, who had been comparatively passive, now broke out into a vehement expostulation, and spoke with a rapidity which was truly amazing, considering that he distinctly enunciated every syllable to which he gave utterance. 'What!' he exclaimed, 'will you then leave me in the hands and at the mercy of these unbelievers? What have I done to deserve this?'

"'Be quiet,' said the Affghan to the boy, in a gentle tone of voice.

"'How can I be quiet?' cried the boy, clenching his fists convulsively, and drawing himself up, whilst his eyes glared, and his nostrils dilated, with uncontrollable passion, and something like foam stood upon his crimson lips. There could be no doubt whose child he was, so wonderful in his wrath was the likeness that he bore to his father, who was very seldom provoked to anger, but who, when it did happen, was 'perplexed in the extreme:' in short, a perfect demon until the paroxysm was over.

"'Baba (child)!' said the Major, 'listen to me.'

"'Don't talk to him now, Sahib,' said the Affghan, compassionately. 'In his anger his senses always leave him, and he cannot hear what you say. Let him exhaust his fury upon me. He will be powerless presently.'

"And so it was. After a brief while, the boy sat down on the carpet, gasped for breath, and was seemingly unable to move or speak. The lady of the house offered him a glass of water, but he shrunk back, and declined to receive it from her hand.

"The Affghan took the Major aside, spoke to him in private, and then left the room. Here another very painful scene ensued. The boy, exhausted as he was, attempted to follow his late master; he was restrained, of course; whereupon he uttered the most heart-rending cries that ever were heard. The Major had him conveyed to his bungalow, where a room was set apart for him, and a servant and an orderly had him in their keeping. It was a month before the boy could be reconciled to his 'fate,' as he called it; and soon afterwards arrangements were made for sending him home to his grandfather and grandmother, who are persons of a lofty position in life and very wealthy. They received him with extreme affection, and on the death of his grandfather, he will succeed to a title and an estate worth eleven thousand a-year. The Affghan, who was very fond of the boy, corresponds with him regularly, and they exchange presents, as well as letters.

"Kelly, of the 62nd, who was killed at Ferozeshah, and who formerly belonged to the 13th Foot, when they were in Affghanistan, told me a more curious story of a little girl, than the one I have related to you of this boy."

"What was it?" I asked.

"My dear fellow," said the Lieutenant, "I cannot talk any more just now. You shall have it some other day. We are not going to part company yet, old boy." With these words he fell asleep, his feet over the dashboard, and his head resting on my shoulder.

THE MARCH CONTINUED.

THE next encampment-ground at which we halted was close to a dâk bungalow; and, during the day, there were several arrivals and departures, the travellers merely halting for an hour or so, while some refreshment was got ready. The Lieutenant, who appeared to know everybody in Hindostan (I never met a person who did not know him), contrived, to use his own phrase, to "screw a small chat out of each of them." On one occasion he returned to the tent richer than he left it. He carried in one hand a small basket containing preserved oysters, crystallized apricots, and captains' biscuits, and in the other a stone bottle of Maraschino. Under his arm was a quantity of gauze, which he wanted for a veil, he said. These contributions he had levied from a lady who was going to Muttra, where her husband was an official of some magnitude. She had just returned from England, the Lieutenant informed me, and was looking as blooming as possible. To my question, "Do you know her?" he responded, "Oh yes; she is one of my sixty!"

"Sixty what?"

"First cousins."

"All in India?"

"Every one of them. My good sir, I have at this moment, in the Bengal Presidency alone, upwards of two hundred and twenty relations and connexions, male and female, and every one of them—that is to say, the men and the boys—in the service of the government."

"Is it possible?"

"Yes. What is more, four-fifths of the number are in the civil service. I should have been in the civil service too, only I was sent away from Haileybury for rebellion and card-playing. It is not an easy matter for me to go to any station in these provinces without finding a cousin in it."

"Do you know the assistant-magistrate of Agra?"

"Yes."

"Is he a cousin of yours?"

"*He* isn't. But his wife's father and my father were own brothers; so it amounts to pretty much the same thing."

"And do you know the judge of Jampore?" This was a gentleman to whom I had letters of introduction.

"Yes. His mother was my aunt."

"It must be dangerous," I suggested, "to express an opinion of any one in India in the presence of a man who has so very many relations."

"Oh, dear no!" said the Lieutenant. "A man with such a frightful lot of connexions has no right to be, and is not generally, very sensitive. Bless me!

if I had nothing to do but to stand up for my relations, I should run the risk of being perpetually knocked down. Life is much too short for that sort of thing. Therefore, when I hear any one abuse or reflect upon any relation or connexion of mine, I am invariably silent; or, if appealed to, express my indifference by a shrug of the shoulders."

Here we were interrupted by the old soubahdar, who came to the door of the tent. He had dined, washed, smoked, slept, and had now got up to grumble. His huge teak-box, which measured four feet by two, and two feet deep, and without which he never travelled, had received a slight injury, and of this he had come to complain. He said, that in the time of Lord Clive or Lord Lake, if such a thing had happened, the men in charge of the hackeries (carts) would have been hanged on the spot; and Phool Singh Brahmin, whose exertions, he alleged, prevented the utter destruction of the box, would have been promoted to the rank of havildar.

"Clive and Lake!" whispered the Lieutenant to me. "He talks like a leading article in a London newspaper." Then, turning to the old man, he inquired, "Would Lord Clive or Lord Lake have sanctioned your carrying about that beastly trunk on a march at all?"

"Yes, Sahib."

"It is not true. Lord Clive and Lord Lake gained their victories by the help of self-denying men, who cheerfully endured any personal inconvenience; not by a parcel of old grumblers like yourself, who have no right to refer to the career of those illustrious men."

"Sahib, I was with Lord Lake's army."

"Then, that's the very reason that you ought not to be here."

"But our present Colonel, Sahib, was with Lord Lake."

"And I wish he was with Lord Lake now!"

"I shall report this, Sahib."

"Very well. Do!"

Whereupon the old officer left the tent, and the Lieutenant assured me that the Colonel, who was as imbecile as the Soubahdar, would cause the matter to be investigated, and that he, the Lieutenant, would, to a certainty, receive a severe reprimand.

"For what?" I asked.

"For not having made arrangements for the safe conveyance of the baggage, and for having treated with a want of courtesy a native commissioned officer of the regiment. I need scarcely say, that this reprimand will not in any way interfere with my night's rest."

"But, the complainant will forget it," said I, "before he gets back to the regiment."

"Forget it!" exclaimed the Lieutenant. "Forget it! A native—especially a native commissioned officer—forget a grievance! Catch that old man forgetting the slightest unpleasantness that has occurred to him during this march. He will, it is true, forget his present grievance to-morrow, when he has a fresh one; but at the end of the journey they will be forthcoming in a lump."

This prophecy was destined not to be fulfilled; for, presently, a Sepoy came to the Lieutenant, and reported that the Soubahdar was very ill. We hastened to the old man's tent, and found him, strange to say, in the last extremity. He was going very fast; but, nevertheless, he continued to gurgle forth a grievance. He demanded, with his last breath—why the East India Company did not give him his pay, as in Lord Lake's time, in *sicca* rupees?

"You shall, in future, receive it in sicca rupees," said the Lieutenant, bending over the old man, whose hand he grasped tightly.

"And will my losses be made good?" he asked, with awful energy.

"Yes," said the Lieutenant.

"It is well!" and the old man slipped almost imperceptibly from one world to another.

That the old Soubahdar, who was upwards of eighty, had died of natural causes, there could be no question; but, clamorous as was the entire company for the interment of the body, the Lieutenant determined on taking it to Agra, for the purpose of a surgical examination. Meanwhile the old man's effects were scrupulously collected and put under seal.

We were now only twenty-six miles from Agra, the capital of the North West Provinces, and it was agreed to perform the distance in one march. We therefore started at sundown, and travelled all night. The moon was shining brightly, the road was in excellent order, and, notwithstanding that the old Soubahdar was lying lifeless on the top of some of the treasure-boxes, the Sepoys were in high spirits, and on several occasions even jocular in respect to the deceased's weakness — that of perpetually grumbling.

Shortly after the day had dawned, I beheld on the distant horizon something like a large white cloud. Had we been at sea, I should have said it was a sail or an iceberg, to which it bore a striking resemblance. I pointed it out to the Lieutenant, who smiled.

"Don't you know what that is?" he said.

"No," I answered.

"Can't you guess?"

"No. What is it?"

"That is the famous Taj Mahal. That is the building that defies the most graphic pen in the world to do justice to its grandeur and its transcendent beauty. Bulwer, in the *Lady of Lyons*, has a passage which sometimes reminds me of the Taj:—

> A palace lifting to eternal summer
> Its marble halls from out a glassy bower
> Of coolest foliage, musical with birds.

But how far short must any description of such a

place fall! How far distant do you suppose we are from that building?"

"About two miles."

"Upwards of nine miles, as the crow flies! Yes; that is the Taj, the tomb of a woman, the wife of the Emperor Shah Jehan. The pure white marble of which it is built was brought from Ajmere. For upwards of twenty-five years, twenty-five thousand men were employed, day by day, on that edifice. I am afraid to say how many millions it cost. The Mahrattas carried away the huge silver gates and made them into rupees. What became of the inner gate, which was formed of a single piece of agate, no one can say. The general opinion is, that it is buried somewhere in Bhurtpore. The original idea was, to build a corresponding tomb on this side of the river for the Emperor himself, and connect the two by a bridge of white marble. A very pretty idea, was it not? Lord William Bentinck was for pulling the Taj down and selling the marble, or using it for building purposes."

"Impossible!"

"Not at all. He thought it was very impolitic to allow these gorgeous edifices to stand—these monuments of folly, extravagance, and superstition, which served none but the worst of prejudices, leading the natives to draw prejudicial comparisons between the simple and economical structures of the British and these stupendous and costly erections of the Mogul

Emperors. And most assuredly our bungalows, churches, and other buildings do present a most beggarly appearance alongside these masses of polished marble and red stone. It looks as though we had no confidence in our hold of the country, and therefore would not go to any expense worth speaking of. Look at our court-houses, in the civil lines, as that part of Agra is called—a parcel of paltry brick and mortar pigeon-holes, not to be compared with the tenements that the menial servants of the Emperors inhabited. Look at the Government House, the Metcalfe Testimonial, and other paltry European edifices.

"Surely," said I, "you would preserve rather than deface or destroy these magnificent works of art—these wonders of the world?"

"Works of art and wonders of the world they doubtless are; but, under existing circumstances, they are eye-sores, and I would pull down every one of them, and convert the material into useful buildings—barracks—splendid barracks for our British and native troops; hospitals, worthy of being called hospitals; court-houses, churches, magazines, and so forth."

"But what barbarians the natives would think us!"

"What does that signify? Are we the conquerors of the country, or are we not? As to what they would think of us, they can't think much worse of us than they do already. Do we not eat swine's flesh? and do not English ladies dance (the natives call it 'jumping about'), and with men who are not their husbands? Barbarians! Why, the very dress that we wear renders us barbarians in their sight."

The sun had now risen high in the heavens, and his rays fell upon the Taj, which we were gradually approaching. I was wrapped in admiration, and wishing in my inmost heart that my talkative companion would cease, and leave me to gaze in silence on that glorious scene, when suddenly the procession halted, and the Lieutenant shouted out the word "Hulloa!" in a voice so loud that I was completely startled.

"What is the matter?" I asked.

"Matter!" the Lieutenant echoed me. "Matter! Look a-head! There is a wheel off one of those rickety carts, and those confounded boxes are scattered all over the road." Here the little officer bounded like an Indian-rubber ball from his seat, and in a towering passion with all the world in general, but no one in particular, rushed to the spot where the disaster had occurred, and there began to fret, fume, and snort most violently.

"Hush, Sahib!" said one of the Sepoys, saluting his officer very respectfully, "or you may wake the Soubahdar, and *then* what will happen?"

This appeal had the effect of restoring the Lieutenant to calmness and good-humour. He smiled, and seemed to feel that matters would certainly have been worse, and the delay more protracted, had the old man been alive and witnessed the accident.

One of the boxes was smashed to pieces, and the rupees were lying about in all directions, the Sepoys picking them up, and searching for others in the dust and sand. I never witnessed a more ridiculous or grotesque scene than this—the native soldiers in their red coats and chacos, but with bare legs and without shoes, kneeling, and sifting the earth through their fingers, the Lieutenant in his pyjamahs and solar hat, a cheroot in his mouth, and in his hand the buggy-whip, which he used as a baton while giving his orders.

"Does this often happen?" I was tempted to ask.

"Constantly," was the Lieutenant's reply. "The Government has a bullock-train for the conveyance of stores; and even private individuals, by paying for the carriage, may have their goods taken from station to station; but, in respect to treasure, we cling to the old system. The military authorities apply to the magistrates, whose subordinates provide these hackeries, which were in vogue some five thousand years ago. And just observe those rotten boxes."

"Why are they not lined with cast iron or zinc?"

"It would be too expensive. The Government cannot afford it."

"But why should not the Government use its own

bullock-train for the conveyance of treasure, instead of hiring these antiquated and rotten conveyances?"

"Because the bullock-train is under the post-office authorities; and the military authorities have nothing to do with the post-office authorities."

"Is that a reason?"

"No—nor is it rhyme; but it is a part of our Indian system, and, what is more, it is Government logic. However, I am not going to stop here all day. We will push on, and get into Agra before breakfast. The treasure will come all right enough, and I will be there to meet it at the office of the magistrate and collector."

We now took our seats in the old buggy. The hood was raised, the syce sat behind, and off we went at a canter, which very soon became a gallop. In the parlance of the Lieutenant, the old horse was indeed "a ripper." When warm there was no holding him, and he went over his seven and a half miles of ground in thirty-seven minutes. At the bridge of boats which crosses the Jumna, we met, by chance, the assistant magistrate (the friend with whom I was going to stay, and the husband of the Lieutenant's first cousin). He was dressed in a pair of large jack-boots, corduroy breeches, a shooting-coat, and a solar helmet, and was riding an immensely powerful Cape horse. He did not recognise either of us at first, but pulled up, and turned round the moment the Lieutenant shouted out his name, with the addition of "Old boy!"—housebold words in the mouth of the Lieutenant, for he not only applied them to things animate, but inanimate ; for instance, his corkscrew, his teapot, his buggy, his watch, his hat, everything with him was an old boy, in common with the Lieutenant-Governor, or the general commanding the division.

After I had been greeted by my friend, who had been at a loss to account for my delay in reaching Agra—the Lieutenant thus addressed him :

"I say, old boy. Look here. I have a lot of treasure for you about seven or eight miles from this ; but there has been a break down. Send out a lot of fellows to give assistance, will you?"

"Yes."

"And look here, old boy. There's a dead Soubahdar."

"A what?"

"A dead Soubahdar. He died suddenly, and I don't wish him to be buried without an examination, because I bullied him mildly only a short time previous to his going out. You will manage that for me, old boy, won't you?"

"Oh, yes."

"He died of old age, and his last grievance ; but still I should like a medical man's certificate ; just to satisfy the colonel who served with him in Lord Lake's time, you know, and all that sort of thing."

"I can manage all that for you," replied the official, riding by the side of the buggy ; "but push on, for the sun is becoming rather oppressive, and I have no hood to my saddle, remember."

My host and hostess made me as comfortable and as happy as any traveller could wish to be made. Of the former I saw little or nothing from eleven in the morning till three or four in the evening, for he was what is called a conscientious officer, and attended strictly to his work. During these hours I used to read, or pay a visit to the mess-rooms of a regiment where a billiard-table was kept. To the officers of the regiment I was introduced by Lieutenant Sixtie, previous to his return to his own corps. He stayed eight days in Agra—upon some plea or other—and sent his company on, in advance of him.

Agra—that is to say, the society of Agra—was at the time split into two sections, the civil and the military. They were not exactly at open war, but there was a coolness existing between the two branches. They did not invite each other, and very seldom exchanged calls. For me, who was desirous of seeing all parties, this was rather awkward, living as I was in the house of a civilian. So I resolved upon taking a small bungalow for a short period, and furnishing it in a mild and inexpensive manner. I was candid enough to confess to my host that, as I was in no way connected with either branch of the service, I was anxious to avoid taking any part in their local differences; and he had the good sense not to press me to remain under his roof.

A few days after I had located myself in my bungalow, I received a call from a native gentleman, a Seik chieftain, who was, and now is, a state prisoner on a handsome stipend. He drove up to my door in a small phaeton, drawn by a pair of large black mules of incredible swiftness and agility. This fallen chieftain—a tall and powerfully-built man—was no other than the renowned Rajah Lall Singh, who commanded the Seik cavalry at the battle of Ferozeshah, and who was subsequently Prime Minister at Lahore, during a portion of the time that the British Government undertook the administration of the Punjab on behalf of Maharajah Dulleep Singh. Lall Singh was now studying surgery. More than one medical officer in charge of the hospitals which he attended, informed me that the Rajah was already a comparatively skilful operator, and could take off an arm or a leg with surprising dexterity. Notwithstanding his previous character—that of a sensualist and faithless intriguer; one, indeed, who had not been constant even to his own villanies—I could not help liking his conversation, which was humorously enlivened with imitations of English officers with whom he had come in contact, and was entertaining to the last degree. His anecdotes, relating to the late Runjeet Singh, were peculiarly interesting; coming as they did from the lips of a man who had been so much in the company of that remarkable monarch, who in many respects resembled Napoleon the First, especially in the selection of the instruments of his power. "All his" (Runjeet's) "chief men," said the Rajah, "were persons of obscure origin: Tej Singh, Sawan Mull, Deenanauth, and the rest of them."

"But you were an exception," said I.

"Indeed not," was his reply. "I began life as a muleteer, and hence my partiality for mules, perhaps."

After a while the Rajah invited me to take a drive with him, to a house about two miles in the country, and situated on the banks of the Jumna. It was not his own house, which was then under repair, he said, but had been placed at his disposal by a friend. I thanked the Rajah, and stepped into his carriage; he followed me, seized the reins, shook the whip, and away we went at the rate of sixteen miles an hour.

The garden-house, at which we soon arrived, was a spacious building of European architecture. It had formerly belonged to a general officer who had married a native woman of considerable wealth. The furniture was all of European make, and was arranged very much in the same manner as that in the Sahib Logue's apartments at Bhitoor. In point of quality it was also very much the same—a portion costly, and the rest of a common description. This house, too, was constantly inhabited by English folks who sought a change of air for a few days. Since his removal to Agra, Lall Singh lived more like an European than a native, and had got into the habit of sitting at ease in a chair, instead of cross-legged like a tailor on the carpet. His dress was of the simplest and most unpretending character imaginable; and, with the exception of a signet-ring on his forefinger, he had no ornament on his person. The table of the apartment to which he conducted me was literally covered with surgical instruments—saws, knives, scalpels of every size and shape. Amongst them I perceived a pair of swords in wooden scabbards covered with rich green velvet, and ornamented with gold and precious stones. Observing that my eyes rested on these swords, he took one up, and remarked, "These have performed some curious operations in their time; but never in a hospital. They have been used chiefly for taking off neads. This once belonged to Dhyan Singh, and that to Heera Singh, who were both assassinated. They are of Damascus steel, and are sharper than any of these knives or scalpels. I have sent a number of swords to England to have them made into surgical instruments." Here our conversation was interrupted by a domestic, who announced—

"THE LALLAH SAHIB;"

and presently a native gentleman walked, or rather limped (for he was lame of the right leg) into the room, and made a very graceful salaam, first to the Rajah and then to myself. He was rather short in stature, but very stoutly built, and about forty years of age. His eyes were full of intelligence and vigour, and his features regular and well-shapen. His manners were easy, affable, unassuming, and modest, and his attire as plain and quiet as possible.

"This gentleman, Sahib," said the Rajah, addressing me, "is a great friend of mine. This house belongs to him. A strange world is this! Only a few years ago, I offered a reward of a lac of rupees (ten thousand pounds) for his head, or two lacs to any one who would bring him alive to my tent."

"Indeed!"

"Yes; and if I had caught him, how changed would have been the whole face of affairs in this country!"

"How so?"

"This gentleman was the contractor for the British army; and, if I had got hold of him, the army could not have been supplied."

"But why was he worth more alive than dead?" I asked, with a laugh, in which the native gentleman heartily joined.

"Because," returned the Rajah, coolly, "if we had secured him alive we would have made him feed us with the supplies bought with his own money; which should also have paid the reward for his capture. This, by the way, was claimed by several who brought in heads, alleging that each was the head of the Lallah the contractor; but the attempted imposition was discovered, and the perpetrators were themselves decapitated."

Unlike Hindoos and Mussulmans, who drink in secret, Lall Singh drank neat brandy openly; and, rising from his chair, he administered unto himself a couple of glasses—or rather a tumbler half-filled—on this occasion. He could take more than two bottles of brandy without being in the least intoxicated. This was owing, of course, to the circumstance that he consumed considerable quantities of bhang; just in the same way that an opium-eater is rarely or never affected by drinking deeply of wine.

The Rajah's visitor, the Lallah Jooteepersâd, had a grievance, and a rather substantial one. He had claimed from the Government fifty-seven lacs of rupees (half a million and seventy-thousand pounds sterling) as the balance due to him for feeding the armies employed during the two Seik campaigns; and the Government had threatened to prosecute him, in one of their own courts, for an attempt to make an overcharge of forty thousand rupees, or four thousand pounds.

"And if they understand the principles of good government thoroughly," said the Rajah, "they will convict you, imprison you for life, and confiscate all your possessions, real and personal. That is the way the Lahore Durbar would have settled so large a claim. But the Indian Government has not the courage to act in that way."

"But I have not attempted to make an overcharge; and if my agents have done so, let it be deducted, if it be incorrect," said the Lallah.

"You are a criminal," said the Rajah.

"How so?" asked the Lallah.

"You say the Government owes you fifty-seven lacs?"

"Yes—and honestly."

"Well, is not that enough to warrant your being transported for life, or hanged? But, as I have told you, the Government has not courage to prosecute you."

In this opinion, however, Lall Singh was in error; for, that very night, the Lallah was informed that he was, to all intents and purposes, a prisoner, and must not leave Agra. The firm belief of every native, not only in the district but throughout India, was, that these proceedings had been taken to evade payment of the contractor's just demands. But the Lallah himself was the first to deny this assertion, and to declare that the prosecution arose out of the circumstance of the Commissary-General being a near relative of the Governor-General of India; that a civilian in power had a quarrel with the Commissary-General, and had represented, semi-officially, that great frauds had been committed, and there could be no question that the heads of the departments were cognisant of such frauds; that the Governor-General, anxious that the honour of a member of his ancient family should be cleared up, had determined upon a strict investigation; and that the civilian in question suggested the public prosecution of the contractor as the speediest and most satisfactory means of arriving at the result!

And such was the opinion of many officers of the Government, civil and military!

The contractor, however, was eventually acquitted, and the Government paid the bill. But, to this day, the natives of India believe that the object of the Government was to cheat their creditor; while the officers, civil and military, are equally sanguine that it was "the honour of the family" that led to the most extraordinary and protracted trial that ever was known in India, and which was emphatically denounced, by the press and public of every country in Europe, as absurd, unjust, and shameful. Nevertheless, Jooteepersâd cannot have harboured any revenge for the wrongs (involving disgrace and dishonour) which were heaped upon him; for it is he who has fed, for several months, the five thousand Christians during their incarceration in the fortress of Agra; and, amongst the number of civilians there shut up, is the gentleman who conducted the prosecution on the behalf of the Government, and who, in the execution of his duty, strove very hard indeed for a verdict of guilty! Without Jooteepersâd we could not have held Agra!

When the sun had gone down, and it was cool enough to walk abroad, Lall Singh led me into the extensive gardens which surrounded his temporary abode. The Lallah had left us, and I was now alone with the ex-Commander of the Seik Cavalry and the ex-Prime Minister of Lahore. I felt much more pleasure in his society than I should have felt had he been in the plenitude of his power; for he bore his altered condition with great dignity and cheerfulness, and discoursed upon all sorts of topics without any restraint or reserve. He even talked about the Ranee of Lahore—with whom his name had been so frequently coupled—and with a chivalrous spirit (whether his assertions were true or not is another matter) assured me that his intrigues with her had been confined exclusively to politics. I asked him where this helpless woman had fled to, after her miraculous escape from Benares, in the garb of a man? He replied that he knew not. He was sure she was not in Nepal—where the authorities supposed her to be—but somewhere in our own provinces.

"Was she a beautiful woman?" I asked.

"No; and never had been," was his reply. "But she had eyes which could charm like those of a snake, and a voice sweeter than that of a bird."

"They say she was the Messalina of the East," and I explained to him what the allusion signified.

"It is not true," he exclaimed vehemently. "She was a vain and clever woman; but the very opposite of the character that she has been described. She was proud of the influence she possessed over men in making them subservient to her will and her caprices."

"Had she great power over Runjeet Singh?"

"None. She was his doll, his plaything, and the only being who could calm him when he had the horrors. Nothing more."

"How the horrors?"

"Runjeet Singh began life as a petty chieftain, with a few hundred followers. He acquired a vast kingdom, and had the most powerful army that the East ever saw, or will see. Whilst he went on conquering, shedding blood, and plundering, he was easy in his mind; but, when he found that he had got as much as he could manage, he stopped; and then came his disquiet. His great fear then was that he could not retain what he had become possessed of—and his chief horror was that the Koh-i-noor would be carried off—that diamond which Runjeet Singh stole, and which the Ranee has worn a thousand times as a bracelet. That diamond which is now in the crown of England."

"Where did it come from originally?"

"No one can say that. The history of the Koh-i-noor has yet to be written. Did you ever see a likeness of Runjeet Singh?"

"Never."

"Then I will show you a very faithful one; a miniature taken by a famous painter who came from Delhi, and spent his life in Lahore. The Maharajah was a diminutive, shrivelled man, frightfully pitted with the small-pox, which had destroyed one of his eyes; but with the other he could gaze for an hour without ever winking. He had a shrill and squeaking voice; but it terrified those who heard it, especially when he was angry. He did not talk much; but he was a great listener. Then, shrivelled and emaciated as he was in his later years, he was possessed of immense physical strength when roused; and upon horseback, where skill could be exercised, few men in his kingdom could have disarmed him."

"Indeed!"

"He inspired all those who approached him—whether European or native—with respect mingled with intense fear."

Our conversation was here interrupted by a gardener, who presented the Rajah and myself respectively with a nosegay; and who volunteered the information, that some workmen, in digging the foundation for a vine trellis had come upon an old house under the earth, and in it had been found several gold and silver coins.

"Where?" asked the Rajah.

"There," said the gardener, pointing in the direction.

We hurried to the spot, and found that the workmen had gone; but sure enough, there were the walls of an apartment, formed of red stone and white marble.

"This quarter of Agra," said the Rajah to me, "was formerly inhabited by persons of the highest rank. Where we are now standing was, no doubt, once the site of a palace; and these walls are those of the ty-khana—a vault beneath the dwelling from which the light is excluded. In these dark places are usually perpetrated what you English call 'dark deeds.'"

I expressed a desire to explore this newly discovered apartment of former days; but the Rajah told me it was then too late, as the workmen had gone; but he promised me that if I would come to him at daylight on the following morning, he would have great pleasure in gratifying my curiosity.

On the following morning, having spent a very dreamy night, I was carried in my palanquin to the Jatnee Bagh. Such was the name of Jooteepersâd's garden-house, in which Lall Singh then resided. The Rajah was dressing. I was confronted by a Seik with an enormous beard, whose hair was a yard long and tied up in a peculiar knot on the top of his head, and who politely inquired if I would take coffee. Ere long the Rajah made his appearance, and we went together to the newly discovered ty-khana, which was now guarded, since gold and silver had been found there. The workmen, some twenty in number, came and commenced their labour: that of clearing away the earth in all directions, in order to get to the bottom of the apartment in the ty-khana. This was accomplished in about two hours, and we then stood upon a stone-floor in the centre of a room, about sixteen feet square. In several of the niches were little lamps, such as are burnt upon the tombs of Moslems, and a hookah and a pair of marble chairs were found in the subterraneous apartment; of which the sky was now the roof. Whilst examining the walls, I observed that, upon one side, there was a ledge about six feet high from the floor (and carried up therefrom), and about a foot in width. This ledge, which was of brick and plaster, resembled a huge mantelpiece, and was continued from one end of the apartment to the other. I asked the Rajah the reason of such a structure in the apartment. He replied that he did not know, nor could any of the workmen account for it; one of them, however, took a pickaxe and dug out a portion, when, to my surprise and horror, I discovered that in this wall a human being had been bricked up. The skin was still upon the bones, which were covered with a costly dress of white muslin, spangled all over with gold; around the neck was a string of pearls; on the wrists and ankles were gold bangles, and on the feet were a pair of slippers, embroidered all over with silver wire or thread; such slippers as only Mahommedan women of rank or wealth can afford to wear. The body resembled a well-preserved mummy. The features were very distinct, and were those of a woman whose age could not at the time of her death have exceeded eighteen or nineteen years. The head was partially covered with the white dress. Long black hair was still clinging to the scalp, and was parted across the forehead and carried behind the ears. It was the most horrible and ghastly figure that I ever beheld.

The workmen appeared to take this discovery as a matter of course; or, rather, to regard it only with reference to the gold and silver ornaments upon the skeleton, and it was with great difficulty that I could prevent them stripping it, forthwith. As for the Rajah, he simply smiled and coolly remarked: "A case of jealousy. Her husband was jealous of her, and thought her guilty, and punished her thus—bricked her up alive in this wall, with no room to move about, only standing room. Perhaps she deserved it,—perhaps she was plotting against his life; perhaps she was innocent: who can say? Hindoos as well as Mahommedans punish their wives in that way."

"You mean that they used to do so in former times, previous to British rule in India. But such a thing could not occur in our time."

"It does not occur so often as it did; but it does occur, sometimes, even in these days. How do you know what happens in the establishment of a wealthy native? Let us look a little further into the wall. It strikes me that we shall find some more of them."

Orders were given accordingly to the workmen to remove with great care the whole of the ledge, in short, to pull away its entire face. This was done; and how shall I describe the awful spectacle then presented? In that wall there were no less than *five* bodies,—four besides that already alluded to. One of the number was a young man, who from his dress and the jewels on his finger-bones must have been a person of high rank; perhaps the lover of one, or both, of the young women; for he had been bricked up between two of them. The others were evidently those of confidential servants; old women, for they had grey hair. They possibly had been cognisant, or were supposed to be cognisant, of whatever offence the others had been deemed guilty.

The sun was now shining brightly on these ghastly remains, covered with garments embroidered in gold and silver. The air had a speedy effect on them, and, one by one, they fell; each forming a heap of bones, hair, shrivelled skin, dust, jewels, and finery. The latter were now gathered up, placed in a small basket, and sent to Lallah. Their value, possibly, was upwards of a thousand pounds. How many years had passed since that horrible sentence had been put into execution? Not less than one hundred and seventy, or perhaps two hundred.

INDIAN SOCIETY.

WHILST I was at Agra, a distinguished military officer of high rank, who had just been appointed as a member of the Council, passed through the station on his way to the seat of government, Calcutta. It was supposed that this general officer would, on the first vacancy, become Deputy-Governor of Bengal; and of course the society of Agra was resolved to do him honour. It would not do for anybody to hang back on an occasion like this; and, for the nonce, both the civilians and the military were of one mind, and actually met on an amicable and pleasant footing, to talk the matter over, and to decide upon what was to be done. After a friendly debate, which lasted for four hours, it was resolved that Sir Gunter and Lady Gallopaway should be invited to a ball and supper, and not to a dinner. It was further determined that the entertainment should take place, not at Government-house (that would be too Civil)—not at any mess-room (that would be too Military)—but at a good-sized hall called the Metcalfe Institution, this being perfectly neutral ground. My friend, the civilian with whom I had been staying, had a perfect contempt for these local squabbles—although he was really compelled to take a part therein ; and, after the meeting was over, he sat down and wrote a metrical squib, ridiculing the whole affair, and sent it for publication to one of the newspapers, the *Delhi Gazette*. For this squib—seeing that it sneered at both the civilians and the military—I unfortunately got the credit, and the consequence was, that, when I made my appearance at the ball, several of the heads of the society who had formerly received me with extreme cordiality, answered me only in monosyllables when I addressed them. Indeed, I learnt afterwards, from my friend's wife, that a meeting had actually been called to consider the propriety of not inviting me, and that I had very narrowly escaped that punishment; for had it not been for the vote of her husband my name would have been omitted, as there were ten for and ten against me, when he held up his hand in my favour.

But to the ball. There were present some twenty civilians, all dressed in black with white cravats ; and each had brought with him his wife, or a sister, or daughter. Of military men (all in full dress uniform) there were about forty-five or fifty; and the ladies who came with them may have numbered thirty. In all, say that there were present—including visitors and stragglers like myself—one hundred and forty. I was rather late, and, on entering the room, beheld one of the oddest sights that I ever witnessed : all the black coats were huddled together, and so were all the reds. They had been unanimous only so far as giving the entertainment was concerned; and it seemed to be distinctly understood by each party that there was to be no mixing; and so the civilians formed quadrilles and danced with the civil ladies, and the soldiers with the military ladies. Had there been a royal regiment in Agra, there would have been three parties, owing to the jealousy that existed formerly between the Queen's and the Company's officers. Besides myself, there were two "interlopers in the East" present at that ball. The one, a French gentleman; the other, a German Baron. They, too, were travelling about in search of the picturesque, and here they had it with a vengeance. The Frenchman could not comprehend this exclusiveness on the part of the blacks; but the German assured us that to him it was a very common sight, and to be witnessed at every ball in every garrison town in his country. "But there," said he, "the military look down on the civilians, while here, it seems to me, that the civilians look down on the military. See, see! See how disdainfully that old Mrs. Revenue Board scrutinizes the dress of Mrs. Lieutenant-Colonel Damzè!"

Sure enough such was the case. "But regard!" said the Frenchman; "how angry is that Mrs. Sudder Adawlut, because that little Mrs. Infantry (whose husband, I am told, is the younger son of a poor English lord) is contemplating her *nez en l'air*. Truly this is a magnificent spectacle! Is it always so, I wonder?"

I was enabled, from experience, to inform him, that in almost every large station—and at Agra especially—it universally occurs; but that in small stations seldom or never.

Here we were approached by Lieutenant-Colonel Damzè himself. After exchanging a few words with the foreign gentlemen on either side of me, he passed on, seemingly proud and happy at having had an opportunity of slighting me in public, on account of the doggerel for which I had the credit.

"Mais, monsieur," said the Frenchman to me, "who, in wonder's name, are all these Damzè gentlemen? There is one Damzè, colonel of such a regiment; another Damzè, major in another corps. There is a Deputy Commissary-General Damzè; there is a Mr. Damzè in the Indian navy; another Damzè is a military secretary; some half dozen Damzès are, I have perceived, on the staff of the Commander-in-Chief. Parbleu! C'est Damzé—toujours Damzè! for here, by Heaven, I meet with still another Damzè! Who *are* all these Damzès?"

I informed him that Damzè was the patronymic of a nobleman in power; and with this explanation he was thoroughly enlightened, and appeared to be perfectly satisfied.

"Let us move up towards the General," said the German Baron, who had been introduced to the old hero. "Let us go and say a few words to him."

It was not easy to do this; hemmed in as was the

General by those who desired to make him remember them in the future. However, it was managed at last; and, somehow or other, we three interlopers contrived before long to monopolize his attention—we, the only people in the room to whom he could not be of any service—for there was nothing that he could give, or get for us, if we had wanted his patronage. We, rather maliciously—so far as the crowd was concerned—stood about the distinguished old man and guarded him; and I have reason to know that he was grateful to us for so doing. Towards the hour of twelve, however, we had to stand back; for Mrs. Lieutenant-Colonel Damzè came and sat upon the sofa on the left side of the General, and talked to him in an animated but somewhat anxious manner, which became even more anxious when Mrs. Revenue Board approached, and taking a seat on the General's right (eyeing Mrs. Lieutenant-Colonel Damzè with a somewhat haughty expression), congratulated the General on his recent good fortune. At this advanced stage of the evening also, Lady Gallopaway was flanked right and left by old Mr. Revenue Board and Lieutenant-Colonel Damzè, C.B. The reader is requested to note that these two letters—C.B.—were Damzè's by right; or, at all events, that he had been recommended for the order, and that the recommendation had been instantly attended to; albeit Damzè had never been within range of an enemy's cannon in the whole course of his life. Lady Gallopaway yawned.

At length a gong sounded, and the band struck up that usual signal that supper is ready, "O, the Roast Beef of Old England, O, the Old English Roast Beef."

The anxiety of the ladies who sat on either side of the General was now at it height. They fanned themselves with fearful vigour; and we, the three interlopers, fancied that we could hear the palpitation of their hearts. Meanwhile their husbands, respectively, by their looks, evinced a corresponding anxiety. Each stood ready to offer his arm to Lady Gallopaway as soon as the General had made his election—of the lady he would lead to the supper table. Each party was equally confident but equally nervous, like the parties to a lawsuit. For weeks past this question of precedence had been debated in Agra, and very warmly debated—namely, whether Mrs. Revenue Board, of the Civil Service, or Mrs. Lieutenant-Colonel Damzè, C.B., was entitled to the *pas*. Now was the moment for a decision, or at all events an authority in support of either position or argument. The old General (upon whom both Mr. Revenue Board and Lieutenant-Colonel Dazmè, C.B., had their anxious eyes) rose, smiled, bowed to the ladies who had flanked him, left them, and wandered about the ball-room, looking to the right and left, as if searching for some one. Presently he stopped short before little Mrs. Infantry, who was talking to a cornet of the 17th Light Cavalry. The General offered her his arm. She took it very graciously, and was led away. But before leaving the room she halted, turned round, and stared very significantly at the two elderly ladies who were still seated on the sofa, overwhelmed in surprise, horror, and indignation. Infantry, who was only a lieutenant in his regiment, observing that the General had recognised the social right of his wife, which she had derived solely from him, instantly rushed up to Lady Gallopaway, and offered her an arm (which she took), led her away in triumph, leaving his own Colonel (Damzè) and old Mr. Revenue Board gasping and gaping at each other in mutual disgust and consternation. Had a shell burst in the building, had the powder magazine exploded and shattered all the windows, the commotion could scarcely have been greater than it was at that moment. No one could account for this extraordinary conduct, or caprice, as it was termed, on the part of the old General. Damzè, who had just been flattering him concerning his wonderful achievements, now declared that "the old fool had become half-witted since eighteen hundred and forty-seven," while Revenue Board, who a quarter of an hour previously had, to the General's face, held forth on the unflinching independence which had marked his character through life, now protested—openly protested—that he had been a time-server throughout his entire career, and had some object in thus truckling before the son of an influential peer! The ladies on the sofa stared at each other; now commiseratingly and in silence for at least two minutes, then simultaneously ejaculated: "What *can* it mean!"

"I thought it would have been me," said Mrs. Revenue Board.

"You?" said Mrs. Damzè.

"Yes; why not? My husband is a civilian of twenty years' standing."

"Is not my husband a Lieutenant-Colonel and a C.B.? If he were only a Major and a C.B. he would take precedence of Mr. Revenue Board."

"You are quite mistaken."

"Indeed not. Do you suppose a C.B. goes for nothing?"

"No; but——"

Here Lieutenant-Colonel Damzè and Mr. Revenue Board, who had been discussing the same question, but in a calmer spirit than their wives, approached, and, making common cause against the upstart enemy (Infantry and his wife), formed a quartette and went into the supper room; where, to their intense mortification, they heard little Mrs. Infantry talking loudly, on purpose to attract the notice of all present. What was even more mortifying still, the old General was paying her marked attention.

The red party, that is to say, the military, were in very high spirits; the black, the civilians, correspondingly depressed. The quartette, consisting of Damzè and Revenue Board, and their wives, ate voraciously, but evidently without appetite. They sipped their wine with an absent formality, which was very entertaining to lookers-on, who were in no way interested in the momentous question which was preying on their very souls.

"It shall not end here," said Damzè, moodily fixing his eyes on the chandelier.

"Not, indeed!" said Mr. Revenue Board.

"I shall put my case to the Governor-General direct," said Damzé. "His Lordship is a near connexion of mine."

"I am perfectly aware of that," said Mr. Revenue Board; "but it is my intention to submit my case to his Lordship through Mr. Bommerson, the Lieutenant-Governor of these provinces, officially; and, if his Lordship's opinion should be adverse, I shall have my appeal to the Court of Directors, amongst whom, thank Heaven! I have several relations and warm friends."

"And you will write, I hope, my dear," said Mrs. Revenue Board, "to Sir John Bobgrouse, who is the President of the Board of Control, and whose secretary married your first cousin—recollect!"

"*We* can write, too," said Mrs. Lieutenant-Colonel Damzè.

"You may write to anybody you please," said Mrs. Revenue Board, defiantly and contemptuously; "but you will remember that the point between us is this—that even if your husband, in consequence of having got, no matter how, a C.B.ship, has the right to precede my husband, a civilian of twenty years' standing—whether you have the right to precede me? That is the question; and I hope, Revenue dear, you will not fail to raise it."

Reader, the question was submitted in all its bearings for the consideration of the Most Noble the Governor-General of India, who, declining to take upon himself so fearful a responsibility, referred the matter to the Home Government. Leadenhall-street had something to say to it, and so had the Board of Control. While the case was pending, the newspapers in every part of India literally teemed with letters on the subject, and their editors were invited to give their opinions thereon. Only one of the number was weak enough to do this, and bitterly did he repent of his rashness; for, having decided in favour of the C.B. and of Mrs. C.B., he lost (so he confessed to me) no less than six-and-twenty civilians, (each of twenty years' standing) in his subscription-list. For more than eighteen months this precedence question formed a leading topic, not only in the public prints, but in private circles. It became, in short, a perfect nuisance. At length the decision of the Home Government came out to India; but, alas! they had only half done their work. They had given C.B. the precedence over the civilian of twenty years' standing, but had been silent about their wives! So, the matter was "referred back." A clerk in the Private Secretary's office told me that he was occupied for three hours in copying only the Governor-General's minute on the Court's despatch, which was a very lengthy one, and signed by the chairman for himself and the other directors, whose names were given in full. He further informed me that the whole of the documents connected with this weighty affair would, if put into type, form a volume five times as bulky as Sir William Napier's *Conquest of Scinde!*

How the matter was settled eventually I do not know; for, when I left India, the question had not been decided. On the great point, when it was referred for a second time to the Home Authorities, there was a difference of opinion between the Court of Directors and the Board of Control, and a long correspondence ensued on the subject, between each of these departments of the Indian Government and the Governor-General, who was required to have the case laid before the Advocates-General of the Supreme Courts at the various Presidencies. These gentlemen differed one with the other in their views of the case, each alleging that the point lay in a nutshell, and was as clear as possible. For all I know to the contrary, it may be in the nutshell at this moment. Both Lieutenant-Colonel Damzè and Mr. Revenue Board laid "cases" before the Calcutta barristers, who pocketed their fees, and laconically expressed their opinions respectively, that the parties who consulted them were in the right—"there could be no doubt on the point," they said. Damzè sent a copy of his case, and the opinion of his barrister thereon, to Revenue Board, who rather triumphantly returned the compliment. I regret to say, that this contest engendered in Agra a great deal of what is called bad blood, and induced many ladies to descend to very unseemly personalities. For instance, Mrs. Damzè one evening, at the band-stand, told Mrs. Revenue Board, that when she (Mrs. R. B.) returned to England, she would have no rank at all, as her husband was not an esquire even—but a "mister" in his own country. To which Mrs. Revenue Board replied:—

"And you, pray? Is not your husband in the Company's service?"

"Yes," rejoined Mrs. Damzè; "but you forget the C.B.!"

Let us now return to the Honourable Lieutenant Infantry. When that officer came up, and led away Lady Gallopaway to supper, Damzè was overheard to say, "I'll take the shine out of that young gentleman." And, if taking the shine meant constantly bullying the subaltern, Damzè certainly kept his word. And when the next hot weather came, and the Lieutenant wished to accompany his sick wife to the Hills, Damzè, when he forwarded the application for six months' leave of absence, wrote privately to the Assistant Adjutant-General, and recommended that it should not be granted. The honourable subaltern, however, was rather too strong for his colonel, in the way of interest. Presuming on the acquaintance which existed between his father and the Commander-in-Chief, he wrote a letter to that functionary, and a few days afterwards found himself in general orders. The wrath of Damzè may be easily imagined, especially as he had boasted to several of his officers of having put a spoke in the Lieutenant's wheel. And by way of throwing salt upon the Colonel's wounds, the Lieutenant called upon him, and, in the politest manner possible, inquired if there was anything he could do for him at head-quarters.

While at Agra, a Bengalee Baboo called upon me. Judging from his appearance, I should have guessed his age to be about fifty years; but he was upwards of seventy. He spoke English with marvellous fluency and accuracy, and could read and write the language as well and as elegantly as any educated European. He was, perhaps, the cleverest Hindoo whom I encountered during my sojourn in the East. His manners were peculiarly courteous and winning, and there was an air of penitence about the man, which, apart from his abilities, induced me to treat him with kindness and consideration. His name was —let us say—Nobinkissen.

The history of Nobinkissen was simply this. He was a Brahmin of the highest caste, and, at the age of eighteen, was a writer in the service of the government, on a salary of ten rupees per month. He ingratiated himself with every civilian under whom he served, and gradually rose, step by step, until he became the Sheristadar, or head clerk, of a circuit-judge of a court of appeal. In this office he acquired riches, and was still adding to his store, when his official career was brought prematurely to a close.

I must here inform the reader that not one civilian in a hundred, no matter what his rank or grade, can read and write Hindostanee or Persian, although the majority of them have some colloquial knowledge of both those languages. Yet, as a matter of course, they append their signatures to every document of which, on hearing it read aloud to them by their native officials, they approve. Their orders they dictate orally; those orders are transcribed by the Sheristadar, who gives them to a native writer to copy. This done, they are read aloud for correction or approval, and then signed in English by the covenanted civilian. Before leaving office every day, such civilian may have to sign fifty, sixty, or a hundred documents; for the rule is, not to sign each of them when read, but to sign them in a mass at the breaking-up of the court. Here Nobinkissen invented his means of money-making. Whenever the judge gave a decree in any case of importance, he made a counterpart of such decree, and when the signing time came, obtained, without any sort of trouble or inquiry, the signature of the Sahib and the seal of the Court to both documents. He was thus, to all intents and purposes—or, at all events, for his own—in possession of something tantamount to the fee-simple of the lands in dispute. He could arm either the appellant or the respondent with the final decree of the Court, under the hand and official seal of the judge. The only question with him now was, which of the litigants would give the most money, and to each, in private, and in the Sahib's name, he exhibited the documents. The highest bidder, of course, gained the day, whereupon Nobinkissen took the coin, handed over one of the decrees, and burnt the other.

It fell out that Nobinkissen was attacked with fever, and, in a state bordering on delirium, he parted with, that is to say, sold, to both respondent and appellant, a decree, under the hand and seal of the judge, such decree arming the holder with the power to take possession of a very large estate in Bengal. Each party, fearful of a disturbance, which often occurs when possession of an estate is sought for, applied to the magistrate of a district, under a certain regulation of government, for assistance, in order to enable him to carry out the judge's decree, which each, as a matter of course, produced. The magistrate was naturally much perplexed, and made a reference to the judge, who could only say he had signed but one decree. There was then a report made to the government by the magistrate. An investigation ensued, and the judge was, meanwhile, suspended, for great suspicion lurked in the minds of many that he was not so innocent as he affected to be. When Nobinkissen recovered from his sickness, and saw the dilemma in which his superior, the judge, was placed, he made a clean breast of it, and confessed that the guilt was his, and his alone. Nobinkissen was tried, convicted, and sentenced to be imprisoned in irons for the term of his natural life. For nine years he was in the gaol at Alipore, near Calcutta. At the expiration of that period he was called upon to furnish some information of which he was possessed, in relation to certain public affairs. He was brought from the prison, confronted with several officials, amongst whom was a member of the council. His altered appearance, his emaciated form, his attitude of despair, and the intelligence and readiness with which he responded to the questions put to him, touched the hearts of those by whom he was examined, and the member of council, who has been since a director of the East India Company, spoke to the Governor-General, and eventually obtained Nobinkissen's pardon and release. The Hindoos and Mussulmans in India (like the Arabs) do not regard being guilty of a fraud or theft as a disgrace. The degrading part of the business is, being convicted, and Nobinkissen, on being set at liberty, could not face his countrymen in Bengal, and therefore retired to the Upper Provinces, where he lived in comparative obscurity, and in easy circumstances; for he had not disgorged his ill-gotten gains. His wife had taken care of them during his captivity.

At the time that Nobinkissen called upon me, the government of India were in considerable difficulty in respect to finance. A new loan had been opened, but it did not fill, and the government had very wisely determined upon closing it. Nobinkissen made this a topic of conversation, and his views—albeit they came from a man who had been convicted of a fraud—are, at the present time especially, entitled to the very gravest consideration.

"Ah, sir!" he remarked, "it is a pitiful thing that the government of a great empire like this should ever be in pecuniary difficulties and put to their wits' end for a few millions annually, in order to make the receipts square with the expenditure."

"But how can it be helped?" I asked.

"Easily, sir," he replied. "Why not make it expedient to do away with the perpetual settlement of Lord Cornwallis, and resettle the whole of Bengal? That is by far the most fertile province in the East; but it is taxed lighter than even these poor lands of the Upper Provinces. Look at the Durbungah Rajah. Nearly the whole of Tirhoot, the garden of India, belongs to him, and he does not pay into the government treasury half a lac (five thousand pounds) per annum, while his collections amount to upwards of twenty lacs. These are the men who get hold of the money and bury it, and keep it from circulating."

"But all zemindarees (lands) are not so profitable in Bengal?"

"No; many are not worth holding—especially the smaller ones, although the land is just as good, and just as well cultivated."

"But how is that?"

"They are so heavily taxed. You must know, sir, that in those days—the days of Lord Cornwallis—the greatest frauds were committed, in respect to the perpetual settlement. The natives who were about, and under, the settlement officers all made immense fortunes, and the zemindars from whom they took their bribes, have profited ever since to the cost of the poorer zemindars, who could not or would not bribe, and to the cost of the British government. It is a great mistake to suppose that the whole of the landholders in Bengal would cry out against a re-settlement of that province. Only men holding vast tracts of country, at a comparatively nominal rent, would cry out."

"And tax the British government with a breach of faith?"

"Yes. But what need the government care for that cry, especially when its act is not only expedient, but would be just withal? In Bengal, all the great zemindars are rich, very rich men. In these provinces, with very, very few exceptions, they are poor, so that the whole of Upper India would be glad to see the perpetual settlement done away with, and the land resettled."

"Why so?"

"That is only human—and, certainly, Asiatic—nature. Few of us like to behold our neighbours better off than ourselves; so that the cry of faith-breaking would not meet with a response in this part of the world."

"Yes; but in Europe the cry would be too powerful to contend against. The Exeter Hall orators and the spouters at the Court of Proprietors would—"

"Ah, sir! India should either be governed in India or in England. It is the number of wheels in the government that clogs the movement of the machine."

"Very true."

"But who are these men—these zemindars with whom you are required to keep an implicit faith? Are they your friends? If so, why do they never come forward to assist you in your difficulties? Did a single zemindar, when, after the battle of Ferozeshah, the empire was shaking in the balance, lift a finger to help the government of India? And, to-morrow, if your rule were at stake, and dependent on their assistance, think you they would render it? Think you they would furnish money if your treasury was exhausted? Not one pice! Think you they would furnish men to protect your stations denuded of troops? No! Although hundreds of them can each turn out a thousand or two of followers, armed with iron-bound bludgeons, swords, and shields, when they desire to intimidate an European indigo-planter, or to fight a battle between themselves about a boundary question. These are the men who, in your greatest need, would remain neutral until, if it so happened, you were brought to your last gasp, when, as one man, they would not fail to rise and give you the final blow."

"Do you believe that? I do not."

"Sir, I know my own countrymen better than you do."

"If such a state of affairs were to come about, and these zemindars remained neutral, of course the cry of breaking faith would be absurd in the extreme. Neutrality, in such a case, would be almost as bad as hostility."

[Nobinkissen's prophecy has been fulfilled to the letter. Our rule has been at stake, in imminent peril, and not one of these men has offered to assist us with men or money. The Rajahs of Durbungah and Burdwan alone, to say nothing of the Newab of Moorshedabad, between them could have furnished an army of, at the very least, five thousand stalwart fighting-men, whereas they have looked upon our difficulties in perfect apathy. It is from the coffers of men of this stamp that large sums should be extracted annually towards keeping up a vast—an overwhelming—European force in India. Faith with such men as these! What claim have they to our faintest consideration! What right to expect that we shall any longer forego the collection of several extra millions annually—several extra millions which, to every intent and purpose, is our just due?]

"There is a line in Shakespeare, sir," Nobinkissen continued, "which the government of India should adopt as its motto, and act up to consistently—

'Cæsar never does wrong without just cause.'"

Our conversation was here interrupted by a noise in the road. I went to the window, and observing a great crowd, inquired of one of my servants who was standing in the verandah:—

"What is the matter?"

"A bullock has fallen down, and they are trying to get him up—that is all, Sahib," was the reply.

I rushed to the spot, followed by Nobinkissen, and there beheld a scene which in no other country would have been tolerated by the crowd assembled.

One of a pair of bullocks, drawing an over-laden cart, had from weakness and fatigue, sank beneath the burden. The driver of the animals (a Hindoo) had broken, by twisting it violently, the tail of the poor beast, which was nothing but skin and bone, and was covered with wounds from ill-treatment. Heavy blows and the tail breaking having failed to make the jaded ox stand upon his legs, the driver—heedless of my remonstrance—collected some straw and sticks and lighted a fire all round him. The poor beast now struggled very hard, but was unable to rise, and presently he resigned himself to be scorched to death.

"I always thought that the cow was a sacred animal with Hindoos?" said I to Nobinkissen.

"Yes," said he.

"And here is a Hindoo who works one of his gods till he drops down with sheer fatigue, and then cruelly puts him to death!"

"Yes, that often happens," said Nobinkissen, smiling.

"Then, what an absurdity and inconsistency for the Hindoos at Benares, and other holy places, to make such a noise if an European only strikes a sacred animal with a whip! Why, it was only the other day that a mob collected around the house of the magistrate and set the authorities at defiance: all because the magistrate had ordered that one of the bulls which crowd the streets should be shut up, on the ground that he had gored several people."

"That is the doing of the Brahmins, who incite the people to such acts; and every concession on the part of the government leads those Brahmins to believe that they have great power, and leads the people also to believe it. If a Mahommedan finds one of those bulls in the way, and gives him a thrashing with a thick stick, or probes him in the side with a sword, the Brahmins say nothing, nor do the people of Benares."

"Why is that?"

"Because it would not be worth while. The strife would be profitless; for, you see, sir, the Mahommedans are not the rulers of this country, but the Sahibs are; and hence the jealousy with which they are watched. In time, the Government of India will see the necessity of forbidding Hindoo festivals in the public streets—abolishing them—just as Suttee was abolished. It is only the dissolute rich and the rabble who take any delight in these festivals, many of which are indecent and disgusting. Sensible and respectable Hindoos take no part in them; on the contrary, they avoid them, and think them a nuisance. Hindooism will never become extinct, so long as this world lasts; but the British Government has the power of doing away with those obnoxious observances in the public thoroughfares, which only disfigure the religion."

"Well, in that case, you would have to do away with the Mahommedan festivals?"

"Most certainly—in the public streets. In private, the Mahommedans as well as the Hindoos might be permitted to keep their festivals in whatever way they thought proper. Do you suppose that the Mahommedans, when in power, suffered the Hindoos to block up the streets continually with their processions, as they do now? Think you that they entertained the same consideration for the bulls and the monkeys at Benares as the British now entertain?

And when, in turn, the Mahrattas overran this part of the country, think you that Agra was ever deafened, as it now is, with the din of the Buckree Ede and the Mohurrum?"

"Perhaps not. But then you see, Nobinkissen, we are a tolerant people, and wish to convince both creeds that we have no desire to interfere with their religious prejudices in any way whatsoever."

"Yes; but then you are inconsistent, and the consequence is, that you not only get the credit of being insincere, but are imposed upon to the utmost."

"How, inconsistent!"

"Why, you declare that you have no desire to interfere with the religious prejudices of the Hindoo and the Mahommedan; but you, nevertheless, encourage missionary gentlemen to go from station to station to preach in the open air concerning the superiority of your religion over all others. Believe me, sir, this does a great deal of harm."

"Ah! but we make converts!"

"How many do you suppose?"

"I cannot say."

"I can. Take India from one end to the other, and you make, annually, one out of fifty thousand."

"No more?"

"No more, sir! That is the result of preaching in the open air, all over the country, and the distribution of thousands and hundreds of thousands of tracts printed in the Hindostanee and Bengalee languages.

"Well, that is something, Nobinkissen."

"And of what class of people are your converts?"

"Respectable men of all classes, I suppose."

"The dregs of both Hindoos and Mussulmans. The most debased and degraded of Indians—men who only assume Christianity in the hope of temporal advantage and preferment—and who fling aside their newly put-on faith, and laugh and scoff at your credulity the moment they find their hope frustrated. I could give you at least one hundred instances; but one will suffice. Not long ago a Mussulman, named Ally Khan, was converted by Mr. Jones, a missionary in Calcutta, and, shortly after his conversion, obtained an appointment with a salary of one hundred rupees a month, in the Baptist Missionary Society. Here he contrived to embezzle sixteen hundred rupees, for which offence he was indicted in the Supreme Court, found guilty, and sentenced to a year's imprisonment in the Calcutta gaol. On hearing the sentence he exclaimed: 'In the name of the devil, is this the reward of renouncing my religion? Farewell, Christianity! From this hour I am a Moslem again!'

"Another very flagrant case occurred in this very station. A civilian took into his service a recently converted Hindoo, as a sirdar-bearer. The fellow had charge of a money-bag, and ran off with it. And where and how do you suppose he was apprehended? At Hurdwar, taking an active part in the Hoolee Festival! The Roman Catholic priests have long since left off asking the natives of India to become Christians. Those who voluntarily present themselves, are, after a strict examination, and a due warning that they must hope for no temporal advantage, admitted into the Church."

"And do they have any applications?"

"Very very few, indeed; but those whom they admit do, really and truly, become Christians."

These last words of Nobinkissen were scarcely pronounced, when a palkee was brought up to my door, and out of it stepped a Roman Catholic priest—an Italian gentleman, a Jesuit—whom I had met a few evenings previously at the house of a mutual friend. Nobinkissen, who appeared to know the reverend father intimately, related to him the substance of the conversation we had just held, or rather the latter part thereof, and the priest corroborated every allegation that Nobinkissen had made.

"Yea," he added, "we now devote our attention, exclusively, to the spiritual wants of the white man who requires our aid—convinced, as we are, of the hopelessness of the task of converting the Hindoo and the Mussulman to Christianity." And, in addition to the instances of false converts afforded by Nobinkissen, he did not scruple to detail several others of an equally atrocious character and complexion.

THE UPPER PROVINCES.

HAVING seen Agra, its edifices, ruins, society, European and native, and having visited Secundra, Futteypore, Sickri, and Muttra, I journeyed upwards to Delhi, where I was received by Mr. Joseph Skinner, the eldest son of the late Colonel Skinner, renowned as the founder and commandant of the famous Skinner's Horse. Mr. Joseph Skinner's house was, at all times, open to all travellers. He was without exception the most hospitable man that I ever met in any part of the world. At his board were to be met daily, either at luncheon or at dinner, civilians and military men of every rank and grade in the service, as well as native gentlemen of position in India—Hindoos and Mahommedans. Even the young princes, sons of the King of Delhi and descendants of the Great Moghul, used frequently to honour Mr. Skinner with their company. The title by which they were usually greeted was Sahiban-i-Alum, signifying "Lords of the World." But the most remarkable native that I ever met at Mr. Skinner's hospitable board was the late Maharajah Hindoo-Rao, a little, fat, round Mahratta chieftain, with small twinkling eyes, and a countenance replete with fun and quiet humour. He was a pensioner of the Gwalior State, and drew therefrom twelve thousand pounds a year, which was guaranteed to him by the British Government. Large as was this income, Hindoo-Rao contrived annually to spend more than double the amount, trusting continually to fate to relieve him from his pressing pecuniary difficulties; not that he ever suffered them to prey upon his mind; on the contrary, he made them a subject of jocularity. In addition to being as hospitable as his friend Mr. Skinner, Hindoo-Rao was addicted to field sports on a large scale, and kept up a very large establishment for the purpose of gratifying this propensity. He was considered—and perhaps justly, by those qualified to form an opinion—the best shot in all India, and with his rifle he had destroyed several hundreds (some say thousands) of tigers. Hindoo-Rao had another very expensive hobby. He desired to possess himself of the Philosopher's Stone, by which he might transmute metals—a mode by which he proposed to improve the state of his finances and eventually pay his debts. On all other points, Hindoo-Rao was sufficiently sensible and shrewd, but on this point he was childish, if not insane. Thousands and thousands of pounds were squandered by him in this absurd pursuit, for he was constantly the victim of juggling forgers, swindlers, and rogues. His house was on a hill immediately overhanging Delhi, and it has recently been made famous throughout Europe as the position of one of our batteries. Night after night in that house would furnaces blaze, while some impostor, who pretended to have the secret, was at work with his chemicals.

I ought to mention that this Mahratta chief was a near relation of the royal family of Gwalior, and that he had been banished and pensioned for having been engaged in some intrigues against the Gwalior State.

The Maharajah Hindoo-Rao was a great gourmand, and those who partook of his dinners never forgot them. It was not often that the old chief could be induced to discuss politics, but on the occasion of the 41st Regiment of Infantry having mutinied at Delhi —a mutiny which, by the way, was hushed up—I heard him very energetically exclaim: "Ah! if you go on humouring your native soldiers in this way, they will never be satisfied until they govern the country!"

The late Sir Charles James Napier visited Delhi while I was there. He came, not as ordinary commanders-in-chief usually come, with a large suite and an escort covering a square mile of encamping ground, but attended only by two aides-de-camp and a military secretary. It was on the morning of his Excellency's arrival that the mutiny in the 41st Regiment, to which I have just alluded, occurred. Sir Charles reviewed the regiments then quartered at Delhi, including the 41st, and complimented them *en masse!* The review over, Hindoo-Rao, who was a great horseman, rode up to the commander-in-chief on his spirited charger, and expressed the happiness it afforded him to see an officer who had so distinguished himself in the military annals of his country. Sir Charles appeared much pleased with the open, frank manner and independent bearing of the old Mahratta chieftain, and accepted, on behalf of himself and his staff, an invitation to dine with him that evening. A large number of gentlemen, European and native, assembled to meet his Excellency; and when Sir Charles returned thanks for the honour that had been paid to him in drinking his health, he made allusion to the pleasure that it afforded him in seeing Christians, Hindoos, and Mussulmen on such good terms, and living together in such amity and concord. What a change since that evening, which to me seems but as yesterday! Several of our party, on that occasion, have become chiefs of the recent rebellion, and were accessory to the massacre of English gentlemen and ladies.

Hindoo-Rao died in eighteen hundred and fifty-four. His funeral was thus described to me by a friend who witnessed it: "They dressed up the old gentleman's corpse in his most magnificent costume, covered his arms with jewelled bracelets of gold, with costly necklaces of pearls and diamonds hanging down to his waist, placed him in a chair of state, sat him bolt upright—just as he used to sit when alive—and thus, attended by his relations, friends, and suite he was carried through Delhi to the banks of the Jumna, where the body was burnt with the usual rites, and the ashes thrown into the river."

Mr. Skinner also is dead. He died in eighteen hundred and fifty-five. When I think of him I am rejoiced that he did not survive to be brutally massacred, as his brothers have been; or to see his house (near the Cashmere Gate) which was always the scene of good-followship and good-feeling, turned into a battery by the rebels; or the church, built by his father, burned and destroyed by the people who had for years and years paid, or affected to pay, unqualified respect and devotion to his family.

I made the acquaintance of another personage at Delhi, for whom I had a very great liking and regard. This was Mirza Futteh Allee Shah Bahadoor, the heir apparent to the throne of Delhi. He was a very amiable and intelligent prince, and had an extraordinary thirst for knowledge. Amongst other things that he was curious to learn was the history of steam power, railroads, and the electric telegraph. For hours together he would encourage me—nay, importune me, to talk with him on these matters. *Apropos* of this prince and his family—while I was at Delhi the festival of the Eed came to pass, and there was an omen which was variously interpreted. The King, in other words the Great Moghul, sacrifices a camel. The King kills (or used to kill) the camel with his own hand, by driving a spear into the breast of the animal. On the occasion to which I now refer, the King, being extremely old and feeble, was assisted by two attendants, and, in attempting to drive the spear, it broke in two pieces. That was the omen. The friends of Mirza Futteh Allee Shah Bahadoor interpreted it as prognosticating the King's death and the speedy succession of the heir apparent to the throne. Others, however, said that it prognosticated the downfall of the King and of his throne for ever. Mirza died about a year ago of an attack of cholera ; and it may not be premature perhaps to say that the throne of the Great Moghul will not in future be recognised. There was another curious prophecy connected with the throne of Delhi, and current for many years in the Punjab. It was implicitly believed that the Sikh soldiery would one day or other, and before long, sack Delhi ; and, in eighteen hundred and forty-five, when the Sikh army crossed our frontier, Delhi was its destination. This prophecy has to some extent been fulfilled. The Sikh soldiers have tasted of the plunder of Delhi. But who could ever have dreamed that their entry into the city of the Great Moghul would be in company with British soldiers ? It is as though, and quite as incredible as if, some one had predicted in eighteen hundred and sixteen that, in eighteen hundred and fifty-five, the Queen of England, a grand-daughter of George III., would be a guest at the Tuileries of an Emperor of the French, and a nephew of Napoleon Bonaparte ; and that such

Queen would be led upon the arm of such Emperor to visit the tomb of the Prisoner of St. Helena.

After leaving Delhi I crossed over to Meerut, which was then, as it always has been since its formation, the favourite station in the Upper Provinces of India. In eighteen hundred and forty-six and forty-seven there were as many as ten thousand troops quartered at Meerut, including two regiments of British foot, a regiment of dragoons, and three troops of horse (European) artillery. Until lately, it has always been deemed prudent to keep a very large European force at Meerut in order to keep Delhi (only forty miles distant) in check; for it was stipulated in one of our treaties with the family of the Moghuls, that no British infantry or cavalry, or other European troops, should ever be quartered in the Imperial City or its immediate vicinity. When, however, the Punjab was annexed, the European force at Meerut was lessened to meet the exigencies of the times; and of late Meerut has not been, in respect to the number of European troops, the station that it was formerly.

There are no ancient buildings to be seen at Meerut. All is of European structure. The church, the barracks, the court-houses, the treasury, the theatre, the bungalows of the civilians and military officers, as well as those of the merchants and "others," are all of brick and mortar, lath and plaster; and they were for the most part thatched, so that the Sepoys had very little trouble in setting fire to them. The reason why houses are commonly thatched instead of tiled and shingled, is that the thatch keeps the interior of the dwelling so very much cooler.

While at Meerut I was a guest of the editor of the journal which used to issue from that station, and as my stay extended over six weeks, during which period I frequently assisted the editor in his work, I gained some knowledge of the practical working of the press in the Upper Provinces. I am authorized to make any use I please of this knowledge.

In the first place I may mention that the order of Government forbidding civilians or military men corresponding with the press, was, to every intent and purpose, a perfect farce and a dead letter. On the staff of the Meerut paper were several gentlemen belonging to each branch of the service. These gentlemen not only wrote, but some of them wrote for pay —for so much per column; while the correspondence columns were filled with letters from covenanted civilians or commissioned officers, judges, and magistrates, and their subordinates; brigadiers, colonels, majors, captains, and subalterns contributed anonymously, whenever the spirit moved them. Ay! and frequently the members of the staff of the Governor-General and of the Commander-in-Chief would not only send items of news, but comments thereon; and I have reason to know that this practice was continued up to the date of the recent outbreak, and is still continued. By the way, the late Major Thomas was virtually the editor of the *Mofussilite* at Agra at the time he received his death wound in the field of battle. The Delhi newspaper was also written for by civilians and military men af all grades.

It was the press that introduced to the notice of the Government many clever and able men, who had no other interest to help them. I could mention scores of instances, but two will suffice. Herbert Benjamin Edwardes, of the Bengal Fusiliers, the "Brahminee Bull" of the *Delhi Gazette*, and Mr. Campbell, of the Civil Service, who was "given up" to Lord Dalhousie as the "Delator" of the *Mofussilite*, and promoted to an office of great responsibility. In the last-mentioned paper there also appeared, in eighteen hundred and forty-seven, forty-eight, and forty nine, a series of leading articles on military reform and other matters, some of which attracted the notice of Sir Charles Napier. They came from the pen of General (then Major) Mansfield, of the Fifty-third Foot, and at present chief of the staff of Sir Colin Campbell. It was not to silence these men, who displayed their ability in the newspapers, that they were placed in staff employ, or promoted. On the contrary, I know that they were expected—and in some instances requested—to use their pens in defence of certain Government measures; and that, on several occasions, they did vigorous battle with their former literary chief, the editor of the paper in which they first made their appearance in print. I remember that on one occasion the editor, on being beaten in an argument, headed his admission of the fact with the following lines :—

> Keen are our pangs ; but keener far to feel
> We nursed the pinion that impels the steel.

There are no newsmen in the Upper Provinces of India, nor, indeed, in any of the Presidencies. Whoever wishes to take a journal must subscribe for a certain period—year or half-year. The rates for the *Mofussilite*, or *Delhi Gazette*, were three pounds twelve shillings per annum, or two pounds per six months. The net profits of both these papers, in eighteen hundred and forty-nine and fifty, were upwards of five thousand pounds per annum. With the exception of the *Friend in India*, when under the control of its original proprietor, these journals of the North-West were by far the most remunerative of any in the East.

There was a native newspaper published at Meerut, called the *Jam-i-Jumsheed*, which title signifies a bowl or glass. into which if you look, you will see what transpires in the whole world. The history of this paper is very curious.

It was founded without the knowledge, privity, or consent of the conductor of the European journal, by the head pressman of his establishment, who was a Brahmin. The editor of this native print, which was lithographed in the Oordoo language, was the moonshee of the English press at Meerut. He was well skilled in English, and his chief employment was translating the native correspondence. Having constant access to the desks of the compositors, this press moonshee acquired a knowledge of every item of news furnished by European as well as native correspondents, and of this knowledge he failed not to avail himself. This, however, was but a small evil, comparatively. Unknown to the conductor of the Meerut paper, a much greater evil arose from the publication of the native print. Availing himself of such sources of information, its editor seized the views of his employer—views intended only for European eyes, and gave his own version of them to his readers in the Hindoostanee language ; and, what was equally mischievous, he published quantities of matter which the conductor of the Meerut paper thought proper to suppress after it was set up in type. These were the morsels in which the native editor took most delight. A single instance will suffice. The following appeared in the leading columns of the *Jam-i-Jumsheed*, the facts having been kept out of the columns of the Meerut paper, at the instance of the friends of the gentleman who was guilty of the indiscretion :—

An act of retributive justice has just been committed by the worthy magistrate of this district. It was supposed that an escaped convict from the jail was secreted in a village about four miles distant from this cantonment. In the dead of the night, the magistrate, at the head of a large body of police, visited the village, aroused the inhabitants from their slumbers, and demanded the culprit. The villagers denied any knowledge of him. The magistrate, with characteristic kindness and consideration, gave them half-an-hour to make up their minds. At the expiration of that time, as the culprit was not produced, he set fire to the village. In those flames, which illuminated the country for miles round, thirteen lives were sacrificed; namely, those of three men, four women, and six children. One of the unfortunate women was in labour at the time. Some malicious natives in the neighbourhood of Meerut give out that the Sahib has been notoriously mad for several years past. Let us hope, however, that the Lieutenant-Governor will not heed such insinuations, but after complimenting the magistrate on his vigour and his zeal, appoint him to the first judgeship that may become vacant. No less than six hundred persons are, by this fire, rendered homeless beggars. But what of that? Must justice be obstructed?

It remains for us to add that the escaped convict of whom the magistrate was in search, has been in Oude for the past month, and that no notice of this affair will appear in any of the papers printed in English and edited by the Sahib Logue. Those gentlemen are far too modest to make known the manifest blessings which arise out of British rule in India.

For upwards of a year and a-half the native paper went on filching news, and writing in the above strain. At length the conductor of the Meerut journal was furnished with some information which led to his discharging his employées, the head pressman and the moonshee, and breaking up their journal, the *Jam-i-Jumsheed.* And more than this was done. The danger of permitting native newspapers to be published without any sort of supervision was elaborately, and from time to time dwelt upon by the English editor, and at length the Government was moved to call for a return of the journals printed in the Hindoostanee language in the Upper Provinces of India, and for an account of the number of copies that each issued. With this return and account the Government was well satisfied; first, because the aggregate circulation was so ridiculously small (comparatively), that it was quite clear that the native press had no power or influence; and, secondly, that the tone of the best conducted and most respectable journals of the native press were loud in their praises of British rule, and firm supporters of the Government. It was overlooked with reference to the first point, that in no country, and in India especially, is the actual circulation of a newspaper any criterion of the number of persons acquainted with its contents, its chief items of intelligence, and its sentiments on the most important questions of the day. Let us take for example, the greatest paper in the world—the *Times*. Compare the number of copies that are struck off daily with the number of hands into which that paper passes, the number of eyes that read it, and the number of ears that listen to hear it read. As to the second point, the praise of the Government of India, it was laughable to hear it mentioned, albeit the subject was of so serious a character. That praise was bestowed very much in the same spirit that Jack Wilkes is said to have conveyed a serious warning, with a humorous grin, to an election mob —"I hear that it is your intention, gentlemen, to take that person (there!) who is interrupting me, place him under that pump, and duck him! Now, if you should do so, no matter how much it may be for his own good, you will—I give you this emphatic warning—incur my most serious displeasure, gentlemen!" They (the native editors) used to wrap up the most bitter irony in the most complimentary phrases, and frequently their allusions, if viewed abstractedly, were both humorous and witty. A case in point. The late Lieutenant-Governor of the North-Western Provinces, a few years ago, presided at an examination of the students of a Government public school. Amongst other questions which his honour put to the boys of the first class was this—"How does the world go round?" The head boy, a very intelligent Hindoo, gave an admirable reply—spoke, as the saying is, like a book. The editor of a native paper, in a notice of the examination, predicted that this boy would come to a bad end for giving such an answer to the Lieutenant-Governor of the North-West Provinces. "He ought," said the native editor, "when so questioned by so potent a ruler, as to the cause of the world's going round, to have flung science into the gutter, and, having assumed the most cringing attitude imaginable, he should have placed his hands together, and then have responded meekly, 'By your honour's grace, favour, and kindness, does this planet revolve upon its axis.'" This same editor once wrote a notice of a ball given by the officers of the Horse Artillery mess at Meerut to the ladies of the Twenty-ninth Foot, on the occasion of that last-mentioned and distinguished regiment coming to the station. When translated, literally, to an Englishman this notice would seem the most flattering account possible; but, if such Englishman took it in the sense in which Asiatics understood and comprehended it, he would, without any sort of doubt, have admitted that it was the most extraordinary and ingenious admixture of satire and obscenity that ever was printed and published!

The same editor, during the second Sikh campaign, burlesqued the despatches of Lord Gough; but so cleverly, that they were taken by English people, who heard them translated, as genuine productions. This was the man who never lost an opportunity of bringing British rule in India into disgrace, ridicule, and contempt amongst his countrymen, and who, eventually, by producing his writings, and having them translated literally, succeeded in obtaining an appointment under the Government worth one hundred and fifty rupees per mensem! The great article on which his good fortune was based, was one descriptive of Lord Dalhousie, on the back of an elephant, proceeding to a spot appointed as the place of an interview between his Lordship and the late Maharajah Goolab Singh. Neither the London nor the Paris *Charivari* ever surpassed this squib, so far as its spirit of ridicule was concerned, while in point of mischief those European journals of fun would never have dreamed of going the lengths of the Asiatic writer. "What became of this native editor?" may be reasonably asked. I hear that he is now aide-de-camp and military secretary to Bahadoor Khan, the rebel, who is at the head of a considerable army, and, according to the latest accounts, in possession of the entire

Bareilly district. He (the native editor) is a Mahommedan, of very ancient and good family; he has an extremely handsome person and plausible manners, and should I again wander in India, it will not at all surprise me to find him in the service of the British Government, and filling some office of considerable dignity and emolument.

I have incidentally spoken of the theatre at Meerut. It was a building about the size of the Adelphi Theatre, and was built by subscription, some twenty-five years ago. The performers were, of course, amateurs, officers in the civil and military services, and now and then an interloper, possessed of histrionic abilities. The ladies were those young gentlemen who could be best made up to imitate the gentler sex. The scene-painters, scene-shifters, prompters, and so on, were men belonging to the various European corps quartered in the station, men who had been about, or connected with, London theatres, and who understood their business thoroughly. On an average, there was a performance once a fortnight. Tragedy was seldom or never attempted; nothing but standard comedies and approved farces. It pains me to think of the last performance I witnessed on the Meerut boards; for, with the exception of myself and another gentleman, every one who had a character assigned to him is now numbered with the dead. The play was *The Lady of Lyons*. Claude Melnotte was an officer in the Governor-General's Body-guard;

his height was under five feet, and his weight exactly eight stone. Pauline was the magistrate of Bolund-Shahur, who was six feet three, and weighed twenty-one stone and some pounds. In short, Claude was about the smallest, and Pauline about the biggest man, in British India. These two died of natural causes within the last three years. The rest have all been massacred or killed in action. Some perished at Cawnpore, and other stations, and some have fallen before Delhi and before Lucknow. And, alas! amongst the audience of that night, how many have since been prematurely despatched from this world—men, women, and children!

There are some matters connected with theatricals in India, in the Upper Provinces, which would strike any gentleman or lady fresh from Europe as very odd. Huge punkahs are suspended from the ceiling, and pulled by natives during the performance. Without the punkahs the heat in the house would be unbearable. Then, there are no boxes, and there is no pit. One part of the house, that nearest to the stage, is set apart for the officers civil and military, and their wives and families. The rest of the house is generally filled by non-commissioned officers and private soldiers. As a matter of course, the greatest order prevails throughout the play, which is usually produced "under the patronage of the officer commanding the station and his lady." The actors are never hissed; but the applause, in which the men always join, is loud, long, frequent, and encouraging.

In most of the large stations, where European troops are quartered—such stations as Meerut, Agra, Umballah, Cawnpore, Lahore—the non-commissioned officers and men of the regiments get up theatrical performances, which are attended by the society. And very creditably, too, do they perform. I have seen a sergeant of the 8th Foot (Colonel Greathead's regiment) play, at Agra, the character of Doctor O'Toole, in *The Irish Tutor*, in a style and with a racy humour which reminded me more of the late Mr. Power than any actor on the metropolitan or provincial boards in England ever did. And at Umballah, I have seen a corporal of the Third Dragoons act the part of *The Stranger* in a way that moved an audience, "unused, albeit to the melting mood," in the literal sense of the phrase, to involuntary tears. But by far the best actor (I am speaking of non-professionals) that I ever listened to, considering the range of characters that he played, was a private in the 9th Lancers. I would have gone night after night, to see him in tragedy, comedy, or farce; or even to hear him sing a sentimental or a comic song. He was a younger brother of an intelligent, influential, rich, and deservedly respected London tradesman, whose name is known in every quarter of the world where the English language is spoken. It behoves me to say that these three men (who, by the way, are all dead) were possessed of great general ability, and had, respectively, received a good education.

It is not for a wanderer and an interloper like myself to make any suggestions to an enlightened (I use the word advisedly) Government; but I do hope that when order is restored throughout our Eastern dominions, when the affairs of the country are a matter of local consideration, the health, comfort, and recreation of the British soldier in those hot plains will command more attention than has hitherto been bestowed upon them. I hope to see barracks in which the men can live in comparative comfort—barracks lofty and spacious, and fitted with punkahs, and other conveniences such as are required for the climate, and such as one always finds in the abodes of officers and gentlemen. I hope to see separate sleeping apartments for the married couples, and separate sleeping apartments for the mass of children above seven and eight years of age. I hope never again to see men, women, young girls, and boys, and infant children, so huddled together that those who escaped demoralization ought to have been exhibited as curiosities of the human species. I hope never again to behold white children, girls of thirteen years of age, the offspring of British soldiers, married, in order that they might remain in the regiment.

"Surely," I once remarked to the Colonel of a

Royal regiment in India, who made some remarks on the painful topic last alluded to—"Surely this might be obviated?"

"Yes, my good sir," was his reply. "But it would cost this Government an outlay of a few thousands of rupees. A little while ago I had a battle with the Government. I insisted on having punkahs hung up in the barracks, and I spoke in a tone so decided that even the frowsy military board—composed of several very old and feeble Company's officers of the last century—was frightened into something like activity. Well, sir, the punkahs were suspended, and I fancied that I had gained an immense triumph; but I was very much mistaken. It was a case of 'There are your punkahs, and now let your men pull them, or employ the natives to do so!' So that the punkahs, after all, instead of promoting a current of fresh air, impeded it, and served only as perches for the flies, and cobweb-booms for the spiders. The idea of the poor men paying for punkah coolies!"

"What would it cost to punkah the whole regiment during the hot season?" I asked.

"I can tell you exactly," said the colonel: "for I have made a correct estimate. The cost for the five hot months would be under three hundred pounds; and by laying out this sum the Government would save some three thousand or four thousand pounds a-year, at the very least."

"How so?"

"Many men cannot bear the heat of these barrack rooms, crowded as they are, and left without punkahs. The consequence is, that they become ill, go into hospital and die there, or spend the greater part of their time there. I should say that if the men had better accommodation, and the same means as *we officers* have of keeping their apartments cool, we should save in every regiment fifty lives annually. Now, every recruit who comes from home and joins a regiment in the Upper Provinces, to fill up a death or casualty in the ranks, costs the Indian Government a hundred and ten pounds sterling. I have pointed all this out; but it is of no use."

"I would report it to the Horse Guards." said I.

"I did so, two years ago."

"And what did the Horse Guards say in reply to your statements?"

"Precisely what the learned world said of poor George Primrose's paradoxes — they said nothing. They treated them with dignified silence, and perhaps contempt. However, I did not stop there. I went further."

"You addressed the Throne, or Prince Albert?"

"No; I did not go so far as that. We had just got the Albert hat out, and after a careful examination of it, I came to the conclusion that his Royal Highness would hardly be disposed to give much ear to my complaint touching the discomfort of the British troops in India. But I wrote to an elder brother of mine, who represents a borough in Parliament, and I begged of him to bring under the notice of the House of Commons the condition of the British soldier in India, and move for a report of the officers in command of the various regiments doing duty in this country."

"And he did so, I hope?"

"Not he. He wrote to me to say that he had never spoken in the House, and never intended doing so, as he had not the faintest ambition to become a public orator; but that he had shown my letter to several friends of his (members of Parliament), who would only be too glad of an opportunity of bringing themselves into notice; and that they, one and all, blew upon it, remarking that the condition of the British soldier in any part of the world was a frightful bore; but that the condition of the British soldier in the East was a bore utterly beyond toleration. 'My dear George,' (he went on to say to me), 'your story would only be received with an ironical hear, hear! followed by a series of coughs, as though the subject had given the House a sudden chill and a very bad cold. Even that garrulous goose, Jamsey, to whom (in despair, and in order to oblige you) I showed your letter—even Jamsey, who is always ready to talk for hours about everything or anybody, shrugged his shoulders, shook his head, sighed, lifted up his hands, groaned, *It wont do*, and left me. Find out some indigo-planter who has been, or is supposed to be, guilty of some sort of oppression towards a sable cultivator of the soil, and we will pretty soon grind his bones to make our bread, my boy; but, for Heaven's sake, and the sake of the House of Commons, don't inflict upon us your British soldiers."

To leave the colonel, and express my further hopes —I hope to see in every large station throughout India two Christian churches erected—one for the Protestants and another for the Roman Catholics. Both erected at the expense of the Government. I hope to see, also, in every large station, a library to which every soldier, at stated hours, shall have access. I hope to see soldiers' gardens—such as the late Sir Henry Lawrence recommended—in which the men may, when they feel disposed, work, or amuse themselves in the cold season. I hope to see a theatre in every large station built and kept in repair, not by subscription from the poor men, but at the cost of the State. I hope, in fact to see the British soldier in the East—not petted, pampered, and made a fuss of, but made as sensibly comfortable as the climate in which he serves will admit of his being made. I hope, from the bottom of my heart, never to see brave men put into such a barrack as that at Loodianah, which fell in upon, and buried in its ruins, the remnant of her Majesty's 50th Regiment of Foot: one of the most gallant regiments in the Army List. They went into the field, during the first Sikh campaign, nine hundred strong. Nine hundred bright bayonets glittered in the sun as they marched away to give the foe (in the words of Lord Gough) "a taste of cold stale." They were at Moodkee, Ferozeshah, Aliwal, and Sobraon. Out of that nine hundred, only three hundred returned to quarters in March, eighteen hundred and forty-six. In three months, six hundred had fallen in battle! The campaign over, they were quartered at Loodianah, and placed in barracks which had been frequently reported rotten, unsound, and dangerous. But of this report—though forwarded by the Commander-in-chief—the military board took no notice. The consequence was, that in a dust-storm on the night of the twenty-first of May, ten years ago, the barracks came down! Beneath that mass of dust and smoke, and unburnt bricks, lay all the men, women, and children, left to represent the glorious 50th Regiment of Foot! Beneath that mass were the heroes who had escaped the carnage of the battle-fields in which three to one of the Regiment had died! Fifty-one men, eighteen women, and twenty-nine children, were killed by the fall of those barracks; one hundred and twenty-six men, thirty-nine women, and thirty-four children, were badly wounded—many maimed and disfigured for life! Well might the Colonel of that regiment cry aloud, "My God! there is no 50th left! The enemy did its worst; but it is the Company Bahadoor that has given us the finishing blow!"

The English reader may possibly doubt the accuracy of these details; but there is a huge grave at Loodianah containing the bones of those men, women, and children of the 50th; and scores of officers still live to bear testimony to the truth of my assertions in respect to this horrible catastrophe.

The engineer at Loodianah was written to by the secretary of the Military Board, and asked why he had not made a report of the state of the barracks which had fallen in? He replied that he had written three letters on the subject, and that his predecessor in office had written seven; and the foolish man was stupid enough to ransack the records of his office, and "had the honour to transmit for information of the Board copies of these documents." For this absurd effort of memory, and ridiculous attempt to clear himself of blame, he was removed from his appointment, and sent to do duty with the Sappers and Miners—a sort of very severe punishment in the East for any engineer officer guilty of an indiscretion.

CHURCHYARDS, ETC.

I CANNOT leave Meerut without taking the reader to the churchyard of that station.

An Indian churchyard presents a very different aspect to a churchyard in England or elsewhere. The tombs for the most part are very much larger. When first erected or newly done up they are as white as snow, formed, as they are generally, of chunam (plaster), which somewhat resembles Roman cement; but after exposure to only one rainy season and one hot weather, they become begrimed and almost black. The birds flying from structure to structure carry with them the seeds of various plants and herbs, and these if not speedily removed take root and grow apace. A stranger wandering in the churchyard of Meerut might fancy that he is amidst ruins of stupendous antiquity, if he were not aware of the fact that fifty years have scarcely elapsed since the first Christian corpse was deposited within those walls which now encircle some five acres of ground, literally covered with tombs, in every stage of preservation and decay. I was conducted in my ramble through the Meerut churchyard by an old and very intelligent pensioner, who had originally been a private in a regiment of Light Dragoons. This old man lived by the churchyard, that is to say, he derived a very comfortable income from looking after and keeping in repair the tombs of those whose friends are now far away; but whose thoughts nevertheless still turn occasionally to that Christian enclosure in the land of heathens and idolators.

"I get, sir, for this business," said the old man, pointing with his stick to a very magnificent edifice, "two pounds a year. It is not much, but it is what I asked, and it pays me very well, sir. And if you should go back to England, and ever come across any of her family, I hope, sir, you will tell them that I do my duty by the grave; not that I think they have any doubt of it, for they must know—or, leastways, they have been told by them they can believe—that if I never received a farthing from them I would always keep it in repair, as it is now. God bless her, and rest her soul! She was as good and as beautiful a woman as ever trod this earth."

"Who was she?"

"The wife of an officer in my old regiment, sir. I was in her husband's troop. He's been out twice since the regiment went home, only to visit this grave; for he has long since sold out of the service, and is a rich gentleman. The last time he came was about five years ago. He comes what you call *incog.*; nobody knows who he is, and he never calls on anybody. All that he now does in this country is to come here, stop for three days and nights, putting up at the dâk bungalow, and spending his time here, crying. It is there that he stands, where you stand now, fixing his eyes on the tablet, and sometimes laying his head down on the stone, and calling out her name: 'Ellen! Ellen! My own dear Ellen!' He did love her, sure*ly*, sir."

"Judging from the age of the lady, twenty-three, and the date of her death, he must be rather an old man now."

"Yes, sir. He must be more than sixty; but his love for her memory is just as strong as ever. She died of a fever, poor thing. And for that business," he again pointed with his stick to a tomb admirably preserved, "I used to get two pounds ten shillings a-year. That is the tomb of a little girl of five years old, the daughter of a civilian. The parents are now dead. They must be, for I have not heard of 'em or received anything from 'em for more than six years past."

"Then who keeps the tomb in repair?"

"I do, sir. When I am here, with my trowel and mortar, and whitewash, why shouldn't I make the outside of the little lady's last home on earth as bright and as fair as those of her friends and neighbours? I have a nursery of 'em, as I call it, over in yonder corner—the children's corner. Some of 'em are paid for, others not; but when I'm there doing what's needful, I touch 'em up all alike, bless their dear little souls. And somehow or other every good action meets its own reward, and often when we least expect it. Now, for instance, sir, about three years, and a half ago, I was over there putting the nursery in good order, when up comes a grey-headed gentleman, and looks about the graves. Suddenly he stopped opposite to one and began to read, and presently he took out his pocket handkerchief and put it to his eyes.

"'Did you know that little child, sir?' said I, when it was not improper to speak. 'Know it?' said he, 'yes. It was my own little boy.' 'Dear me, sir!' I answered him. 'And you are, then, Lieutenant Statterleigh?' 'I was,' said he; 'but I am now the colonel of a regiment that has just come to India, and is now stationed at Dinapore. But tell me, who keeps this grave in order?' 'I do, sir,' says I. 'At whose expense?' says he. 'At nobody's, sir,' says I. 'It is kept in order by the dictates of my own conscience. Your little boy is in good company here; and while I am whitening the tombs of the other little dears, I have it not in my heart to pass by his without giving it a touch also.' Blest if he didn't take me to the house where he was staying, and give me five hundred rupees! That sort of thing has happened to me more than five or six times in my life, not that I ever hope or think of being paid for such work and labour when I am about it."

"That must have been a magnificent affair," said

I, pointing to a heap of red stone and marble. "But how comes it in ruins?"

"It is just as it was left, sir. The lady died. Her husband, a judge here, took on terribly; and ordered that tomb for her. Some of the stone was brought from Agra, some from Delhi; but before it was put together and properly erected, he married again, and the work was stopped. I was present at the funeral. There was no getting him away after the service was over, and at last they had to resort to force and violence—in fact, to carry him out of the yard. But the shallowest waters, as the proverb says, sir, always make the most noise, while those are the deepest that flow on silently. Yonder is a funny tomb, sir," continued the old man, again pointing with his stick. "There! close to the tomb of the lady which I first showed you."

"How do you mean funny?" I asked, observing nothing particular in the structure.

"Well, sir, it is funny only on account of the history of the two gentlemen whose remains it covers," replied the old man, leading me to the tomb. "One of these young gentlemen, sir, was an officer—a lieutenant—in the Bengal Horse Artillery; the other was an ensign in a Royal Regiment of the Line. There was a ball, and by some accident that beautiful lady of our regiment had engaged herself to both of them for the same dance. When the time came, both went up and claimed her hand. Neither of them would give way, and the lady not wishing to offend either by showing a preference, and finding herself in a dilemma, declined to dance with either. Not satisfied with this, they retired to the verandah, where they had some high words, and the next morning they met, behind the church there, and fought a duel, in which both of them fell, mortally wounded. They had scarcely time to shake hands with one another when they died. In those days matters of the kind were very easily hushed up; and it was given out, though everybody knew to the contrary, that one had died of fever and the other of cholera, and they were both buried side by side in one grave; and this tomb was erected over them at the joint expense of the two regiments to which they belonged. I get ten rupees a year for keeping this grave in order."

"Who pays you?"

"A gentleman in Calcutta, a relation of one of them. I'll tell you what it is, sir. This foolish affair, which ended so fatally, sowed the seeds of the fever that carried off that beautiful and good woman yonder. She was maddened by the thought of being the cause of the quarrel in which they lost their lives. I knew them both, sir, from seeing them so often on the parade ground and at the band stand; very fine young men they were, sir. Yes; here they sleep in peace."

"Whose tombs are those?" I asked, pointing to

some two or three hundred which were all exactly alike, and in three straight lines; in other words, three deep.

"Those are the tombs of the men of the Cameronians, sir. These graves are all uniform, as you observe. Fever made sad havoc with that regiment. They lost some three companies in all. Behind them are the tombs of the men of the Buffs, and behind them the tombs of the men of other Royal Regiments of Infantry—all uniform you see, sir; but those of each regiment rather differently shaped. To the right, flanking the Infantry tombs, are the tombs of the men of the Cavalry, 8th and 11th Dragoons, and 16th Lancers. In the rear of the Cavalry are the tombs of the Horse and Foot Artillerymen—all uniform you see, sir. Egad! if they could rise just now, what a pretty little army they would form, of all ranks, some thousands of 'em, and well officered, too, they would be; and here a man to lead them. This is the tomb of Major-General Considine, one of the most distinguished men in the British army. He was the officer that the Duke of Wellington fixed upon to bring the 53rd Foot into good order, when they ran riot in Gibraltar some years ago. This is the tomb of General Considine, rotting and going rapidly to decay, though it was only built in the year 1845. A great deal of money is squandered in the churchyards in India. Tombs are erected, and at a great expense frequently. After they are once put up it is very seldom that they are visited or heeded. Tens of thousands of pounds have been thrown away on the vast pile of bricks and mortar and stone that you now see within this enclosure, and with the exception of a few all are crumbling away. A Hindoo —a sweeper—said to me the other day in this graveyard, 'Why don't you English burn your dead as we do, instead of leaving their graves here, to tell us how much you can neglect them and how little you care for them? What is the use of whitening a few sepulchres amidst this mass of black ruin?' I had no answer to give the fellow, sir; indeed the same thought had often occurred to me while at work in this wilderness. Do you not think, sir, that the government, through its own executive officers, ought to expend a few hundred pounds every year on these yards, in order to avert such a scandal and disgrace? I do not speak interestedly. I have as much already on my hands as I can perform, if not more; but I do often think that there is really some reason in the remarks of that sweeper. All these graves that you see here so blackened and left to go to ruin, are the graves of men who have served their country and died in its service. Very little money would keep the yard free from this grass and these rank weeds, and very little more would make all these tombs fit to be seen; for neither labour nor whitewash is expensive in this part of the world. One would hardly suppose, on looking about him just now, that the sons and daughters of some of the best families in England are buried here, and that in a very short time no one will be able to distinguish the spot where each is lying; so defaced and so much alike will all the ruins become. What, sir, I repeat, is the use of throwing away money in building tombs, if they are not kept in repair? Instead of laying out fifty or a hundred pounds on a thing like this, why not lay out only five pounds on a single head-stone, and put the rest out at interest to keep it up?"

"Or a small slab with an iron railing round it?"

"Ah, sir; but then you would require an European to remain here, and a couple of native watchmen to see that the railings were not carried off by the villagers. As it is, they never allow an iron railing to remain longer than a week, or so long as that. They watch for an opportunity, jump over this low wall, and tear them down, or wrench them off and away with them."

"But surely there is some one to watch the yard?"

"Yes, two sweepers—men of the lowest caste of Hindoos. And when it is found out that a grave has been plundered of its railings, or that the little marble tablet, which some have, has been taken away, they deny all knowledge of the matter, and are simply discharged, and two others of the same caste are put into their places. It would not be much to build a comfortable little bungalow for an European—a man like myself, for instance—and give the yard into his charge, holding him responsible for any damage done, and requiring him to see that the grave of every Christian—man, woman, and child—is kept in good order. But horrible as is the condition of this churchyard—looking as it does, for the most part, more like a receptacle for the bodies of felons than those of good and brave soldiers and civilians, and their wives and children—it is really nothing when compared with the graveyard of Kernaul. Kernaul, you know, sir, was our great frontier station some twenty years ago. It was, in fact, as large a station as Umballah now is. It had its church, its play-house, its barracks for cavalry, infantry, and artillery, its mess-houses, magnificent bungalows, and all the rest of it. For some reason or other—but what that reason was I could never discover, nor anybody else to my knowledge—the station was abandoned with all its buildings, which cost the government and private individuals lacs and lacs of rupees. You may be pretty sure that the villagers were not long in plundering every house that was unprotected. Away went the doors and windows, the venetians, and every bar, bolt, nail, or bit of iron upon which they could lay their fingers; not content with this, the brutes set fire to many or nearly all of the thatched bungalows, in the hope of picking up something amongst the ruins. The church—the largest and best in the Upper Provinces, with no one to take care of it—was one of the first places that suffered. Like the other buildings, it was despoiled of its doors, windows, benches, bolts, nails,

&c., and they carried away every marble tablet therein erected, and removeable without much difficulty. And the same kind of havoc was made in the burial-ground—the tombs were smashed, some of the graves, and especially the vaults, opened; and plainly enough was it to be seen, that the low caste men had broken open the coffins and examined their contents, in the hope of finding a ring, or an ear-ring, or some other ornament on the person of the dead. I went there a year ago on some business connected with the grave of a lady, whose husband wished her remains to be removed to Meerut, and placed in the same vault with those of his sister, who died here about eighteen months since. I was not successful, however. There was no trace of her tomb. It was of stone, and had been taken away bodily, to pave the elephant shed or camel yard, perhaps, of some rich native in the neighbourhood. Looking around me, as I did, and remembering Kernaul when it was crowded with Europeans, it seemed to me as though the British had been turned out of the country by the natives, and that the most sacred spot in the cantonment had been desecrated out of spite or revenge. And it is just what they would do if ever they got the upper hand."

[Whilst I write, it has just occurred to me that this old soldier and his family perished in the massacre at Meerut on the 10th of May. He was in some way related to, or connected by marriage with,

Mrs. Courtenay, the keeper of the hotel, who, with her nieces, was so barbarously murdered on that disastrous occasion.]

"Why, bless my soul!" exclaimed the old man, stooping down and picking up something, "if the old gentleman hasn't shed his skin again! This is the skin of a very large snake, a cobra capella, that I have known for the last thirteen years. He must be precious old from his size, the slowness of his movements, and the bad cough he has had for the last four or five years. Last winter he was very bad indeed, and I thought he was going to die. He was then living in the ruins of old General Webster's vault and coughing continually, just like a man with the asthma. However, I strewed a lot of fine ashes and some bits of wool in the ruin to keep him warm by night, and some fine white sand at the entrance, upon which he used to crawl out and bask, when the sun had made it hot enough; and when the warm weather set in he got all right again."

"Rather a strange fancy of yours, to live upon such amicable terms with the great enemy of the human race?"

"Well, perhaps it is. But he once bit and killed a thief who came here to rob a child's grave of the iron railings, which its parents, contrary to my advice, had placed round it, and ever since then I have liked the snake, and have never thought of molesting him. I have had many an opportunity of killing him (if I had wished to do it) when I have caught him asleep on the tombstones, in the winter's sun. I could kill him this very day—this very hour—if I liked, for I know where he is at this very moment. He is in a hole, close to the Ochterlony monument there, in that corner of the yard. But why should I hurt him? He has never offered to do me any harm, and when I sing, as I sometimes do, when I am alone here at work on some tomb or other, he will crawl up, and listen for two or three hours together. One morning, while he was listening, he came in for a good meal which lasted him some days."

"How was this?"

"I will tell you, sir. A minar was chased by a small hawk, and in despair came and perched itself on the top of a most lofty tomb at which I was at work. The hawk, with his eyes fixed intently on his prey, did not, I fancy, see the snake lying motionless in the grass; or if he did see him he did not think he was a snake, but something else—my crowbar, perhaps. After a little while the hawk pounced down, and was just about to give the minar a blow and a grip, when the snake suddenly lifted his head, raised his hood, and hissed. The hawk gave a shriek, fluttered, flapped his wings with all his might, and tried very hard to fly away. But it would not do. Strong as the eye of the hawk was, the eye of the snake was stronger. The hawk for a time seemed suspended in the air; but at last he was obliged to come down, and sit opposite to the old gentleman (the snake) who commenced, with his forked tongue, and keeping his eyes upon him all the while, to slime his victim all over. This occupied him for at least forty minutes, and by the time the process was over the hawk was perfectly motionless. I don't think he was dead. But he was very soon, however, for the old gentleman put him into a coil or two, and crackled up every bone in the hawk's body. He then gave him another sliming, made a big mouth, distended his neck till it was as big round as the thickest part of my arm, and down went the hawk like a shin of beef into a beggarman's bag."

"And what became of the minar?"

"He was off like a shot, sir, the moment his enemy was in trouble, and no blame to him. What a funny thing nature is altogether, sir! I very often think of that scene when I am at work here."

"But this place must be infested with snakes?"

"I have never seen but that one, sir, and I have been here for a long time. Would you like to see the old gentleman, sir? As the sun is up, and the morning rather warm, perhaps he will come out, if I pretend to be at work and give him a ditty. If he does not, we will look in upon him."

"Come along," said I.

I accompanied the old man to a tomb, close to the monument beneath which the snake was said to have taken up his abode. I did not go very near to the spot, but stood upon a tomb with a thick stick in my hand, quite prepared to slay the monster if he approached me; for from childhood I have always had an instinctive horror of reptiles of every species, caste, and character.

The old man began to hammer away with his mallet and chisel, and to sing a very quaint old song which I had never heard before, and have never heard since. It was a dialogue or duet between the little finger and the thumb, and began thus. The thumb said:

"Dear Rose Mary Green!
When I am king, little finger, you shall be queen."

The little finger replied:

"Who told you so, Thummy, Thummy? Who told you so?"

The thumb responded:

"It was my own heart, little finger, who told me so!"

The thumb then drew a very flattering picture of the life they would lead when united in wedlock, and concluded, as nearly as I can remember, thus:

THUMB.

"And when you are dead, little finger, as it may hap,
You shall be buried, little finger, under the tap."

LITTLE FINGER.

"Why, Thummy, Thummy? Why, Thummy, Thummy? Why Thummy, Thummy—*Why*?"

THUMB.

"That you may drink, little finger, when you are dry?"

But this ditty did not bring out the snake. I

remarked this to the old man, who replied: "He hasn't made his toilet yet—hasn't rubbed his scales up, sir; but he'll be here presently. You will see. Keep your eye on that hole, sir. I am now going to give him a livelier tune, which is a great favourite of his; and forthwith he struck up an old song, beginning

> "'Twas in the merry month of May,
> When bees from flower to flower did hum."

Out came the snake before the song was half over! Before it was concluded he had crawled slowly and (if I dare use such a word) rather majestically, to within a few paces of the spot where the old man was standing.

"Good morning to you, sir," said the old man to the snake. "I am happy to see you in your new suit of clothes. I have picked up your old suit, and I have got it in my pocket, and a very nice pair of slippers my old wife will make out of it. The last pair that she made of your rejected apparel were given as a present to Colonel Cureton, who, like myself, very much resembled the great General Blücher in personal appearance. Who will get the pair of which I have now the makings, Heaven only knows. Perhaps old Brigadier White, who has also a Blücher cut about him. What song would you like next? 'Kathleen Mavourneen?' Yes, I know that is a pet song of yours; and you shall have it."

The old man sung the melody with a tenderness

and feeling which quite charmed me, as well as the snake, who coiled himself up and remained perfectly still. Little reason as I had to doubt the truth of any of the old man's statements, I certainly should have been sceptical as to the story of the snake if I had not witnessed the scene I have attempted to describe.

"Well, sir," said the old man, coming up to me, after he had made a salaam to the snake and left him, "it is almost breakfast-time, and I will, with your permission, bid you good morning."

I thanked him very much for his information, and suffered him to depart; and then, alone, I wandered about that well-filled piece of ground. I have always had a melancholy pleasure in strolling from tombstone to tombstone, and reading the various epitaphs, and on that morning, after all that I had heard from the old pensioner, I was just in the humour for gratifying this morbid desire.

Some miles to the northward of Meerut is the station of Burnampore. No troops are quartered here; it is what is called in India a purely civil station, containing only a magistrate (who is also the collector of the revenue), an assistant (a covenanted civilian), the establishment of the office, and a small police force. To these two gentlemen and their few subordinates were entrusted the care and the collections of a district as large as Lancashire or Yorkshire, and containing, possibly, as many inhabitants. The idea of two gentlemen keeping in order a district of such dimensions was simply absurd; but they did their best, and that was all that could be expected of them. I remained four days and nights at Burnampore, and during that time was a guest of the assistant magistrate, whose acquaintance I had made at Meerut. Anything more monotonous and dreary than the existence of a gentleman stationed at such a place it would be very difficult to imagine. My host assured me that if it were not for an occasional visit paid by some traveller on his way up or down the country, both himself and his superior officer would have died of ennui. "If it were not for the shooting, which is very good in this district," he added, "I would rather be a permanent passenger on board ship, or the inmate of a debtors' prison in London, or any other part of England—in either case, one would have something like company, and one would have, at all events, a somewhat cooler and more congenial climate."

In the district of Burnampore there are a great number of wolves, and during my short stay, even, two were brought in, and the Government reward (two rupees a-head) claimed upon them. These ferocious creatures often carry off the young children of poor people and devour them. It was in this district that "a wolf child," as the natives of India express it, was found some years ago, and taken to Meerut, where it was exhibited as a curiosity. "There can be no question," said my friend and host, when I spoke to him one morning on this subject, "that the male wolf, in all these cases, seizes and runs off with the infant, and that when he has carried it alive to the den, the female, especially if she happens to have cubs at the time, instead of killing and devouring, suckles and fosters the little human being. So, after all, the story of Romulus and Remus may not be a mere fable."

"No," said I. "But what is that Greek epigram from the Anthology of Bland and Merivale? The she-goat that suckled the whelp of a wolf, which wolf, when she had no more milk to give it, killed her and eat her. Something about

> 'Be kind, be gentle, and do what you will,
> A stubborn nature will be nature still.'"

"Yes," replied my host. "I do remember something about it; and by and bye we will talk the matter over, and refer to the volume, which I have amongst my books; but at present you must excuse me, for I have a duty to perform. You may come with me and witness the operation, if you like; but understand me, I shall not be offended if you decline to do so."

"What operation?"

"That of hanging."

"What? Hanging! Hanging what?

"A man—a culprit—a murderer. Is is a part of my duty to see this operation performed. Come," he added energetically, and slapping me on the shoulder. "Come, be a sort of Selwyn for once in your life."

Whilst I was hesitating, the magistrate approached in his buggy. He had been taking his morning drive, and had dropt in upon his assistant to have some friendly conversation. He had forgotten all about the forthcoming execution; and, on hearing that we were just about to start for the spot, he very kindly offered to take us there — an offer which was accepted by his assistant with many thanks. So, off we drove, three in a gig, like so many men going to witness a pugilistic encounter in England during the beginning of the present century.

When we had arrived at the place of execution, a field some distance from the gaol, in which had been erected a temporary gallows, I was surprised at not finding a mob. There was no one there but the culprit—who was eating as much rice as he could, and as fast as he could—a couple of native policemen with drawn swords guarding him; the gaoler, who was a Mahommedan, and a Bengalee writer (clerk), who stood with pen, ink, and paper in hand, ready to dot down the official particulars of the scene, preparatory to their being forwarded to Government, according to a certain regulation.

"Is everything ready?" said the assistant magistrate to the gaoler.

"Yes, Sahib," he replied; "but he has not yet finished his breakfast."

"In one minute, Sahib," cried the culprit, who overheard the conversation; and hastily taking into his stomach the few grains of rice that remained upon the dish, and drinking the remainder of his half-gallon of milk, he sprang up, and called out the word "Tyear!" signifying "I am ready." He was then led up to the scaffold, the most primitive affair that I ever beheld. It was only a piece of woodwork resembling a large crock or crate in which a dinner-service is packed for exportation. Upon this crock, which was placed under the beam, he was requested to stand. Having obeyed this order, the rope was adjusted around his neck. The assistant magistrate then called out to him in Hindostanee, "Have you anything to say?"

"Yes, Sahib," was the reply. And he began a long story, false from beginning to end, but every word of which the Bengalee writer took down. He spoke, and with vehemence, for about thirty-five minutes, when, having stopped, either finally, or to take breath, the assistant magistrate gave the signal to the gaoler, by waving his hand. The crock was then pulled from under the culprit by the two policemen, and down dangled the culprit's body, the feet not more than eighteen inches from the ground.

They are not adepts in the art of hanging in India; it took the culprit at least ten minutes to die.

At times I feared, so desperate were his struggles, that he would break the beam, snap the rope, or bring down the whole apparatus. In the days of Henry Fielding, the vulgar used to speak of hanging as "dancing on nothing," and this horrible idea the Indian culprit on that morning amply realised. The reader must not, however, sympathize with his sufferings. He had been justly convicted, and was justly put to death for murdering, in that very field where he expiated his offence, a little girl of seven years of age, in order to possess himself of a single bangle she wore—a bangle valued at one rupee four annas—half-a-crown of English money. I cannot accuse myself of a cruel or brutal disposition; but, if the monster whom I saw hanged had had a thousand lives instead of one, I could have witnessed the taking of every one of them without a single atom of a desire to save him.

The cutting down of the culprit, as soon as it was discovered that life was extinct (for as there was no crowd of pickpockets and vendors of cakes and ginger-beer to take a moral lesson, the prescribed hour was unnecessary) was quite as primitive as the foregoing part of the operation. One of the native policemen with his blunt sword, severed the rope by sawing it just above the tie, and down came the corpse. I was tempted to jump out of the buggy in which, sitting between the magistrate and his assistant, I had witnessed the execution, and examine, or rather look attentively at, the deceased. A finer head, in a phrenological point of view, I had never seen, and across the naked chest was suspended the sacred thread, indicating that the culprit was a Brahmin.

"Is it not very odd," said I, on my return to the buggy, "that most of the diabolical crimes committed in this country are committed by Brahmins?"

"Not at all odd," replied my host. "Do you not know that they believe nothing can hurt their pure souls after death; and hence their comparative recklessness in this world? There was a Brahmin hanged here, about a year ago, who, just before he was turned off, made a speech such as that made by Napoleon on paper to Sir Hudson Lowe—'You may convict me of what you please; you may make me a prisoner; you may, if you like, shackle these limbs, and consign me to a dungeon; but you will find that my soul will be just as free, just as proud, as when it awed all Europe!'"

"Ah, but that was the emanation of ——"

"What the deuce is that?" cried the magistrate, who was driving us rapidly towards home. "See! That thing in the road." And coming up to it, he reined in the horse.

The syce (groom), who was running behind the buggy, picked up the object, at his master's bidding. It was a cloak—a lady's cloak—made of most costly materials—satin and silk, and wadded throughout. It had evidently fallen, unobserved, from some palanquin during the night, and an examination of the foot-prints showed that the last traveller who had moved along the road was journeying upward, and was then most probably staying at the dâk bungalow, at Deo-bund, a halting-place some twelve miles distant. The assistant magistrate, after we had breakfasted, proposed that he and I should drive to Deobund, and make inquiries. I was nothing loth, and a swift mare having been harnessed and put to the buggy, off we started, two sowars (native horsemen or mounted police) cantering behind us.

About two miles from the bungalow to which we were proceeding, we overtook a tribe of large monkeys. I should say there were as many as four hundred, and each carried a stick of uniform length and shape. They moved along in ranks or companies, just, in short, as though they were imitating a wing of a regiment of infantry. At the head of this tribe was an old and very powerful monkey, who was no doubt the chief. It was a very odd sight, and I became greatly interested in the movements of the creatures. There could be no question that they had either some business or some pleasure on hand, and the fact of each carrying a stick led us to conclude that it was the former upon which they were bent. Their destination was, like ours, evidently Deobund, where there are some hundreds of monkeys fed by a number of Brahmins, who live near a Hindoo temple there, and perform religious ceremonies. They (this monkey regiment) would not get out of the road on our account, nor disturb themselves in any way, and my friend was afraid to drive through their ranks, or over any of them, for when assailed they are most ferocious brutes, and armed as they were, and in such numbers, they could have annihilated us with the greatest ease. There was no help for us, therefore, but to let the mare proceed at a walk in the rear of the tribe, the members of which, now that we were nearing Deobund, began to chatter frightfully. Just before we came to the bungalow, they left the road, and took the direction of the temple. Fain would we have followed them; but to do so in the buggy would have been impossible, for they crossed over some very rough ground and two ditches. My friend, therefore, requested the sowars to follow them, and report all they might observe of their actions. Meanwhile we moved off to the bungalow, in search of the owner of the cloak. The first person whom we saw was an ayah, who was sitting in the verandah, playing with a child of about five years of age.

"Whose child is that?" asked the assistant-magistrate of the ayah.

"The mem-Sahib's."

"What is the mem's name?"

"I don't know," she replied, with a smile which seemed to say that she was not warranted in being communicative. While travelling, few servants who know their business will tell strangers the name of their master or mistress.

"What is *your* name?" he then inquired of the boy, in English.

"I don't understand you," was the reply, in Hindostanee, accompanied by a shake of the head. It is wonderful how rapidly the children of Europeans in India take a cue from a native servant of either sex. Not always, but in very many cases, it is in deceit and falsehood that children are first schooled by the servants. The reader must understand that deceit and falsehood are not regarded as immoralities in the eyes of Asiatics. A man or woman who, by fraud and perjury wins a cause, or gains any other point, is not looked down upon as a rogue, but up to as a very clever fellow. Several other experiments were made in order to extract from the ayah the name of her mistress, but to no purpose. The only information we could learn was, that the lady was much fatigued, and was sleeping. We said nothing about the cloak, by the way.

The servants of the bungalow, and at Deobund (there were four of them) now came up to make their most respectful salaam to one of the lords of the district, the assistant-magistrate, and on questioning them in private as to the name of the lady, we were in no way successful. All that the ayah would tell them, they said, was, that she had come from Calcutta, and was going to Simlah. "She is a burra beebee, however, Sahib," added the Khansamah; "for all along the road, after she left the steamer at Allahabad, until she arrived at Meerut, she was escorted by two sowars; and when she reaches the Saharunpore bungalow, she will find sowars ready. This is the only district in which she has had no escort."

This was a mystery that my friend could not unravel: why, if other magistrates had been indented upon (as magistrates very frequently were, when ladies were nervous and travelling with only an ayah), he should be omitted; especially as his district was as dangerous to pass through as any other (not that there was much or any danger in those days), was more than he could understand; and he very naturally became all the more curious (apart from the ownership of the cloak) to know the name of the lady who had broken the link of her escort when she came into his district. "Perhaps," said he to me, "either I have or my chief has given her husband some offence, and, possibly, he is small-minded enough to decline asking me to do what after all is only a matter of duty, or of civility and compliment, which amounts to pretty much the same thing. However, we shall see."

My friend now mentioned to the Khansamah, a very old but very active and intelligent man, the sight we had seen on the road—the regiment of monkeys.

"Ah!" exclaimed the old man, "it is about the time."

"What time?"

"Well, Sahib, about every five years that tribe comes up the country to pay a visit to this place; and another tribe comes about the same time from the up-country—the hills. They meet in a jungle behind the old Hindoo temple, and there embrace each other as though they were human beings and old friends who had been parted for a length of time. I have seen in that jungle as many as four or five thousand. The Brahmins say that one large tribe comes all the way from Ajmere, and another from the southern side of the country, and from Nepal and Tirhoot. There were hundreds of monkeys here this morning, but now I do not see one. I suppose they have gone to welcome their friends."

The sowars who had been deputed to follow the tribe now rode up, and reported that in the vicinity of the old temple there was an army of apes—an army of forty thousand! One of the sowars, in the true spirit of Oriental exaggeration, expressed himself to the effect that it would be easier to count the hairs of one's head than the number there assembled.

"Let us go and look at them," I suggested, "and by the time we return the lady may be stirring."

"But we will not go on foot," said my friend; "we will ride the sowars' horses. In the first place, I have an instinctive horror of apes, and should like to have the means of getting away from them speedily, if they became too familiar or offensive. In the second place, I do not wish to fatigue myself by taking so long a walk in the heat of the day."

We mounted the horses, and were soon at the spot indicated by the sowars. There were not so many as had been represented; but I am speaking very far within bounds when I state that there could not have been fewer than eight thousand, and some of them of an enormous size. I could scarcely have believed that there were so many monkeys in the world if I had not visited Benares, and heard of the tribes at Gibraltar. Their sticks, which were thrown together in a heap, formed a very large stack of wood.

"What is this?" my friend said to one of the Brahmins; for since his appointment he had never heard of this gathering of apes.

"It is a festival of theirs, Sahib," was the reply. "Just as Hindoos at stated times go to Hurdwar, Hajipore, and other places, so do these monkeys come to this holy place."

"And how long do they stay?"

"Two or three days; then they go away to their homes in different parts of the country; then attend to their business for four or five years; then come again and do festival, and so on, sir, to the end of all time. You see that very tall monkey there, with two smaller ones on either side of him?"

"Yes."

"Well, sir, that is a very old monkey. His age is more than twenty years, I think. I first saw him fifteen years ago. He was then full-grown. His native place is Meerut. He lives with the Brahmins at the Soorj Khan, near Meerut. The smaller ones are his sons, sir. They have never been here before; and you see he is showing them all about the place, like a very good father."

Having seen enough of these "sacred animals," we returned to the bungalow; we were only just in time, for the lady was about to depart, albeit the sun was very high in the heavens, and the day, for the time of year, was extremely hot. We caught sight of her in the verandah. My friend became deadly pale, and exclaimed: "Is it possible!"

"What?" I asked him.

"I will tell you on our way home. I must see her—speak to her—painful as our meeting must be. Only fancy, if that cloak should be hers!"

The lady, who must have learnt from the servants at the bungalow the name of my friend, the official, evidently desired to avoid an interview with him; for upon our approach she retired from the palanquin, which she was arranging, and entered hastily the room she had occupied. We (my friend and myself) went into the other room of the bungalow, which happened to be vacant. Presently we heard the voice of the ayah. She was very angry and was accusing the servants of the bungalow of being thieves. She had now, for the first time since they were lost, missed several articles, and amongst them the cloak of her mistress. She was perfectly ready to swear that she had seen them all since their arrival at the bungalow; that she had removed them from the palkees with her own hands; and if the servants had not stolen them who had?—who could have done so? Distinctly did we hear the lady command the ayah to be silent—to say nothing of the loss, and enter her palanquin; but the ayah, too much enraged to hear or to heed the command, repeated her accusation; whereupon the servants in a body rushed into the apartment in which we were standing listening, and after protesting their perfect innocence of the theft, referred to the character for honesty which every one of them had borne for many years. Strange to say, frequent as are the opportunities which the servants at these bungalows have of pilfering from travellers, they rarely or never avail themselves of such opportunities; and, whenever it has happened that a lady or gentleman has died in one of them, the money and effects have always been forthcoming, with nothing whatever missing.

The lady now forced the ayah to depart, and enter her palanquin, in which the little boy was sitting; she was about to follow, when my friend rushed into the verandah, and, seizing her by the hand, detained her. She was as agitated as he was; and quite as pale. He held her hand in his with a firm but withal a gentle grasp, and looked into her face, which must have been beautiful when she was a few years younger. As it was, she had still a charming profile and countenance, and a skin as white as snow. From the window, or rather looking through the venetians, I beheld the scene, which reminded me of that exquisite picture of Mr. Frank Stone—*The Last Appeal.* There was a look of agony and despair in the face of the man; while the woman, who appeared to sympathise with his sufferings, did not for awhile raise her eyes from the ground. But at length she did so, and, looking mournfully into my friend's face for a few seconds, burst into tears, and presently her head, involuntarily as it were, rested on his shoulder. Suddenly recollecting herself, she again attempted to take her departure; but my friend, now grown desperate seemingly, placed her arm beneath his, and walked with her to a clump of shade-giving mango trees, in front of the bungalow, and there they held a conversation which lasted some ten minutes. The lady then tore herself away from my friend, and after bidding him farewell, she threw herself into her palanquin, which was speedily lifted by the bearers and borne away, followed by the two sowars, who were commanded to escort the fair traveller to the next station. My friend, from the verandah of the bungalow, watched the procession till it was out of sight, and then, seating himself on the steps, covered his face with his hands, and wept like a child.

"Come!" I said, after a time, laying a hand on

his shoulder. "I am not very impatient to know your secret, but it is time that we thought of returning. What about the cloak? You have not restored it to the owner."

"No, my dear fellow, and I never intend to do so. She has consented to my retaining it. That cloak has warmed her dear limbs, and the sight of it shall warm my heart till the last hour of my existence."

On the way home my friend (who was accidentally drowned in the river Jumna, about two years ago) spoke as follows:

"Ten years have now elapsed since that lady and I were fellow-passengers on board of a ship bound from London to Calcutta. She was then seventeen years of age, and I twenty. On the voyage we became very much attached to each other, and eventually loved each other devotedly. And, what was more, we were betrothed. It was arranged that as soon as practicable we should be married. I was compelled, on arrival, to remain at the college at Fort William for a year, to pass an examination; she was obliged to proceed to a large station in Bengal, to join her family. Her father was a member of the civil service; previous to her arrival he had promised Alice (that is her name) to an old man, a judge, who had been twice married, and who was then a widower. This old man was very rich, and had—as he still has—a great influence with the government. A brother of his was one of the lords of Leadenhall-street, and of this country. For some time after our unhappy separation we corresponded regularly; but suddenly the correspondence ceased. Her letters to me, and mine to her, were intercepted. Meanwhile, the old judge, to whom she had been promised, paid his addresses to her. She refused him. Many devices were resorted to in order to wean her affections from me. They all failed. At length they hit upon one which had the desired effect. They caused a paragraph to be inserted in one of the Calcutta journals, to the effect that I had married the daughter of a half-caste merchant. Alice was permitted to see this paper, but none of those containing my indignant denial of the truth of the announcement.

"In disgust at my imagined faithlessness, and in despair and recklessness, Alice at length accepted the hand of the old judge. They were married. When made acquainted with this horrible fact, I became half-mad. I drank very hard, had an attack of *delirium tremens*, and was sent home for change of air and scene, to recruit my health. On my return to India, after an absence of eighteen months, I was sent to Dacca, where there was not the slightest chance of my ever seeing Alice. Subsequently, I was, at my own request, transferred to these provinces, but sent to Banda—a sort of penal settlement for refractory civilians; not that I ever committed any offence beyond that of loving Alice and being beloved by her. You must understand that, owing to the influence of his brother, her old husband, shortly after his marriage with Alice, became the great man he now is; and he had only to express a wish in this country, touching the appointment or *dis*appointment of any junior in the service, to have such wish instantly realised. My only surprise is, that when it became necessary for her to pass through this district, I was not ordered away to Scinde, on some trumpery business, alleged to be special. Had there been any idea that we should meet—as by the merest chance we have met—again in this world, I should certainly have been removed, and ordered to some other station miles away. I have never seen her since we parted in Calcutta, now more than nine years ago, until this very day. But, thank Heaven! she loves me still!"

"I was afraid, when I saw you talking to her beneath that clump of trees, that——" I was about to make some observations.

"Ah, no!" he interrupted me. "There is no danger. Great and lasting as my love for her is, I could not bear the thought of taking the slightest advantage of her feelings; or to see her fall from the sphere in which she holds a lofty and proud position. She is not happy, neither am I. But spirits will recognise each other, and be united for ever and ever. Ours is not a solitary case; sometimes when ladies in India fall they deserve far more of pity than of blame."

THE HIMALAYAS.

I HAVE already spoken of a German Baron and a French gentleman whom I met at Agra, and I have said that they, like myself, were travelling in search of the picturesque, and with a view to become acquainted with Oriental character from personal observation.

While staying with my friend at Barnapore, I received a letter from the former, proposing that we should meet on a certain day at Mussoorie, in the Himalaya mountains, and travel into the interior together. I agreed with all my heart; and my friend, the assistant magistrate, was tempted to apply for six weeks' leave, in order that he might accompany us.

Let me describe these foreign gentlemen. They were respectively about my own age—thirty-two—had seen a great deal of the world, and of the society at every court and capital in Europe. They were both possessed of considerable abilities, and of the most enviable dispositions; always good-natured and good-tempered; patient and cheerful under those innumerable little difficulties that almost invariably beset a wanderer in the East, or, in fact, a wanderer in any part of the world. They had, moreover, a keen sense of humour; and, each in his own peculiar way, could relate a story, or an incident in his life, in such a manner as to make it wonderfully mirth-provoking. They were men of refined understanding and of very refined manners: take them all in all, they were the most charming companions I ever encountered. They were utterly devoid of vulgar nationalities—of any enthusiastic admiration of their own fatherlands, and would just as soon ridicule the foibles peculiar to their own countries, respectively, as the foibles of a man of any other country. My friend the assistant magistrate was also a desirable companion. He, too, was a good-tempered, good-humoured being, with a keen sense of humour, and some wit. He had read a great deal of late years, in that out-of-the-way station to which he had been appointed, and he had profited by his reading.

It was beginning to be very hot in the plains, and my friend and myself were not a little glad when we found ourselves on the road to a colder clime. We drove as far as Deobund in the buggy; and, at three P.M. threw ourselves into our palanquins (palkees), bound for Dehra Dhoon at the foot of the hills; at which place we arrived at about nine o'clock on the following morning, and were deposited—both of us fast asleep—in the verandah of the hotel, kept by a Mr. William Johns, who had been formerly a professional jockey in the North-West Provinces of India.

So much has been written of Dehra Dhoon and Mussoorie, that even a brief sketch of these places would be unwarranted in this narrative.

As soon as we arrived at Mussoorie we began to collect coolies (hill-men), to carry our baggage and stores. We required in all about one hundred and fifty for the expedition, and by the time that we had got these people together, and made arrangements with them, and the guides whom we required, and had laid in our stock of provisions, &c., the foreign gentlemen joined us, and expressed their readiness to start at any given moment. We lingered, however, for two days, in order that they might take some rest, and make the acquaintance of the gentlemen at the club, who, at the instance of my friend, had made them as well as myself honorary members of the institution.

On the third morning, in the front of the club-house, our marching establishment was collected, and the one hunded and fifty men of whom it was composed were laden with the baggage and stores. There were tents, the poles thereto belonging, camp tables, chairs, beds, bedding, leather boxes of every kind, containing our clothing, &c., deal chests, containing all sorts of provisions, dozens of cases of wine—port, sherry, claret—beer, ducks, fowls, geese, guns (rifles and others), umbrellas, great-coats, &c., &c., &c. Having seen this train fairly off, we, the four of us, followed shortly after on foot, and overtook them at the Landour Hill, a mountain about nine thousand feet above the level of the sea. We were all in high spirits—including my friend the assistant magistrate—notwithstanding he put on his lady love's cloak as soon as we were out of sight of the club, and began to quote in a melancholy but very loud voice, which reverberated through the valleys on either side of us, those glorious lines of the poet Thomson :—

> "There is a power
> Unseen, that rules th' illimitable world—
> That guides its motions, from the brightest
> Star to least dust of this sin-tainted mould;
> While man, who madly deems himself the lord
> Of all, is nought but weakness and dependence.
> This sacred truth, by sure experience taught,
> Thou must have learnt, when wandering all alone:
> Each bird, each insect flitting through the sky,
> Was more sufficient for itself than *thou!*"

Our first halting-place was about nine miles from Mussoorie. It was a flat piece of ground, some distance down the southern face of the peak over which the road wound. The place was called Sowcowlee, and here and there were to be seen a few patches of cultivation and a cowshed. Our course lay in the direction of Almorah, another Hill Sanatarium for the English in India. The tents pitched, and all made snug and comfortable, we threw ourselves down upon our beds, not to sleep, but to take some rest after a long walk. Meanwhile our servants busied themselves in preparing the dinner, for which the exercise and the change of air had given us all a keen appetite.

"Well!" exclaimed my friend (whom in future we

will call Mr. West), raising to his lips a bumper of claret, and quoting from the Sentimental Journey, "the Bourbon is not such a bad fellow, after all."

Neither the Frenchman nor the German understood the allusion; but when it was explained they relished it amazingly. We were rather a temperate party; and after the second bottle of wine was emptied, we caused the glasses to be removed from our small table, and a green cloth spread over it. We then began to play at whist—a game of which we were all equally fond; and, what was of great consequence, we were all equal as players. We did not gamble exactly; but the stakes were sufficiently high to make either side attend very carefully to the game. The whist over, we each took a tumbler of warm drink, and turned in for the night, and slept, as the reader may imagine, very soundly.

On the following morning, at sunrise, we were awakened, and informed that upon a hill opposite to our encampment there were several large deer. We arose, and went in pursuit of them. After dodging them for some time we came within range, and each of us, selecting his animal, fired. One shot only took effect, and that was from the Baron's rifle. During our ramble we discovered that there were plenty of pheasants in the locality, and so we agreed to remain for the day, and, after breakfast, see what we could do amongst them. Under the circumstances we should have been compelled to halt, for, as is usual on such occasions, our servants had forgotten several little matters essential for our comfort, if not necessary for our journey, namely, the pickles and the sauces, the corkscrew, the instrument for opening the hermetically sealed tins containing lobsters, oysters, and preserved soups. Amongst other things that had been left behind was the Baron's guitar, and without it he could not, or would not, sing any of his thousand and one famous German songs. And such a sweet voice as he had! So, while we were amongst the pheasants, five coolies were on their way back to Mussoorie, to bring up the missing articles above enumerated.

By two o'clock, we had bagged eleven noble birds, and returned to our encampment, sufficiently hungry to enjoy the refreshments which the Khansamah (butler), who was a great artist in his way, had prepared for us. Our repast concluded, we had our camp bedsteads brought into the open air, and threw ourselves down on them.

Holding his cigar between the thumb and forefinger of his left hand, the Baron thus went off:—

"Who can explain the inscrutable mystery of presentiments? Who can fathom the secret inclinations of the human heart? Who can lift the veil of sympathy? Who can unravel the web of magnetic natures? Who can fully comprehend that link which unites the corporeal with the spiritual world? Who can explain that terrible symbol which pervades so many of our dreams? The sweet anxiety that seizes us when listening to some wonderful tale; the voluptuous shiver which agitates our frame, the indefinite yearning which fills the heart and the soul. All this is a guarantee that some invisible chain links our world with another. Let no one condemn as idle nonsense that which our shallow reason may refuse to accept. Can the most acute understanding explain, or even comprehend, its own growth; or even the growth and colouring of a mere flower? Is not Nature herself a perfect mystery unto the minds of thinking men?"

"What is the matter, Baron?" asked the Frenchman. "Have you a nightmare in this broad daylight?"

"No, no," returned the Baron, with good-natured impetuosity. "It is not so. I wish to tell you something—a little story, if you will listen."

"Pray go on," we (his three companions) cried out, simultaneously.

"Some ten or twelve years ago," the Baron proceeded, "I was travelling from Munich to Berlin. Tired by the continual rumbling of my carriage, I resolved upon taking a day's rest at Augsburg. It was the day of All Souls. The autumnal sun was shining brightly, and a large procession went its way towards the cemetery, a mile distant from the town. Wherefore, I know not; but I was instinctively led to join this procession. On arriving at the cemetery we found it, comparatively, crowded. All the graves were decked with flowers and sprigs of young cypress, and near every stone there sat or knelt, at least, one mourner. Tears of love and regret wetted the sacred earth. In a singularly agitated frame of mind, I wandered through the cemetery. The recollection of departed friends, and of dear ones far away, made me sad, unhappy, miserable. And I could not help thinking that if I had been then entombed, no friendly hand would on that day have deposited a wreath or a flower upon my grave, no beloved eye shed a tear of sorrow, no faithful heart sent up to Heaven a fervent prayer for the eternal rest of my soul. Haunted by such gloomy thoughts, I wandered on, and at last came to a newly-made grave. An hour previously had been buried in that spot a young girl of seventeen years of age. The parents and the lover of the girl stood weeping near her grave, and her young friends adorned the mound with freshly gathered flowers. In a fit of profound melancholy, I bent down, mechanically picked up a half-opened rose-bud, and walked on. Approaching the gate of the cemetery, with the intention of returning to my hotel, my eyes fell upon a tablet upon which were engraved the following words :—'Respect the property of the Dead. Flowers are the property of the Dead.' These simple words made a very great impression on my already excited mind : and glancing, involuntarily, at the rose-bud which I still held in my hand, my heart smote me for having carried it away from the girl's grave. I was on the point of returning to re-deposit the flower, when an indescribably false shame prevented my doing so, and I left the cemetery with the rose in my hand. On returning to my hotel, I put it in a glass of water, and placed it on a small table near the head of my bed, upon which I threw myself, and soon fell into that state which all of you must have experienced: a state in which the senses hover between sleep and wakefulness, as though undecided which to choose. Suddenly my apartment was filled by a bright but soft light, without my being able to perceive whence it came. Be it known that I had extinguished my candle. Ere long, the door of my room was opened; and in glided, noiselessly, a pale spectral figure, clad in a white robe, and wearing a garland of flowers. It was the figure of a young girl, and the face was angelic. With motionless eyes and outstretched hand she approached my couch, and in plaintive voice asked me: 'Why hast thou robbed the Dead? Why hast thou taken that flower which a faithful lover threw upon my last resting-place on earth?' Seemingly my pulses ceased to beat, and I could scarcely breathe. The phantom then stretched forth the left hand, and took the rose out of the glass; and with the right hand she beckoned to me, saying: 'Come! Come, and give back the property of the Dead. Respect the property of the Dead. Come! Follow me!' In vain I tried to resist. I arose, and followed the figure out of the room and into the deserted streets. It was not dark; for the moon was at her full and shining brightly. Onward stalked the figure, I followed her towards the cemetery. We arrived at the gate. She touched it. It opened noiselessly. We entered. She led me to the grave—the grave from which I had taken the flower. With trembling hand I received from hers the rose, and placed it on the very spot whence I had removed it. And then—"

Here the Baron paused—and relighted his cigar.

"Well—and then?" we all asked.

"Then," replied the Baron, "I awoke—that is to say, if I had ever been asleep. And looking in the tumbler in which I had placed the rose, I discovered that it was gone."

"The chambermaid, possibly; or the waiter, who may have entered your apartment for orders, may have seen, admired, and carried it away while you were slumbering," suggested the lively Frenchman; "and a very lucky fellow you were, not to have missed your watch and your purse at the same time and place."

"No," said the Baron, shaking his head.

"Perhaps," said Mr. West, "you had taken more wine than usual?"

"No," was the reply. "The truth is that the story I have related to you was written by that great Austrian wit and satirist, Saphir. It was one of his earlier compositions, which, strange to say, were all of a very melancholy cast. Saphir, however, to this day asserts that his story of 'The Death Rose' is a fact, and that it happened to himself."

One by one, we dropped off to sleep, and slept for about an hour and a-half. On awakening, the Frenchman, West, and myself, almost simultaneously exclaimed, "Confound your Death Rose, Baron!" for the truth was that the story had taken possession of our senses, while we were asleep.

"I thought it would," said the Baron laughing. "Everybody dreams of the Death Rose after I have told the story. But, ah! See in the distance! Here are the coolies returning! I can make out my guitar-box on the head of one man. Ah! to-night we will sing plenty of songs!"

And in the evening the Baron sang for several hours (we could have listened to him all night) some of the most sentimental, and some of the most humorous songs that I had ever heard. Fortunately I knew enough of German to appreciate them; and my friend, Mr. West, was equally fortunate. As for the Frenchman he understood and spoke—albeit very imperfectly—every language current in Europe. On that night we retired before twelve, for we had agreed to rise and proceed early on the morrow.

In pursuance of such agreement, as soon as the day dawned we struck our tents, packed up our traps, loaded the coolies, and set out for a place called Demooltee, distant some fourteen or fifteen miles. The road, which had been very, very seldom travelled over by Europeans, was a narrow and bad road, winding round and leading over lofty peaks, some ten or eleven thousand feet above the level of the sea. Above us and below us we frequently saw herds of Ghooral and other deer ; but as we could not, or would not rather, have stayed to pick up any that we might kill, we suffered them to graze on, and preserved our ammunition. By the way we saw an animal which none of us had ever seen before—an animal called the Seron. It is a species of chamois, but larger and stronger. Its colour was reddish, and it had a quantity of stiff, short hair on the neck, which gave it the appearance of a hogged mane. The native guides told us that it was a very shy animal, and only to be found where there was a great quantity of wood. The scenery of this part, in March, was exceedingly beautiful and varied. At times we had a good view of Mussoorie and the surrounding country. At other times we moved through vast forests of pine, and woods of oak, rhododendron, and other magnificent trees. In the midst of one of these woods our halting-place was situated, a large grassy flat, bounded on either side by a deep and steep precipice, while in every direction the surrounding mountains, which locked us in, were covered thickly with trees.

"What fools men are," exclaimed the Baron, whilst the servants were unpacking, "to huddle themselves together in old countries when lands like these remain uncultivated and unenjoyed! And what fools are those travellers who go, year after year, gazing on comparatively paltry mountains and lakes which the eyes of the vulgar of all nations have beheld, when such fresh and gorgeous scenery as this may be looked at! Travelling in Switzerland and Italy—bah!"

"But, my dear Baron," said the Frenchman, "you forget that the Peninsular and Oriental Company demand four pounds a day for conveying you from England to India, in consequence, they say, of the dearness of coals."

"Ah! well," laughed the Baron, opening with his own hand a bottle of hock, and emptying the contents into a silver tankard, "if you regard the matter in an economical point of view, you at once cut short my argument and my sentiment. Egad! what grapes could be grown on yonder hill, in that warm valley! What wine could be grown there! I will come out to this country with a few German peasants. I will have vineyards. I will make a fortune so colossal that Rothschild, when he is in difficulties, will have to write to me. Yes, I will. The thing is to be done, and I will do it."

"But you forget," said Mr. West, "that you are now some twelve or thirteen hundred miles from the nearest sea-port, Calcutta, and that there would be some little difficulty in transmitting the produce to Europe."

"Europe! Europe! Why do you talk of Europe? Does not British India contain enough of Europeans to make a market? This bottle of good wine which we are going to drink costs twelve shillings in this country. I could grow it, make it, and sell it for one shilling a bottle! Ah! you may laugh; but I tell you this is the fact. I am a proprietor of vineyards, and do not speak at random like a schoolboy, or an enthusiast. The natives of the country would soon learn that art—for an art it is—of wine-making; and as for the soil, it is superb. Yes! Grow wine, which would do your soldiers good. Generous wine, instead of that blood-drying, brain-consuming, soul-destroying arrack—your horrible grogs, and your bile-making beers."

"But we have no roads, Baron."

"True! But is there a scarcity of labour in India? Are pickaxes, shovels, spades, saws, and gunpowder to blast rocks, so expensive that a government cannot procure them? Roads! My good sir, only a few years ago there was no road over the Splügen! The time was when you had no road from Calcutta to Benares. You have no roads! Well, make them. The wine and the tea that you grow will more than pay for them, as well as remunerate the growers."

"The tea?" asked Mr. West.

"Yes, the tea, I said!" returned the Baron. "You have discovered that you can grow tea in the lower range of these mountains, and you do grow it in small quantities; now why not, having made the experiment, grow it in *large* quantities? I would say to Mr. Chinaman, 'I thank you very much, but I do not want any more of your tea. You are insolent, overbearing, and insulting in your dealings with me, and now you may drink your own tea, and I will drink *my* own tea; and, if you like, you may stir yours with your own pigtail. We will bring China into our own dominions, for God has given to this climate and to this soil the same properties as your soil and climate possess.' I do not say it, as you know, with any sort of intention to offend, but the result of my experience leads me to believe that the government of this country is, in all matters (save annexation), as slow as the government of the Dutch was in by-gone days. There is a listlessness and a languor about its movements; a want of everything in the shape of society and enterprise, and seemingly such an earnest desire to discourage the efforts of those who would in reality develope the resources of India, that I am astonished any man unconnected with the services should persevere in the attempt to make a living in the Eastern British dominions."

"I quite agree with you," said Mr. West, "especially as regards that portion of your remarks which relates to the obstacles thrown in the way of enterprising Englishmen. I have been a member of the Civil Service for nearly ten years, and have always been impressed with the idea that the policy of the government in respect to settlers in India, was and is a very erroneous policy."

The conversation here was brought abruptly to a close by the approach of one of the guides, who, in a very confidential manner, imparted to us that there was a kakur (a barking deer) grazing on a crag not far from the encampment. So we seized our guns, went in pursuit, and were fortunate enough to kill the animal. His bark resembles exactly that of a Skye-terrier when very much excited. On our return to the encampment we encountered a huge bear, and succeeded in killing and carrying him to the door of our tent, where the natives skinned him and deprived him of his fat, which they boiled down and used in the lamps instead of oil. And very brightly did it burn ; but the aroma was not a peculiarly pleasant one. I am afraid to say how much grease was taken from this enormous bear ; but I know that I am speaking within bounds when I assert it was in excess of two gallons and a half.

We dined at dusk, and then, as usual, betook ourselves to whist, but so cold did it become shortly after dark, that we were forced to put on our great coats, notwithstanding there was an enormous wood fire in front and at the back of our tent. These fires had been lighted to serve another purpose beyond that of giving warmth—namely, to scare away the leopards which abounded in that locality. It was a very picturesque scene ; the white tents standing out in relief from the dark wood, lighted up by the fires, and here and there groups of coolies wrapped up in blankets, and sitting as closely as possible to the blaze.

At daylight on the following morning our march was recommenced. We had a distance of ten miles to travel before we could reach the next halting-place, named Kanah Tall. During this march we did not go out of our way for game, but only took such as chanced to cross our path. All we killed was ghooral, (which we did not stop to look at even) and two braces of partridges of very peculiar plumage. They were remarkably handsome birds, with a red mark round the eye and down each side of the neck, olive-coloured feathers on their backs, and their wings and breasts covered with white and red spots. We could not fail to admire the beauty of the flowers which flourished in this locality. The ground on either side of the narrow and wild road was literally covered with violets, dog-roses, and a lily of the valley, and other little decorations of the earth, of which I know not the name. Throughout the whole march the scene was truly fairy-like. Kanah Tall was only five thousand feet above the level of the sea, and therefore very much warmer than our last halting-place. Of this we were by no means sorry, not only for our own sakes, but for the sakes of our personal servants, who had never before travelled out of the plains. Here, at Kanah Tall, we found the English holly growing. Botanists may tell me what they please about this holly of the

Himalayas bearing a distinctive character; but I say it was the English holly—the same sort of holly that I saw last Christmas in almost every house in London and in the country.

Here, at Kanah Tall, we shot no less than seven elks. These deer are very plentiful hereabouts, and do a great deal of damage to the crops of the poor villagers at harvest time. Ghooral and kakur also abound here. We were so tired on the evening that we stopped at Kanah Tall that we could not sit up to play at whist! We actually fell asleep over our second rubber, and by general consent threw our cards upon the table and sought our beds.

The next day, at three P.M., we arrived at a place called Jullinghee, ten miles distant from Kanah Tall. Jullinghee is a large village situated on the right bank of the Bhagaruttee, a stream that flows direct from Gungootrie, and is in consequence one of the most sacred streams that compose the mighty and holy Ganges. We were encamped beneath a clump of apricot and walnut trees, but it was frightfully hot; for we were now not more than a couple of thousand feet above the level of the sea. The woods, however, were exceedingly beautiful and diversified. Not only were there apricot, walnut, rhododendrons, oaks, hollies, and other trees of the higher altitudes, but also the tamarind, the fig-peepul, the pomegranate, and others of the plains. At this village we procured some honey, which is taken from its makers in a very singular manner. The bees build in cavities in the walls of the houses, which are closed within by a moveable board, and are only entered by the bees, by a small aperture from without. When the owners of the houses want honey they darken the interior of the house, and removing the board, which forms the back part of the hive, extract as much as they require. The bees during this process fly out into the light to discover their enemies, who then close the back part of the hive, and remain safely within doors until the wrath of the bees has subsided.

In the evening we took a walk in the village of Jullinghee, which appeared to be rich and populous, but very dirty. Our arrival had caused a great stir, and there was a large concourse of people near our tents to look at us. A short distance from the village were the ruins of several houses which once formed a separate hamlet, but which had been deserted for fear of a ghost which was said to haunt it. The same effect of superstition is by no means uncommon in the plains of India. There is a very curious instance in the Meerut district. A village had long been deserted under the idea that it was haunted by a fakir. The settlement officer, however, with much difficulty prevailed upon a neighbouring Zemindar to farm the land at something like a nominal revenue. Shortly afterwards the Zemindar presented himself to the settlement officer, and represented that he had been very ill, and that the visitation was ascribed by his friends and by himself to his impiety in interfering with haunted lands. The settlement officer, however, talked to him and insisted on his keeping his engagements, and once more did he venture to brave the ghost. So complete was his success that the village shortly became one of the most flourishing in the district, and the very relatives who had been foremost in reproaching the zemindar for his impiety, brought a suit against him in one of the local courts, to recover a share of his large profits!

On the day following we marched to a place called Teree, a large straggling village, situated on a plain of some extent, at the junction of the Billung and Bhagaruttee rivers. A regular hot wind was blowing here, and our tents were unbearable; so we threw ourselves beneath the shade of a huge tree which grew on the banks of the Billung, and which served also as a shelter for a party from Srinugger, who were celebrating the marriage festival of a Bunneah (corn-merchant) of some twenty-two years of age, with a young lady of eight. The little damsel was on the ground, and did ample justice to the marriage dinner, which consisted of rice, butter, sweetmeats, and a goat roasted whole—a goat which had been decapitated by one blow, and cooked without any sort of preparation beyond the removal of the entrails; it was not even skinned. Portions of this feast were distributed on plantain leaves to each guest by the Brahmins, who officiated as cooks and waiters.

Teree is the residence of a Rajah, named Soodersain Saha, whose family, before the Goorkha invasion, ruled over the provinces of Gurhwal and Sirmoor, and indeed over the whole hill country as far as Simlah, and from the snowy range to the plains. Expelled by the Goorkhas, he sought refuge with the British : and after defeating the Goorkhas, was replaced by us in the greater part of his territories ; a part of them we retained as the price of our assistance, namely, a portion of Gurhwal, the whole of Dehra Dhoon, and a part of the Terai. And we hold Landour and Mussoorie from him at a nominal annual rent. The Rajah is extremely civil to Europeans, and the moment he heard of our arrival he sent a deputation to wait upon us. The deputation brought with them a variety of presents, consisting of milk, sweetmeats, dried flour, dried fruits, and a couple of goats. The deputation gave us to understand that it would afford the Rajah very great pleasure to make our personal acquaintance ; and we were just on the point of starting for his Highness's abode, when his arrival was unexpectedly announced to us. At Srinugger, in a portion of the country we took from him, is situated the family palace, a handsome and substantial building. This is rather a sore point with the old Rajah, and as he considers the more modern abode which he now inhabits beneath his dignity, he prefers going to see any one with whom he is desirous of having an interview.

Having caused chairs to be placed in the front of our tents, we advanced to meet the Rajah, who, dismounting from a large Cabul horse, joined us, shook hands with us very cordially, and remained with us for upwards of an hour. He was a very small and rather an old man; active and intelligent. He talked to us about the Goorkha war, of which he had been a spectator in the British camp; and he was very eloquent on Punjab politics, and greatly praised Lena Singh, whom he described as "very far in advance of any of his countrymen in point of humanity, civilization, and prudence." The little man told us, amongst other things, that he was thinking of having an iron suspension-bridge over the Bhagaruttee, but that he could not find an engineer; and that his applications to the Government, although he was ready to defray every expense, had not met with any reply. The present bridge is a sling or swing, and constructed in the following manner. Two lines of coir rope, each consisting of a number of smaller ropes, are suspended from the rocks on either side of the stream, and apart from each other about four feet. From these ropes depend, at intervals of about two feet, smaller lines or ropes about three or four feet deep. These support slight wooden ladders, the ends of which are lashed firmly to one another. The whole affair has a very frail appearance, and at first it requires no small amount of nerve to step from ring to ring of the ladder, over that roaring torrent beneath.

Of course this bridge is only passable by men. Cattle and mules swim across the river much higher up, where the torrent is not so rapid.

We asked the Rajah where he had got his idea of an iron suspension bridge, and he replied: "From a picture-book which was given to me by a gentleman who was out on a shooting excursion some years ago in these hills."

We stayed two days at Teree, and, despite the heat, enjoyed ourselves amazingly. Our next encampment ground was at a place called Pon, a march of eleven miles. Our route at first lay along the south bank of the Billung river, and then up a deep glen at the foot of a mountain, whose summit was some five thousand feet above the level of the ocean. The monotony of this day's journey was broken by meeting with another marriage party, some of whom carried parasols of evidently Chinese manufacture, and made out of painted paper. We shot also several green pigeons —a very different bird from the green pigeons of the plains, and much better eating. By-the-by we also met a pilgrim and his wife on their way to Gungootree, the source of the Ganges: both of them were painted and bedaubed after the most grotesque fashion. The Frenchman took a sketch of this couple, and I have heard that it now adorns an album in the possession of the Empress of the French.

Our next march was to a place called Tekowlee, where we halted beneath the shade of some large trees, and near the banks of a clear stream of water. On one side of the stream there grew a quantity of wild mint, some of which we gathered and cooled, preparatory to using it for "cup." There is a moderate-sized village near Tekowlee, and a Gosains' house or monastery, which is inhabited by a large number of this sect: we visited, and entered into conversation with them. The building was composed of a large square court-yard, surrounded by a range of two-storied barracks, or rather cells, the lower story of which is protected by a verandah. The place was full of men, women, and children: the Gosains being the only monastic order who are permitted by their tenets to marry.

We had been out sixteen days before we reached Loba, near to which place the Commissioner of Kumaon resides during the rains and the autumn. His bungalow is built upon the spur of a hill of considerable length, and there is a good quantity of flat ground in the vicinity. Not far from the bungalow is an old fort, a Goorkha stronghold, which commanded the pass leading to Almorah. It is chiefly celebrated, however, as the place where Moorcroft and Hearsey were discovered on their return from the Munsarowar lake, whither they had gone disguised as Bairagis; and so well had they sustained their characters, that they would have returned undetected, had not a rumour of their attempt reached the ears of the authorities and excited their vigilance. They were harshly treated for some days, but eventually released on a promise that they would return direct, and without delay, to the British territories.

The Commissioner was not at the bungalow when we arrived. Mr. West, however, knew him sufficiently well to warrant our taking possession of it for the day. After a residence for some time in tents, a house is a very agreeable change.

On leaving Loba we came upon the Pilgrim road, constructed by a former Commissioner of Kumaon to facilitate the progress of the pilgrims to the sacred places within the British Himalayas. It was a very humane project, for many of the unfortunate pilgrims used formerly—overcome by the difficulties of the route—to lie down and perish by the way-side. Of these pilgrims we met swarms—hundreds, if not thousands—and with some we occasionally stopped to converse.

Our encamping ground, at which we arrived at four in the afternoon, was a short distance from a village called Guniah. Our tents were pitched beneath a clump of trees, and close to a clear stream called the Ram Gunga, in which we caught a quantity of fish with a casting-net. There are some mines between Loba and Kumaon, but we did not go out of our way to visit them. Here an accident happened to the Baron. He sprained his ankle and could not walk; so the next morning we put him into a Dandi, and he was carried along the road by four of the coolies.

A Dandi is a pole, upon which is hung by its two ends, which are gathered together, a piece of cloth or canvas, open in the centre. This forms a hollow seat, not a particularly comfortable one, until you get accustomed to it, when the motion is rather pleasurable than otherwise. During this day's march we shot a quantity of black partridge, a hill fox, a deer, and a wild dog of enormous size.

On the third day after leaving Loba we sighted our (then) destination—the town of Almorah. On nearing the place we came upon a hill to the right, which bears the name of Brown's Hill; so called after an officer of the 31st Native Infantry, who, in the Ghoorkha war, volunteered to take it with his company, though it had a stockade on the top which was obstinately defended. And he did take it, after a very severe loss. A monument is erected on this hill to the memory of those who fell in the engagement. A little further on is a large tree now used as a gallows. This tree was the scene of a well-remembered occurrence, just after the above-mentioned battle. A Goorkha, shot through the leg, had fallen here. The fighting over, a British officer was standing over him, and giving directions to a party of Sepoys to have him taken to the hospital; when, raising himself with his left hand, with his right he cut the officer down with his kookeree—a deadly weapon with which the little Goorkhas now chop up the rebels.

Apropos of a kookeree in the hands of a Goorkha,

I must relate a little matter which I now know to be a fact, but which I could scarcely credit when it was first told to me. A party of Goorkhas—say fifteen or twenty—will proceed to a jungle in which they know there is a huge tiger. They will surround the jungle, form a circle, and closing in gradually, hem in the ferocious beast. Every man will then drop down on the right knee, as soldiers do forming a square, and, kookeree in hand, wait for the spring of the tiger, who becomes somewhat bewildered and anxious to make his escape. After moving about for a brief while in this den, of which the bars are human beings (about five feet high), and glaring first at one and then at another, he lashes himself into a fury and makes his spring: then the nearest Goorkha delivers a blow with his kookeree which divides the tiger's skull. Wonderful as this feat is, I once saw at Jutog, near Simlah, a sight that struck me as even more wonderful. A Goorkha battalion was (and now is) quartered at Jutog. There was a festival at which the Goorkhas sacrifice an ox. The adjutant of the battalion asked me if I should like to witness the ceremony; as it was something new to me, I replied in the affirmative, and we walked to the parade ground, where the whole regiment, in undress, was assembled, and surrounding the victim and the executioner. The ox was forced to kneel, and by the side of him knelt the little Goorkha, armed with the kookeree, which is nothing more than a huge curved knife, but very heavy, and as sharp as a razor. At a given signal he struck the ox immediately behind the hump over the shoulder, peculiar to all Indian cattle; and the body was divided into two parts. He had, with a single blow, gone though the ox just as completely and as cleanly as a butcher with his hatchet would remove a chop from a loin of mutton. They are a very odd race of people, those little Goorkhas; wonderfully honest even among themselves; light-hearted almost to childishness; capable of enduring any amount of toil; obedient and respectful, without cringing to, fawning on, or flattering their superior, the white man. The great blot upon their characters is their frightful jealousy of their wives. Woe betide the woman who gives her Goorkha husband the faintest reason to suspect her of infidelity! He at once takes the law and the kookeree into his own hands, and slays both the wife and her (real or supposed) gallant. I am glad to say this is not a frequent occurrence, though it does happen now and then. As a body, the Goorkha women are as virtuous as their husbands are honest and brave.

The Commissioner of Kumaon received us at Almorah, his head quarters, with great cordiality and kindness, and offered us rooms in his house. This offer we declined, inasmuch as our party consisted of four, and his house was not a large one. Besides, he had other visitors who were putting up at his bungalow. We accepted, however, his invitation to dine, and on our way rode through the town, which is considered the best in the British hill possessions. Bishop Heber writes that Almorah reminds him of Chester. It consists of one street about a mile and a half long, and about sixty feet wide, paved with large slabs of slate, and closed at either end by a gate. One half of the town is much higher than the other, and the street is divided in the middle by a low flight of steps on which the ponies pass up and down with extraordinary self-possession. The houses are small, but neat and whitewashed. They all consist of two or more stories. The lower ones are shaded by wooden verandahs more or less carved. At one end of the town is the old Goorkha fort; at the other end Fort Moira, a small English fortification, near to which were the Sepoy lines. A neat little church has just been erected at Almorah. The people of the place are all fair-complexioned, and some of the children as white as those born of European parents.

RETURNING.

At Almorah I parted company with my foreign friends. They intended crossing the mountains—the snowy range—to pay a visit to Kanawur. This was a journey for which I had not much inclination; besides I was doubtful whether I could breathe at an elevation of eighteen thousand feet above the level of the sea. As it was, several of the coolies died of cold and the rarity of the atmosphere. In fact, both of my friends themselves had, as they informed me afterwards, a very narrow escape. On several occasions they were compelled to huddle themselves amongst the coolies in their tent, and the sheep which they were taking with them for food were kept alive for the sake of the warmth they could impart in the canvas abode. The grandeur of the scenery, they said, would defy any attempt at describing it. What they most wondered at was the impudence of that insect, man, in daring to climb up into such regions.

My friend, the assistant magistrate, had still a fortnight of unexpired leave, and proposed to me that we should pay a visit to a friend of his at an out-of-the-way station, called Bijnore. I had not the least objection, and thither we went. We were most hospitably received, partly out of regard for ourselves in particular, but chiefly because our host had not seen a white face for five weeks.

The cutcherry, or court-house, was undergoing repair, and the magistrate, therefore, was obliged to administer the duties of his office in his own abode, or rather in the verandah; for a large number of half-clad natives in a hot country do not impart to a confined space an agreeable perfume by any means. To me this scene—the native court—was particularly interesting. There sat the covenanted official in an arm-chair, with his solah hat on and a cheroot in his mouth, listening very attentively to the sheristadar, or head clerk, who was reading or singing aloud the entire proceedings in the case then pending.

The prisoner, surrounded by half-a-dozen native policemen, all with drawn swords, was standing ten paces off. Ever and anon he interrupted the court by protesting his innocence, and assuring the Sahib that the whole of the depositions were false from beginning to end. This interruption was usually—I may say invariably—rebuked by the words, "Choop raho, suer!" ("Hold your tongue, you pig!") And, not unfrequently the nearest policeman accompanied this mandate by giving the culprit a smart blow on the back or a "dig in the ribs." I have seen prisoners well thrashed in our Indian courts of justice by order of the presiding magistrate for talking out of their turn; but that was not the case in the present instance. No more violence was resorted to than was absolutely necessary for the maintenance of order and the progress of the trial. The offence of which the prisoner stood charged was that of forging a bond for five hundred rupees, and suing thereon for principal and interest. The defence was, that the signature to the bond was not a forgery, and that the money had been advanced to the prosecutor; to prove which, no fewer than seven witnesses were called. Each of them swore, point black, that, upon a certain day and at a certain place, they saw the prisoner pay over the money, and saw the prosecutor execute the deed. To rebut this, the prosecutor called eleven witnesses who swore, point blank, that, upon the day and at the hour mentioned as the day and hour on which the deed was executed, they met the prosecutor at a village forty miles distant from Bijnore. In short, if their testimony was to be relied upon, the eleven witnesses had proved an alibi.

This was one of those cases which happen continually in courts of justice in India; where the magistrate or judge must not be, and is not, guided by the oaths of the witnesses, but entirely by circumstances. It is one of those cases, too, in which it would be dangerous to consult the native officers of the court; for having received bribes from both parties, their advice would be dictated entirely by pecuniary considerations. With them the question would be simply out of which party—the accused or the prosecutor—could most money be got in the event of "guilty" or "not guilty." With regard to the characters of the witnesses, they are pretty equal, and generally very bad on both sides. Indeed, in nearly all these cases, the witnesses are professionals; that is to say, men who are accustomed to sell their oaths, and who thoroughly understand their business. They know exactly what to say when they come into court, just as an actor, who is letter perfect in his part, knows what to say when he comes on the boards. In fact, a case is got up exactly as a play is. Each man has his particular part and studies it separately; before the day of trial comes they meet and rehearse, and go through "the business" till they verily believe (such is my opinion) that they are not perjured, but are speaking the truth. As for shaking the testimony of men so trained to speak to a certain string of facts, I would defy the most eminent nisi prius advocate in Europe. Besides, even if you should reject one part of a statement, it does not follow, in a native court, that you should reject the whole. The price paid to these professional witnesses depends, in a great measure, on the nature and magnitude of the cause. It is about twelve per cent. out of the sum in dispute. I believe it is distributed amongst the witnesses, and the like sum amongst the native officers of the court. This, of course, does not include little extra presents given secretly to those who are supposed to have the greatest amount of influence with the Sahib, and who pretend that they will speak to him favourably. The personal servants, also, of the European magistrate or judge expect some gratuity, and hang about a client like the servants of badly regulated hotels where attendance is not charged in the bill. It is this that makes litigation so expensive in India that even the successful party is often ruined before the suit is half concluded.

"Tiffin is ready, Sahib," said the khansamah, coming into the verandah, and placing his hands together in a supplicating attitude. "It is on the table, Sahib."

"Then we will adjourn," said the magistrate, bowing to me, and rising. This was at once the signal for breaking up the day's proceedings.

The tiffin over, we began to play at whist, and continued to do so until the sun had lost his power, when the buggies were ordered, and we took a drive in couples along a very bad road. It fell to my lot to be the companion of the magistrate, a very able and excellent man: one of the most efficient officers in the East India Company's civil service. He was, moreover, an admirable linguist, and spoke Hindostanee as well as any native.

"You understood the proceedings to-day?" he asked me.

"I followed them; yes."

"And you heard the evidence?"

"Yes."

"What would you say? Is he guilty or not?"

"I cannot say, although I have thought a good deal on the point. Even while we were playing whist, to-day's proceedings were uppermost in my mind. Nothing can be clearer than that either one side or the other is perjured."

"Both sides are perjured. If the bond be genuine, the men who really witnessed the execution and who subscribed their names as witnesses will not come forward, or else they are such fools that the native lawyer for the defence will not trust to them lest they should be confused and commit themselves."

"But what do you think? Is the bond a genuine document or not?"

"That is the very question. And when there is no evidence to weigh, how are you to act?"

"I suppose that in those cases you give the prisoner the benefit of the doubt?" I remarked.

"Not always. If I did that, I should acquit almost every culprit that is brought before me, and so would every judge throughout the length and breadth of the land. By the way, about a year ago, I sent a case to the sessions judge—a case of murder. I fancied there could be no doubt as to the guilt of the accused; which was the opinion of the sessions judge and of the Sudder Court of Appeal. The man was hanged about six weeks ago; and now I have discovered, beyond all question, that he was hanged for the offence of which his prosecutor was guilty! It may be all very well for people in England to rail at the administration of justice in this country; but they would be less severe upon some of us if they could only come out here and see the material with which we have to deal. The administration of justice may be, I confess, very much reformed and improved, but where the great bulk of the people are corrupt, it can scarcely be in anything like a perfect state." This statement, remember, was made by a magistrate who speaks as well as writes the native language as well as the natives themselves. But conceive the confusion and injustice in those courts, where the magistrates solely depend on corrupt moonshees for what they know of the evidence.

There is but very little twilight in India; and by the time that we had returned from the drive it was dark. Shortly afterwards, dinner was announced. Dinner over, we resumed our whist, and played until midnight.

The following day was a native holiday—a Hindoo holiday. What with Hindoo holidays and Mahommedan holidays, nearly a third of every year is wasted: for, upon these days public business is suspended and the various offices closed. It is devoutly to be hoped that, when our rule in India is completely re-established, these absurd concessions—these mere pretexts for idleness—will no longer be suffered to prevail. It is only the pampered native servants of the Government, civil and military, who are clamorous for the observance of these "great days," as they call them. Go into the fields or ride through a bazaar on one of these holidays and you will see the people at their work, and the shopkeepers pursuing their respective avocations. You pass the court-house, the treasury, the magistrate's office, and observe that they are all shut up. You ask the reason, and are informed that it is a native holiday. You go to an establishment founded and conducted by private enterprise—a printing-office, for instance—and you observe Hindoos of every caste, and Mussulmans also, at their daily labour. Why? Because the head of such an establishment stipulates that those who wish for employ must work all the year round, and they prefer employ on such terms to no employ at all. So it is in some mercantile firms in Calcutta, and at the other Presidencies; albeit such firms experience very great inconvenience from the circumstance of the Government banks being closed on these holidays; if a merchant wishes to get a cheque cashed, or a bill discounted, he must wait sometimes for days together. Even the doors of the Queen's courts are often closed, and the judges and the counsel left unemployed, notwithstanding that the litigants are British subjects; and this because the native writers in these courts and the officers attached to them, are paid by the Company's Government, which recognises absence from duty on these holidays.

It would be hard to deprive either of the great

sects of certain holidays in every year. The Doorgah-Poojah, for instance, or the Mohurrum; but it is sheer folly, and profitless withal, to sanction these constantly repeated interruptions to public business. The idlers of the covenanted civil service in India are, naturally, in favour of closing the doors of the various offices as often as possible; but the hard-working portion, those men who take some interest in the discharge of the duties for which they draw their pay, regard the native holidays as an intolerable nuisance which ought, long since, to have been abolished.

Whilst we were enjoying ourselves after dinner, on the evening of the Hindoo holiday, the khansamah came in, and announced that two Sahibs had arrived.

"Two Sahibs?" said our host. "Who are they?"

"They are strangers to me, Sahib," said the khansamah, "and they do not speak Hindostanee; but their bearers say that they are Lord Sahibs."

"Who on earth can they be?" said the magistrate of Bijnore (loudly) to himself; and, rising, he left the table to make inquiry in person, and offer the travellers every hospitality.

"O, I beg your pardon," said a voice from one of the palanquins. "But would you be good enough to tell me where I am?"

"You are at Bijnore," said the magistrate, blandly.

"Bij-what?"

"Bijnore."

"Then, how far am I from Meerut?"

"A very considerable distance—forty miles at least."

"How the deuce is that?"

"Well, sir—in the words of the Eton Latin Grammar—I may reply:—

Felix qui potuit rerum cognoscere causas.

But where have you come from?"

"From Seharry something or other; but confound these nores, and pores, and bores! There's no recollecting the name of any place, for an hour together. The magistrate—I forget his name just now; but it was Radley, Bradley, Bagley, Ragley, or Cragley, or some such name—told me he would push me on to Meerut, and here am I, it seems, forty miles out of my road! Well, look here. I am Lord Jamleigh."

"Indeed! Well, you are welcome to some refreshment and repose in my home, in common with your friend; and whenever you desire to be 'pushed on,' I will exert my authority to the utmost to further your views."

"O, thank you. My friend is my valet. Here, Mexton, jump out and take my things into a room."

While Mexton is obeying this order, and while his lordship is following his host, let us inform the reader who his lordship was, and what was the object of his mission to India.

His lordship was a young nobleman, who was about to enter Parliament, and, being desirous of acquiring information concerning India in order to be very strong when the question for renewing the charter came on in eighteen hundred and fifty-two or fifty-three, he resolved on travelling in the country for a few months: the entire period of his absence from home, including the journey overland, not to exceed half a year. After a passage of thirty-four days—having already seen the Island of Ceylon, and approved of it—his lordship landed at Madras, was carried up to Government house, where he took a hasty tiffin, and was then carried back to the beach, whence he reembarked on board the steamer, and was, three days afterwards, landed at the Ghaut in Calcutta, where he found a carriage ready to convey him to the viceregal dwelling. After two days' stay, he was "pushed on," at his own request, to the Upper Provinces: his destination being Lahore. The newspapers got hold of his name, and came out with something of this kind:—"Amongst the passengers by the *Bentinck* is Lord Jamleigh, eldest son of the Right Honourable the Earl of Dapperleigh. His lordship leaves Calcutta this evening, and will pass through the following stations." Then came a list. At many of the stations he was met—officiously met, by gentlemen in authority, who dragged—literally dragged—him, in their anxiety to have a lord for a guest, to their houses, and kept him there as long as they could: taking care to have the north-west journals informed of where and with whom his lordship had put up. He was not allowed to stay at a dâk bungalow for an hour or two, and then proceed, taking—in the strictest sense of the phrase—his bird's-eye view of India, its people, its institutions, and so forth. Some of them threw obstacles in the way of his getting bearers, so that he might remain with them for four-and-twenty hours, and thus thoroughly impregnate and air their houses with an aristocratical atmosphere. Others lugged him to their courts and collectorates, albeit he had seen one of each at Burdwan and Bengal, and consequently had seen the working of the Indian judicial and revenue departments, and knew all about them! This sycophantic importunity of a few government officials soured his lordship's temper, which imparted to his manners a rudeness which was perhaps foreign to his nature. His lordship was led to believe that *all* Indian officials were a parcel of sycophants—progress-impeding sycophants—and hence he grew to treat them all alike: and he did not scruple, at last, to extract his information from them much in the same way that a petulant judge who has lost all patience with a rambling witness, takes him out of the hands of counsel, and brings him sharply to the point. For instance, "I know all about that, but tell me this,"—note-book in hand—would Lord Jamleigh in such wise frequently interrogate his civil hosts, who insisted on doing themselves the honour of entertaining his lordship. The fact was that, in his own opinion, he knew all about India and its affairs long before he touched the soil, for he had read a good deal in blue books and newspapers. His object, as we have before hinted, was simply to see the country and travel in it, or through it, and thus arm himself with a tremendous and telling weapon in a contested debate, should he take part therein. And therefore when his lordship asked questions it was not so much with a view to obtain information as to test the accuracy of that already acquired by reading, over the fireside in the library, of his father's mansion in Bagdad Square. Thus, the entries in his lordship's note-book were, after all, merely a matter of form.

Having divested himself of the dust with which he was covered, and having restored himself to his personal comforts, his lordship joined our little party, and partook of some dinner which the khansamah had prepared for him. His repast concluded, his lordship moistened his throat with a glass of cool claret, and proceeded, in his own manner, to interrogate his host, who was not only an accomplished scholar, but a ready and refined wit. It was thus that the dialogue was commenced and continued :—

"What is the number of inhabitants in this district?" asked the noble guest.

"Upon my word I don't know; I have never counted them," said the host.

"But have you no idea? Can't you give a guess?"

"Oh, yes; some hundreds of thousands."

"Ah! And crime—much crime!" his lordship persevered.

"Very much. But we are going to reduce it, during the ensuing half-year, exactly thirty-three and a-half per cent.," answered the magistrate, looking uncommonly statistical.

"How?"

"Well, that is what my assistant and myself have decided upon."

"I do not understand you. How can you possibly say at this moment whether, during the next six months, the amount of crime shall be greater or less?" His lordship was puzzled.

"How? Why just in the same way that the directors of a joint-stock bank determine in their parlour what shall be the amount of dividend payable to shareholders. My assistant wanted to make a reduction of fifty per centum on the last returns; but I think thirty-three and a-half will be a very fair figure."

"You intend, perhaps, to be more severe?" said the young legislator.

"Nothing of the kind. On the contrary, we intend to be less energetic by thirty-three and a-half per cent.—to take matters more easily, in short."

"I wish I knew what you meant."

"I will explain it to you."

"As briefly as possible, please." His lordship did not want to be bored, evidently.

"By all means."

"I only want facts, you see."

"And I am about to give you facts—dry facts."

"Well?"

"The facts are these. There is a district in these provinces nearly twice the size of this, and it contains nearly double the number of inhabitants."

"Yes."

"During the past half-year, the number of convictions in that district has been very much less than the number of convictions in this district. And the Sudder Court of Appeal has come to the conclusion, on looking at the figures in the official return, that the proportion of CRIME to population, in this district, is greater than it is in that district."

"Very naturally."

"Indeed? But suppose that the magistrate of that district only attends his court once or twice a-week, and then only for an hour or two on those days; and suppose that his assistant is a young man who makes sport his occupation and his business, and business his recreation and his sport. And suppose that I and my assistant work hard, and do our best to hunt up all the murderers, thieves, and other culprits, whom we hear of, and bring them to justice and to punishment. What then? Are the figures in the official returns, touching the convictions, to be taken as any criterion of the crime perpetrated in our respective districts?" His worship delivered these questions triumphantly.

"In that case, certainly not."

"Well, the Sudder have looked at the convictions, and the consequence has been, that in the last printed report issued by that august body (composed of three old and imbecile gentlemen) to the Government, the magistrate of that district and his assistant have been praised for their zeal, and recommended for promotion, while the magistrate and assistant of this district have been publicly censured; or, to use the cant phrase of the report, 'handed up for the consideration of the Most Noble the Governor-General of India.'"

"Is it possible?" asked the Lord, throwing up his hands.

"You ask for dry facts, and I have given you dry facts."

"May I make a note of this?" (pulling out an elegant souvenir). "Not that I should think of mentioning your name."

"You may make a note of it; and, so far as mentioning my name is concerned, you may do as you please. I have already written to the Sudder what I have stated to you," was the answer.

"What! about the thirty-three and a-half per cent?"

"Yes; and, what is more, I have insisted on a

copy of the letter being forwarded to the Governor-General."

"And what will be the result, do you suppose?"

"I neither know nor care. I have just served my time in this penal country; and, being entitled to both my pardon and my pension, I intend to apply shortly for both."

The reader will be glad to hear that a long correspondence ensued on this subject between the Sudder, the Government, and the mutinous magistrate. The upshot was, that the imbecile old men who had too long warmed that tribunal were pushed off their stools by the Governor-General (Lord Dalhousie), who, very meritoriously, bullied them into resigning the service; threatening, as some say, to hold a commission on their capacity for office. In their stead were appointed three gentlemen, whose abilities and vigour had hitherto been kept in the back settlements of India. The crowning point of all was, that the mutinous magistrate was one of the illustrious three!

Lord Jamleigh informed us that he had seen Lahore, and that he was about to go across the country to Bombay, and that he should then have seen all three Presidencies, as well as all the Upper Provinces, and the Punjab. He regretted, half apologetically, that he had not been able to take a look at the Himalayas, Simlah and Mussoorie; but the fact was, "he was so much pressed for time."

"Poor devils!" exclaimed our host, smiling. "But, as they wont know anything about it, they wont feel it much—indeed, not at all."

"To whom are you alluding?" asked my lord.

"The Himalayas," sighed our host, passing the claret to his lordship, who, by this time, had discovered that he had not got into a nest of sycophants, who worshipped a title, no matter how frivolous or how insolent the man might be who wore it; but that he had accidentally fallen into the company of persons of independent character; and albeit, they were desirous of giving him a welcome and making him comfortable—being a stranger who had lost his way—nevertheless, were determined to make him pay in some shape for the want of courtesy he had exhibited when the bearers set his palkee down at the door of the bungalow. This discovery made his lordship a little uncomfortable, and rather cautious in his observations. He felt, in short, as one who knows that he has committed an error, and that some penalty will be exacted; but what penalty, and how exacted, he cannot imagine. Had he been able to get away, he would probably have taken a hasty farewell of us. But that was impossible. His jaded bearers were cooking their food, and, until twelve o'clock, there was no hope of getting them together.

The khansamah came in with a fresh bottle of wine. Our host, withdrawing his cigar from his lips, inquired of him if the wants of the gentleman's servant had been attended to.

"Yes, Sahib," was the reply.

"And have you given him any champagne?"

"No, Sahib."

"Then do."

"Oh, pray do nothing of the kind!" exclaimed his Lordship. "He is not accustomed to it."

"Then he will enjoy it all the more," said our host. "I hope he is taking notes, and will write a book on India. I should much like to see his impressions in print; and he may possibly dignify me by devoting a few lines to the character of my hospitality. It is to be hoped, however, that, should his travel inspire him with a thirst for literary distinction, he will confine himself to a personal compilation of his experience, and not go into judicial or revenue matters; for, should he do so, you may find yourself clashing with him, and that would be awkward. His publisher's critic might be inclined to break a spear with your publisher's critic, in their respective reviews of your respective works, and it would be quite impossible to conjecture where the controversy might end. Indisposed as I am, generally, to obtrude my advice upon any one, and much less on a perfect stranger, I nevertheless feel that I am only doing you a kindness when I say that, if I were you, I would regard Hindostan as a sort of Juan Fernandez, myself the Crusoe thereof, and this valet as my man

Friday; and then, with a due observance of that line of demarcation which should always be drawn between civilised man and the savage, I would not permit him to keep even a stick whereon to notch the day or time of any particular event that occurred during my residence in the country, lest he should some day or other—in consequence of my having discharged him, or he having discharged me—rise up and instigate some man or other to call in question the accuracy of my facts. The wine is with you; will you fill, and pass it on?"

Lord Jamleigh became very red in the face, and rather confused both in manner and speech. As for myself and the two assistant-magistrates, there was something so benignant in the expression of our host's handsome and dignified countenance—something so quaintly sarcastic in the tone and manner of his discourse, that, had we known that death was the penalty of not maintaining the gravity of our features, our lives would certainly have been forfeited.

A silence for several minutes ensued; and then Lord Jamleigh spoke to our host as follows:—

"Most of the young noblemen who come to this country, come only to travel about and amuse themselves. I come on business—I may say, Parliamentary business. My time is short, and I must make the most of it. I dare say, when you saw my name in the papers, as having arrived in India, you little thought that I was not a man of pleasure and excursion?"

"Upon my word, the subject never once became a matter of speculation with me," said our host.

After some further conversation, in which our host spared his visitor as little as was consistent with good breeding, Lord Jamleigh, who had been "sitting upon thorns," rose and said :—

"I am afraid I have already trespassed on your goodness too long. I will not attempt to apolo—apolo—or to express how much—how much; nor to assure you that—assure you—that when—"

"Oh, pray don't mention it!" said our host, smiling. "You desire your palkee?"

"If you please," said Lord Jamleigh.

The palkee was ordered, and we were standing in expectation that it would be instantly announced as "ready," when the sirdar-bearer (head personal attendant) came into the room, in a state of excessive trepidation, and informed us that the Sahib's Sahib (Lord Jamleigh's valet) was drunk, asleep, and refused to be disturbed on any pretence whatever.

This announcement, which caused general merriment, induced Lord Jamleigh to ejaculate :—

"That's the champagne, I suspected as much!"

"Where is he?" inquired our host of the sirbar-bearer. "In his palkee?"

"No, Sahib," was the reply. "He is lying on that Sahib's bed," pointing to me.

Here, again, everybody laughed, except myself. I was rather angry, being somewhat particular on this point. So I suggested that he might he put into his vehicle at once. The native servants, of course, were afraid to touch him, lest he should awake and "hit out;" so we, the five of us, Europeans, the magistrate, the two assistant magistrates, Lord Jamleigh, and myself, had to lift, remove, and pack in his palkee, the overcome, and perfectly unconscious valet. He must have been sipping brandy-and water before he came to the bungalow, for he had only half finished his bottle of champagne. Lord Jamleigh now got into his palanquin, and composed himself for the night, or, rather, the remainder of it, and in order that there might be no mistake as to his Lordship's destination, the magistrate sent a horseman to accompany the cortège, with directions that "the Sahibs" were to be taken to Durowlah, on the road to Meerut, and to the house of the magistrate, by whom Lord Jamleigh had been invited, or rather, "petitioned," to stay with him, should he pass through that station, and (to use his Lordship's own terms), as he had promised to do so, he supposed that he must keep his word. When a palanquin is escorted by a sowar, the sowar when the destination is approached, rides on and gives notice that a lady, or gentleman, as the case may be, is coming; and, as the natives of India can never pronounce European names properly, the precaution is usually taken of writing down the name of the traveller on a card, or a slip of paper, and giving it to the sowar. In this case, "Viscount Jamleigh" was written down for the guidance and information of the Durowlah functionary.

It was about seven A.M. when this card was put into the hands of the gentleman who had invited Lord Jamleigh; whom, by the way, he had never seen. The bungalow was immediately all life and in commotion; the servants ordered to prepare tea and coffee; the best bed-room vacated by the present occupants; hot water in readiness; and ere long a palkee —a single palkee—loomed in the distance; theot her palkee was a long way, some three miles, behind. One of the bearers who was carrying it, had fallen and injured himself, and thus was a delay of an hour and a half occasioned. And during that hour and half a pretty mistake was committed. The first palkee was that containing the valet, and the one behind was that of his lordship. The valet had not recovered the effects of his potations; and, on being awakened, seemed, and really was, bewildered and stupified—so much so, that he could not inform the magistrate that he was "only a servant," and not entitled to the attentions that were showered upon him. With trembling hand, he took the cup of tea from the silver salver, and gazing wildly round, murmured, rather than said—

"Brandy! Little Brandy!" which was at once brought and administered. He then had his warm "wash," sat down on the best bed, and suffered himself to be punkahed by two domestics in snow-white garments. This revived him somewhat; but still he felt far too ill to talk. He simply shook his head, and there was a good deal of meaning in that shake, if the magistrate could only have understood it.

"Take some brandy and soda-water, my lord," said his host.

The valet nodded assent.

The magistrate mixed the dose, and administered it with his own hands.

The valet sighed, and again shook his head.

"You will be better presently, my lord," said the magistrate.

"Drunk as a lord!" hiccuped the valet.

"O, no, my lord! It was the jolting along the road."

"In that coffin?" said the valet, who now began to regain the use of his tongue.

"Yes, my lord."

"Am I a lord? He, he, he! Where am I?"

"At Durowlah, my lord."

"And who are *you?*"

"Your host, my lord."

"Then this is not the station-house?"

"Not exactly, my lord."

"Give us a little drop more of that last brew."

"Yes, my lord."

"Ah! Thank you! I feel better now—much better. It was that champagne. Good it was, though. What place was that we were at?"

"Bijnore, my lord."

"I'm not a lord."

"Would that I were in your place, my lord!"

"Well, it isn't a bad place," grinned the valet. "Plenty to eat and drink, little to do, and good wages. But hang this Hindyer! It was a mistake altogether!"

The magistrate took this for fun, laughed immensely, and then said:—

"We had Lord Frederick Pontasguieure staying with us for a week, last winter. A very amusing character he was."

"O, had you? Was he amusing? O! We don't keep his company. Don't know him. I'd give a five-pound note to be in Piccadilly at this moment. This is a nice mess. But the traps are all right, I see. There's the dressing-case, and the writing-desk, and the little medicine-chest."

"Recline upon the bed, my lord, and have a gentle sleep. The punkah, you will find, will very speedily lull you to repose."

"Well, I will," said the valet; and soon fell fast asleep. The venetians were then closed, and the house kept as quiet as possible.

When Lord Jamleigh himself arrived, and established his identity, the scene that ensued may be easily imagined.

The magistrate, with a marvellous want of tact, acknowledged the mistake that he had made: told, in fact, the whole uncomplimentary truth. Lord Jamleigh, and perhaps with reason, was dreadfully annoyed at the idea that the servant should have been mistaken for himself; but he let out, however, that that was the third time the thing had happened, and that in future he should insist upon the fellow wearing livery, instead of plain clothes, and a black wide-awake hat.

The valet was speedily lifted out of the best bed, and transferred to another apartment, where he slept himself sober, and arose at about half-past one to explain to his lordship that he was not much in fault.

I would advise all noblemen and gentlemen who, like Lord Jamleigh, would take a bird's-eye look at India, not to travel with an European servant, who, in that country, is as helpless as an infant, and quite as troublesome, besides being in the way of everybody in every house. It is, moreover, cruel to the servant. He can talk to no one, and becomes perfectly miserable.

MISCELLANEOUS.

THE house of a civilian (a magistrate and collector) in the heart of a district, such as Bijnore, is really worthy of contemplation. With the exception of a bungalow, which is usually occupied by the assistant, and which may, therefore, be said to belong to the magistrate's house, there is no other Christian abode within five-and-thirty or forty miles. The house is usually well, but not extravagantly, furnished; the walls are adorned with prints and pictures, and the shelves well stored with books. In a word, if the punkahs and the venetian blinds, the therm-antidotes, and sundry other Indian peculiarities were removed, you might fancy yourself in some large country-house in England.

There was at Bijnore a native moonshee who was a very good scholar; and, as I was anxious to read Hindostanee and Persian with him (the more especially as I much enjoyed the society of mine host and his assistant), I was induced to accept an invitation to remain for a month. During this period I studied for several hours a-day, besides attending the Court House regularly, to listen to the proceedings, and acquire some knowledge of a most extraordinary jargon, composed of a little Hindostanee, a little Persian, and a good deal of Arabic. This jargon is known in India as the language of the courts. A good Persian and Hindostanee scholar cannot understand it, unless he is accustomed to it. Many magistrates and judges have insisted upon having pure Hindostanee spoken; but to no purpose. Up to a recent period, Persian mixed with Arabic was the language in which legal proceedings were conducted, —Persian and Arabic being as foreign languages to the people of India as English, German, or French. And, when the order went forth that Hindostanee was to be used, the native officers of the courts, and the native lawyers who practised therein, complied with it by putting a Hindostanee verb at the end of each sentence, and using the Hindostanee pronouns, retaining in all their integrity (or rascality) the Persian and Arabic adverbs, prepositions, nouns, adjectives, and conjunctions. An indigo planter in Tahoot, who spoke Hindostanee perfectly, having lived amongst the natives for upwards of twenty years, assured me that he did not comprehend a single sentence of a decree in court Hindostanee, that he heard read out to him—a decree in a case to which he was a party. What is even more absurd, each court has its own peculiar jargon, so that the magistrate or judge, who from long experience has acquired a thorough knowledge of the jargon of his own court, has very great difficulty in comprehending the jargon of another court. This might be altered by fining any officer of court, or native lawyer, who, in matters connected with a suit, used words and phrases unintelligible to the mass of the people; but the order would have to emanate from Government. No magistrate or judge would venture on even an attempt to bring about so desirable a reform

Whilst at Bijnore, I was seized with an attack of tic-douloureux, and suffered all its extreme agonies. One of my host's servants informed me that there was a very clever native doctor in the village, who could immediately assuage any pain —tooth-ache, for instance—and he begged permission to bring him to see me. I consented.

The native doctor was a tall, thin Mussulman, with a lofty forehead, small black eyes, long aquiline nose, and finely chiselled mouth and chin. His hair, eyebrows, and long beard were of a yellowish white, or cream colour. Standing before me in his skull-cap, he was about the most singular looking person I ever beheld. His age did not exceed forty-four or forty-five years. He put several questions to me, but I was in too great pain to give him any replies. He begged of me to sit down. I obeyed him, mechanically. Seating himself in a chair immediately opposite to me, he looked very intently into my eyes. After a little while, his gaze became disagreeable, and I endeavoured to turn my head aside, but I was unable to do so. I now felt that I was being mesmerized. Observing, I suppose, an expression of anxiety, if not of fear, on my features, he bade me not to be alarmed. I longed to order him to cease ; but, as the pain was becoming less and less acute, and as I retained my consciousness intact, I suffered him to proceed. To tell the truth, I doubt whether I could have uttered a sound. At all events, I did not make the attempt. Presently, that is to say, after two or three minutes, the pain had entirely left me, and I felt what is commonly called, all in a glow. The native doctor now removed his eyes from off mine, and inquired if I were better. My reply, which I had no difficulty in giving at once, was in the affirmative; in short, that I was completely cured. Observing that he placed his hands over his head, and pressed his skull, I asked him if he were suffering.

"Yes, slightly," was his reply ; "but I am so accustomed to it, it gives me but little inconvenience."

I then begged of him to explain to me how it was that he had the power to afford me such miraculous relief. That, he said, he was unable to do. He did not know. I then talked to him of mesmerism and of the wonderful performances of Dr. Esdaile, in the Calcutta hospital. He had lately heard of mesmerism, he said ; but, years before he heard of it, he was in the habit of curing people by assuaging their pain. The gift had been given to him soon after he attained manhood. That, with one exception, and that was in the case of a Keranee—a half-caste—no patient had ever fallen asleep, or had become beehosh (unconscious), under his gaze. "The case of the half-caste," he went on to say, "alarmed me. He fell asleep, and slept for twelve hours, snoring like a man in a state of intoxication." I was not the first European he had operated upon, he said; that in Bareilly, where he formerly lived, he had afforded relief to many officers and to several ladies. Some had toothache, some tic-douloureux, some other pains. "But," he exclaimed, energetically, "the most extraordinary case I ever had, was that of a Sahib who had gone mad—'drink delirious.' His wife would not suffer him to be strapped down, and he was so violent that it took four or five other Sahibs to hold him. I was sent for, and, at first, had great difficulty with him and much trembling. At last, however, I locked his eyes up, as soon as I got him to look at me, and kept him for several hours as quiet as a mouse, during which time he had no brandy, no wine, no beer; and, though he did not sleep, he had a good long rest. I stayed with him for two days, and whatever I told him to do he did immediately. He had great sorrow on his mind, poor man. Three of his children had died of fever within one short week, and he had lost much money by the failure of an agency-house in Calcutta. There was a cattle serjeant, too, an European, whom I also cured of that drinking madness by locking up his eyes."

"What do you mean by locking up his eyes?"

"Well, what I did with you; I locked up your eyes. When I got his eyes fixed on mine, he could not take them away—could not move."

"But can you lock up any one's eyes in the way that you locked up mine?"

"No; not everybody's. There was an artillery captain once who defied me to lock up his eyes. I tried very hard; but, instead of locking up his, he locked up mine, and I could not move till he permitted me. And there was a lady, the wife of a judge, who had pains in the head, which I could not cure, because she locked up my eyes. With her I trembled much, by straining every nerve, but it was of no use."

"Do you know any other native who has the same power that you possess?"

"Only three; but, I dare say, there may be hundreds in these provinces who have it, and who use it. And now, Sahib," said the native doctor, taking from his kummerbund (the cloth that encircles the waist) a bundle of papers, "I desire to show you some of my certificates, at the same time to beg of you to pardon my apparent want of respect in appearing in your presence in this skull-cap instead of a turban; but the fact is, that when I heard you were in such great pain, I did not think it humane to delay until I had adorned myself."

I proceeded to examine very carefully every one of his many certificates; not that I was in any way interested in them, but because I knew it would afford him great pleasure. In all, they were quite as numerous as those which English charlatans publish in testimony of their skill in extracting corns. They were more elaborate however; for it is by the length of a certificate that a native judges of its value—just in the same way that Partridge, when Tom Jones took him to see *Hamlet*, admired the character of the King, because he spoke louder than any of the company, "anybody could see that he was a king." As for myself, I sat down and covered a whole sheet of foolscap in acknowledgment of my gratitude to Mustapha Khan Bahadoor, for having delivered me from unendurable torments. To my certificate I pinned a cheque on the North-West Bank for one hundred rupees (ten pounds), and, presenting both documents to the doctor, permitted him to take his leave. Some months afterwards, on discovering that this cheque had not been presented for payment, I wrote to the assistant-magistrate, and asked him, as a favour, to send for the native doctor, and obtain some information on the subject. In reply, I was informed that the doctor preferred keeping the cheque appended to my certificate as an imperishable memorial of the extraordinary value in which his services had been held by an European gentleman, and that he would not part with it for ten times the amount in gold or silver. Such a strange people are the natives of India! Their cupidity is enormous certainly, but their vanity (I am speaking of the better class) is even greater. One hundred rupees was equal to half a year's earnings of the native doctor, and yet he preferred holding the useless autograph of an insignificant Sahib like myself for the amount rather than realize it. The native doctor evidently reasoned thus :—"I might spend the one hundred rupees, might not be believed if I made the assertion that I had received it; but here is the voucher." Some may imagine that he kept it as a sort of decoy-duck; but this I am perfectly satisfied was not the case.

I was now about to leave Bijnore, and, as time was of no object to me, I made up my mind to travel no more by palkee, or horse dâk, but in the most independent and comfortable manner. I therefore provided myself with two small tents, and two camels to carry them, two bullocks to carry the tent furniture, my baggage, and stores; a pony for my own riding, and a similar animal for a boy khitmutghur, who was also my personal servant or bearer.

I engaged also a cook and a sweeper, or general helper; so that, when the sawans (camel drivers), the bullock-man, and the syces (grooms), were included, my establishment numbered, in all, eight servants, whose pay in the aggregate amounted to fifty rupees (five pounds) per mensem. This, of course, included their "keep," for they provided themselves with food. The expense of keeping the camels, the bullocks, and the ponies, was, in all, thirty-five rupees (three pounds fifteen shillings) per mensem; while my own expenses, including everything (except beer and cheroots), were not in excess of fifty rupees per month; so that I was thus enabled to travel about India at a cost of not more than two hundred pounds per annum, or two hundred and twenty-five pounds at the very outside. The reader must remember that in almost every one of the villages in India, fowls, eggs, rice, flour, native vegetables, curry stuff, and milk are procurable, and at very small prices, if your servants do not cheat you, and mine did not; for I made an agreement with my boy khitmutghur to that effect; indeed, I entered into a regular contract with him previous to starting, touching the purchase of every article that would be required during my journey. This boy was, in short, my commissariat department. His name was Shumsheer (a word signifying in the Persian language, "a sword"), but he generally went by the name of Sham. He had been for several months in the service of the assistant magistrate of Bijnore; who, as a very great favour, permitted the boy to accompany me on my travels; he was so clever, so sharp, so intelligent, and so active a servant. He was not more than sixteen, and very short for his age; but stoutly built, and as strong as a young lion. He was, moreover, very good-looking, and had, for a native of Hindoostan, a very fair complexion. He had been for several years the servant, or page, of an officer on the staff of a governor-general, and he spoke English with considerable fluency, but with an idiom so quaint, that it was amusing in the last degree to listen to him. He had been "spoilt," in one sense of the word, while at Government House, not only by his own master, but by the whole staff, who had encouraged him to give his opinions on all subjects with a freedom which was at first very disagreeable to me. But, ere long, I too encouraged him to do so; his opinions were so replete with such strong common sense, and were expressed in such an original fashion. If an inquiry touching a certain administration had been called for by Parliament, what an invaluable witness would that boy have been before a Committee of either house—provided he had not been previously "tampered with!"

When all my preparations had been completed, I took leave of my friends, and left Bijnore at three o'clock one morning. My destination was Umballah. I did not take the main road; but a shorter cut across the country, conducted by a guide who knew the district well, and who was enjoined to procure for me another guide as soon as his information failed him.

By seven o'clock we had travelled over twelve miles of ground, and as the sun was beginning to be very warm, I commanded a halt. Our tents were then pitched beneath a tope (cluster) of mango-trees whose branches formed a dense shade. Having bathed, breakfasted, smoked, and read several pages of a Persian book, I fell asleep, and was not awakened until noon, when Sham came into my tent and reported that there was an abundance of black partridge in the neighbourhood: he then proposed that I should dine early—at one P.M.—and at half past four take my gun; and, permitting him to take another, sally forth in search of the game. To this proposal I at once assented, and removing my camp stool to the opening of my little hill tent, I looked out into the fields, where I saw some men ploughing. For the first time during my travels I was struck with the appearance of the instrument which the natives use for tilling the soil; an instrument which, in fact, closely resembles that used by the Romans, according to the directions laid down in the Georgics:

"Curvi formam adcipit ulmus aratri," &c., &c.,

and at first I felt some surprise that an implement so apparently ill-fitted for the purpose for which it is designed, should answer all the requirements of the cultivator. The substitution of the English plough for this native hùr has been several times projected by gentlemen who were zealous in the cause of agriculture; but without any success, or reasonable hope thereof; for when we consider the cheapness, and the great amount of labour always available, the general lightness of the soil, the inaptitude of the natives of India for great or continued physical exertion, the inferiority of the cattle, all of which are the marked characteristics of India, it would not only be undesirable, but impossible to introduce the English plough generally as an implement of husbandry—an implement requiring physical strength, manual dexterity, and a superior breed of cattle for draught. Rude and simple as the native hùr is, or as it may seem to the casual observer, cursorily viewing the operation of ploughing, it has still many good qualities which render it peculiarly suited to the genius of the Indian cultivator; and it is not in any immediate endeavour to improve it or alter it that any real benefit can be conferred on the cause of Indian agriculture. All the efforts, therefore, that have been made in that direction have been time and trouble expended to no purpose. It has been said that all improvement to be real must be spontaneous, or take rise within itself; and it would seem to be more reasonable to improve such means and appliances as the natives use and understand, without running counter to the ideas and shocking the prejudices which they entertain, by endeavouring to compel their adoption of European modes of culture, which, however well suited to the land of their origin, have not the quality most necessary to their practicability, that of being comprehensible to the people of India. The true end of agriculture:

> "with artful toil
> To 'meliorate and tame the stubborn soil,
> To give dissimilar yet fruitful lands
> The grain, or herb, or plant, that each demands,"

is best to be attained by aiding and assisting the development of those resources of the soil which have already been made visible by the people themselves.

Here it is that the duty of the Government begins. The precariousness of the land tenure is one of the greatest impediments to the outlay of capital by the tenant in the improvement of the land; and as there is but little prospect of the removal of this objection, the Government should fulfil what would, were the case different, be the obvious plans of the landholder in developing the resources of the soil. Irrigation and manure are the two great points most deserving of attention. On both points the resources of the country are incalculable; the advantages evident and immediate; both require system and an outlay of capital, which the zemindar (native landholder) is often unable, and oftener unwilling, to adopt and incur—from want of confidence in the administration of the law and the law itself. With the ryot, or cultivator, the case is very different. The law, or the administration thereof, affects him in a very slight degree compared with the zemindar. The land tenure matters very little to him; his rights have been secured; he profits by the outlay of capital on the land. Risk he has none. His advantage is immediate. But he does not possess the means of improvement in any way. He may build a well, dig a tank, or plant a grove to the memory of a departed ancestor, and by so doing enhance the value of the land to the zemindar; but he almost always ruins himself by the act, leaving his debts to be paid by his descendants, and the well, tank, or grove mortgaged to the banker for the extra expenses incurred in its establishment! It behoves an enlightened Government to do for the people and the country what they are unable to do for themselves. An inquiry properly set on foot, and undertaken by competent persons on the part of the Government, to investigate all particulars regarding the state of agriculture, would bring to light many facts, which, if made fitting use of, would not only greatly redound to the honour but adduce greatly to the advantage and profit of the State. The information thus acquired, and not founded on the reports of native (Government) collectors, police officers, and peaons (messengers), but ascertained by the personal inspection of European officials, and from the opinions of the zemindars and cultivators themselves, would enable the Government to know and devise remedies to obviate the evils arising out of the gradual decline of the agricultural classes in our earliest occupied territories. It would show the Government many places where the expenditure of four or five thousand rupees (four or five hundred pounds) in the repairs or erection of a dam, for the obstruction of some rain-filled nullah (a wide and deep ditch), would yield a return yearly of equal amount, besides affording employment, and the means of livelihood to hundreds of persons. It would show where the opening of a road, or the building of a bridge, involving but a small expenditure, would give a new life to a part of the country hitherto forgotten, and render the inhabitants flourishing and happy, by throwing open to them a market for their produce—a market at present out of their reach. It would prove incontestably that the means of irrigation—the true water-power of India, has been even more neglected than the water-power of that (in comparison with the United States) sluggish colony, Canada. The initial step once taken—the march of improvement once fairly set on foot—private enterprise, duly encouraged, will follow in the wake of the Government; and capital once invested, land in India will become intrinsically valuable, and thus obtain the attention it merits. Agricultural improvement would induce lasting and increasing prosperity of the cultivating classes (the bulk of the population) and of the country itself.

"What! Sham! Dinner ready?" I exclaimed, on observing the boy approaching the tent with a tray and a table-cloth.

"Oh, yes, sir; quite ready. And very good dinner."

"What have you got?"

"Stewed duck, sir—curry, sir; pancake, sir. And by the time you eat that, one little quail ready, sir, with toast. I give dinner fit for a governor-general, sir; and the silver shining like the moon, sir."

(It was in this way that he ran on whilst laying the table.)

"But why are you preparing covers for two, when I am dining alone?"

"Yes, sir. But only poor mans has table laid for one. That place opposite is for company sake. And suppose some gentleman come—not likely here, but suppose? Then all is ready. No running about—no calling out, 'Bring plate, knife and fork, and spoon, and glass,' and all that. And if two plates laid, master, if he like—when I am standing behind his chair keeping the flies off while he eats—may fancy that some friend or some lady sitting opposite, and in his own mind he may hold some guftoogoo (conversation). That's why I lay the table for two, sir."

I had been warned by the gentleman who permitted Sham to accompany me, that he was such an invaluable servant, it was only politic to let him have his own way in trifling matters; and therefore instead of objecting to his proceeding, I applauded his foresight.

Whilst discussing the stewed duck, which was excellent—as was indeed every dish prepared by Sham, when he had "his own way—" and while he was standing behind me, keeping the flies off with a chowrie (a quantity of long horsehair fastened to a handle), I talked to him without turning my head:

"You say you wish to take a gun. Have you ever been out shooting?"

"Oh, yes, sir. When my master went up from Calcutta to Mussoorie and Simlah with the Governor-General, I went with him. And I often went out shooting in the Dhoon, with my master, who was a great sportsman, sir. And I was out with my master—on the same elephant—when the Governor-General shot the tiger."

"What! Did the Governor-General shoot a tiger?"

"Oh, no, sir. But my master and the other gentlemens make him think he did, sir."

"Explain yourself."

"Well, sir, the Governor-General said he had heard a great deal of tiger shooting, and should like to see some for once. So my master, who was a very funny gentleman, went to an officer in the Dhoon—another very funny gentleman—and between them it was agreed that his lordship should shoot one tiger. And so they sent out some native shikarees (huntsmen), told them to wound but not kill one big tiger in the jungle, and leave him there. And the native shikarees did shoot one big tiger in the jungle, and they came and made a report where he was lying. Then next morning when all the elephants and gentlemens was ready, and the Governor-General had his gun in his hand, they all went to the jungle; and when they got to the place and heard the tiger growl very angrily, my master called out: 'There, my lord—there he is; take your shot!' and my lord fired his gun, and my master cried out very loud: 'My lord, you've hit him!' And my lord, who was very much confused—not being a sportsman—said, 'Have I?' And all the gentlemens cried out: 'Yes, my lord!' And then some of the gentlemens closed round the tiger and killed him, by firing many bullets at him. And my lord had the tiger's skin taken off, and it was sent to England to be make a carpet for my lord's sitting-room. And for many days all the gentlemens laughed, and asked of one another, 'Who shot the tiger?' And the Governor-General was so happy and so proud, and wore his head as high as a seesu-tree. But he had enough of tiger-shooting in that one tiger; for he was not a sportsman, and did not like the jolting of the elephant in the jungle."

My repast ended, and the table-cloth removed, I lighted a cigar, and took my camp-stool once more to the opening of the tent, when, to my surprise, and somewhat to my dismay, I found myself besieged by a host of ryots, cultivators of the soil, each bearing a present in the shape of a basket of fruit or vegetables, or a brass dish covered with almonds, raisins, and native sweetmeats. These poor creatures, who doubtless fancied that I was a Sahib in authority (possibly, Sham had told them that I was a commissioner—a very great man—on a tour of inspection), prostrated themselves at my feet, and in the most abject manner imaginable craved my favour and protection. I promised each and every one of them, with much sincerity, that if ever it lay in my power to do them a service, they might depend upon my exerting myself to the utmost; and then I made a variety of inquiries touching their respective ages, families, circumstances, and prospects, in order to prove that I had already taken an interest in them. I then asked them some questions touching the game in the locality, and was glad to hear the report made by Sham confirmed to the letter. I was assured that the light jungle in the rear of my tents literally swarmed with black partridges.

It was now nearly time to go out, and in the course of two hours I brought down no less than seven brace, while Sham distinguished himself by killing five birds. By the time I returned to my tent I was weary, and retired to rest, having previously given orders that I was to be called at two A.M., insomuch as at that hour I intended to resume the march. It is one thing, however, to retire to rest, but it is another thing to sleep. What with the croaking of the frogs in a neighbouring tank, and the buzzing and biting of the musquitoes in my tent, I could not close an eye. I lay awake the whole night, thinking—thinking of a thousand things, but of home chiefly; and right glad was I when Sham approached my bed, holding in one hand a cup of very hot and strong coffee, and in the other my cigar-case, while the noise outside, incident on the striking of the tents and the breaking up of the little camp, was as the sweetest music to my ears.

FORWARD.

I WAS twelve days marching from Bijnore to Umballah, and, by keeping away from the high-road, I did not see during my journey a single European face. I moved entirely amongst the people, or rather the peasantry, of the Upper Provinces of India—a very poor and very ignorant peasantry, but, comparatively speaking, civil and honest. Sham made a much greater impression upon them than I did; mounted on his pony, and dressed in very gay attire—a purple velvet tunic, pyjamahs of red silk trimmed with gold lace, a turban of very gorgeous aspect, and shoes embroidered all over with silver. He had more the appearance of a young rajah or prince than a gentleman's servant. And Sham talked to his countrymen—if the wretched Hindoos could be so called—in a lofty strain which vastly amused me, though I did not approve of it. I said nothing, however. As for the camp arrangements, he had completely taken them out of my hands, and he was so much better manager than myself that I was well content that it should be so; all that was left to me was to name the hour for departing from an encampment-ground, and the next spot whereon I wished my tents pitched.

It was past six o'clock on the morning of the 20th of April, when I came within a few miles of Umballah. The mornings and the nights were still cool; but, in the day the heat was beginning to be very severe. However, after taking my coffee and making my toilet, I caused my pony to be re-saddled, and, followed by Sham mounted on his pony, rode into the cantonments, inquiring my way, as I went along, of the various servants who were moving about. I eventually found myself at the door of a bungalow, which was tenanted by a very old friend and distant connexion of mine. He was an officer in one of her Majesty's regiments of foot, then stationed at Umballah.

"You will sleep here, of course, during your stay," he said; "but you are the guest of the mess, remember. We have settled all that, and we will go up in the buggy presently to deposit your pasteboard in the mess reading room. I will point out to you where you will always find your knife and fork, and I will introduce to you all the servants—the mess-sergeant especially."

I must now digress for a brief while, in order to give the uninitiated reader some idea of Indian etiquette as it exists amongst Europeans, members of society. In other countries, or at all events in England, when a gentleman goes to take up his abode, for a long or a short period, in a strange locality, it is usual for the residents, if they desire to show him any civility, or make his acquaintance, to call upon him in the first instance. In India the reverse is the case. The stranger must make his round of calls, if he wishes to know the residents; and, what is more, he must leave his cards on the mess, "for the colonel and officers of her Majesty's —— Regiment." You may leave a card on every officer in the regiment, from the senior colonel down to the junior ensign; and each of them may, and possibly will, invite you to his private board; but, if you omit to leave a card on the mess, it would be a gross breach of decorum in any member of the mess to invite you to dine at the mess-table, because you have "not left a card on the mess." And not only to the royal regiments does the rule pertain, but to every regiment in India, and to every brigade of artillery.

Having left my cards at the mess of the regiment to which my friend belonged, I was driven to the mess-house of the —— Dragoons, where another expenditure of cards was incurred; then to the mess-houses of the two native infantry regiments, and the mess-house of the native cavalry regiment. I was then whisked off to the house of General Sir Doodle Dudley, G.C.B., who commanded the division. The General was very old, close upon eighty; but he was "made up" to represent a gentleman of about forty. His chesnut wig fitted him to perfection, and his whiskers were died so adroitly, that they were an exact imitation of their original colour. The white teeth were all false; likewise the pink colour in the cheeks and the ivory hue of the forehead. As for the General's dress, it fitted him like a glove, and his patent leather boots and his gold spurs were the neatest and prettiest I had ever seen. In early life Sir Doodle had been a rival and an acquaintance of Beau Brummell. When a Colonel in the Peninsular war, he had been what is called a very good regimental officer; but, from 1818 until his appointment to India, in 1847, as a General of Division, he had been unattached, and had never done a single day's duty. He was so hopelessly deaf, that he never even attempted to ask what was said to him; but a stranger, as I was, would scarcely have credited it; for the General talked, laughed, and rattled on as though he were perfectly unconscious of his infirmity. I ventured a casual remark touching the late dust-storm which had swept over the district, to which the General very vivaciously replied:—

"Yes, my good sir. I knew her in the zenith of her beauty and influence, when she was a lady patroness of Almack's, and the chief favourite of his Royal Highness the Prince Regent. Oh, yes! she is dead, I see by the last overland paper; but I did not think she was so old as they say she was—eighty-four. Only fancy, eighty-four!" Then darting off at a tangent, he remarked, "I see they give it out that I am to have the command-in-chief at Bombay. The fact is, I don't want Bombay, and so I have told my friends at the Horse Guards at least a dozen times. I want the governorship and the commander-in-chief at the Cape; but, if they thrust Bombay upon me, I suppose I must take it. One can't always pick and choose, and I fancy it is only right to oblige now and then."

"We shall be very sorry to lose you, General," said my friend, mechanically; "very sorry indeed."

"So I have told his Excellency," exclaimed the General, who presumed that my friend was now talking on an entirely different subject. "So I have told him. But he will not listen to me. He says that if the court-martial still adheres to its finding of murder, he will upset the whole of the proceedings, and order the man to return to his duty; and the court *will* adhere to its original finding; for the court says, and I say, that a private who deliberately loads his firelock, and deliberately fires at and wounds a serjeant, cannot properly be convicted of manslaughter only. Well, it cannot be helped, I suppose. The fact is, the commander-in-chief is now too old for his work; and he is, as he always was, very obstinate and self-willed." And the General continued, "For the command of an army or a division in India, we want men who are not above listening to the advice of the experienced officers by whom they are surrounded!"

When we were leaving the General, he mistook

me for my friend and my friend for me, and respectively addressed us accordingly (his eyesight was very imperfect, and he was too vain to wear glasses). He thanked me for having brought my friend to call upon him, and assured my friend that it would afford him the greatest pleasure in the world if the acquaintance, that day made, should ripen into friendship.

"He is an imbecile," I remarked, when we were driving away from the General's door.

"Yes; and he has been for the last six or seven years," was the reply.

"But he must be labouring under some delusion with respect to being appointed to the command-in-chief of an Indian presidency?"

"Nothing of the kind. He is certain of it. He will go to Bombay before six weeks are over, you will see."

The General *did* go to Bombay, where he played such fantastic tricks before high heaven, that the angels could not have "wept" for laughing at them. Amongst other things, he insisted on the officers of the regiments buttoning their coats and jackets up to the throat, during the hottest time of the year. He would have nothing unmilitary, he said, "hot climate or no hot climate." He was quite childish before he relinquished his command, and was brought home just in time to die in his fatherland, and at the country-seat of his aristocratic ancestors. Although utterly unfitted, in his after life, to command troops, he was a very polished old gentleman, externally; and, having enjoyed a very intimate acquaintance with Blücher, and other celebrated commanders, he could repeat many anecdotes of them worthy of remembrance. "Blücher," he used to say, "generally turned into bed all standing, jack-boots included; and, if his valet forgot to take off his spurs, and they became entangled with the sheets, woe betide the valet. The torrent of abuse that he poured forth was something terrific." I also heard the General say that Blücher, having seen everything in London, remarked with great earnestness, "Give me Ludgate Hill!" and on being asked to explain why, replied, with reference to the number of jewellers' and silversmiths' shops which in that day decorated the locality,

"Mein Gott! what pillage!"

After leaving the General's house, we called upon some six or eight other magnates of Umballah for the time being; and on returning to the mess-house at the hour of tiffin, I was rather fatigued. The scene, however, revived me considerably. There were seated round the large table, in the centre of the lonely room, some seventy or eighty officers of all ranks, from the various regiments in the station. There was to be a meeting held that day at the mess-room, to discuss some local matter, and the majority of those present had been invited to "tiff" previously. No one was in uniform—at least, not in military uniform; all wore light shooting-coats and wide-awake hats, covered with turbans. The local question, touching the best means of watering the mall, where the residents used to take their evening ride or drive, having been discussed, the party broke up. Some went to the different billiard-rooms to play matches (for money, of course); others retired to private bungalows to play cards, or read, while reclining on a couch or a bed, or a mat upon the floor. Every one smoked and sipped some sort of liquid. It was to a room in my friend's bungalow that eleven of the party, inclusive of myself, repaired, to while away the time until sundown, by playing whist.

Never did the character of an officer's life in India strike me so forcibly as on that afternoon. There was an air of lassitude and satiety about every one present. The day was hot and muggy, and the atmosphere very oppressive. It was a fatiguing bore to deal the cards, take up the tricks, mark the game, or raise to one's lips the claret cup which Sham had been called upon to brew. Sham was well known to most of the officers of the regiment to which my friend belonged. He had made their acquaintance (to use his own words) when he was on the Governor-General's staff.

The three men who had not cut in at whist were

lounging about, and making ineffectual attempts to keep up a conversation. The shooting-coats and the waistcoats were now discarded, and the suspenders, and the shoes, or boots; in short, each person only wore strictly necessary clothing, while the native (coolie) in the verandah was ever and anon loudly called upon to pull the punkah as strongly as possible. That room that afternoon presented a perfect picture of cantonment life in India during the summer season, between the hours of two and half-past five, P.M. The body is too much exhausted to admit of any serious mental exertion beyond that which sheer amusement can afford; and it is by no means uncommon to find your partner or yourself dropping off to sleep when called upon to lead a card, or follow suit. The three men who were sitting (or lying) out, soon yielded to the influence of the punkah, closed their eyes, and got up a snore, each holding between his fingers the cheroot he had been smoking.

Ah, yes! It is very bad to have to endure the frightful heat—to feel one's blood on the broil, even under a punkah, and with doors and windows closed, to exclude the hot air of the open day. But what must it be for the men, the privates and their wives and children? They have no punkahs, though it has been shown that they might have them at a trifling cost. They have no cold water, much less iced water to sip—though they might have it, if the authorities had the good sense (to put humanity entirely out of the question) to be economical of that invaluable commodity in India, British flesh and blood. They, the men of the ranks, and their wives and children, have no spacious apartments (with well-fitted doors and windows), to move about in, though there is no reason why they should not have them, for the land costs nothing, and labour and material is literally dirt-cheap in the Upper Provinces of India.

"But the Royal Infantry Barracks at Umballah is a fine, large building!" it may be suggested. I reply, "Not for a regiment one thousand strong"—a regiment mustering one thousand bayonets, to say nothing of the numerous women, and the more numerous children. In a cold climate, it would be ample for their accommodation; but not here, where in a room occupied by an officer, the thermometer frequently stands at ninety-three degrees, and sometimes at one hundred and five degrees. In the matter of ice, the reader must be informed how it is manufactured. During the "cold weather," (as the winter is always called,) small earthenware vessels of shallow build, resembling saucers in shape, are filled with water, and placed in an open field, upon a low bed of straw. At dawn of day there is a coating of ice upon each vessel, of about the thickness of a shilling. This is collected by men, women, and children (natives), who receive for each morning's, or hour's work, a sum of money, in cowries, equal to about half of a farthing When collected, it is carried to an ice-pit, and there stored. The expenses are borne by a subscription, and the amount for each ticket depends entirely on the number of subscribers. In some large stations, an ice-ticket for the hot season costs only three pounds. In smaller stations it will cost six pounds. The amount of ice received by each ticket-holder is about four pounds, and is brought away each morning at daylight, in a canvas bag, enveloped in a thick blanket, by the ticket-holder's own servant. It is then deposited in a basket made expressly for the purpose. In this basket is placed the wine, beer, water, butter, and fruit. The bag of solid ice is in the centre of all these, and imparts to each an equal coldness. These four pounds of ice, if properly managed, and the air kept out of the basket, will cool an inconceivable quantity of fluids, and will last for twenty-four hours—that is to say, there will be some ice remaining when the fresh bag is brought in. If a bewildered khansamah, or khitmutghur, in his haste to bring a bottle, leaves the basket uncovered, the inevitable consequence is, that the ice melts, and there is an end of it for the day. I have scarcely known a family in which corporal punishment was not inflicted on the servant guilty of such a piece of neglect. But, great as was the privation, it was always cheerfully endured by the society, when the doctors of the various departments indented on them for their shares of ice respectively. And this occasionally happened, when the hospitals were crowded with cases of fever. Scores and scores of lives were often saved by the application of ice to the head, and the administration of cold drinks.

Ice is not manufactured below Benares. Calcutta and its immediate neighbourhood revels in the luxury of American ice, which may be purchased for three half-pence per seer (two pounds). The American ships, trading to India, take it as ballast, which by the time it arrives in the river Hooghley becomes a solid mass.

The sun has gone down, and it is now time to bathe and dress for our evening drive. The band is playing. We descend from the buggy, languidly; and languidly we walk first to one carriage and then to another, to talk with the ladies who are sitting in them. They, the ladies, wear a very languid air, as though life, in such a climate, were a great burden—and it is, no doubt, a great burden from the middle of April to the first week in October. There is a languid air even about the liveliest tunes that the band plays. Then we languidly drive to the mess-house for dinner. The dinner is more a matter of form than anything else. But the wines, which are well iced, are partaken of freely enough—especially the champagne. There is, of course, no intoxication; but as the evening advances the company becomes more jovial, and by the time the dessert is placed on the table, that dreadful feeling of languor has, in a great measure, taken its departure. It is now that the evening commences, and many very pleasant evenings have been spent in that Umballah mess-room, despite the heat. The colonel of the regiment to which my friend belonged was a man of very good sense; and during the hot season he sanctioned his officers wearing, except when on parade, a white twill jacket, of a military cut, with the regimental button; and he had not the slightest objection to a loose neck-tie instead of a tightly-fitting black stock. This matter ought to have been sanctioned by the highest military authority, the commander-in-chief; or rather, it ought to have been stated in a general order that such rational attire was approved of, instead of being left to the caprice of a colonel, or brigadier, or general of division. The regiment of royal cavalry, too, were equally fortunate in their colonel. He was also of opinion that the comfort of the officers under his command was worthy of some consideration, and he could not see the necessity of requiring a gentleman to sit down to dinner in a thick red cloth jacket (padded), and buttoned up to the very chin. But before I left Umballah, the old General altered this, and insisted on "this loose and unsoldierlike attire being instantly abandoned." He had overlooked it for several months, or, at all events, had expressed no objection; but suddenly the major-general commanding was aroused to observe with great regret that the dress in some regiments was fast becoming subversive, &c., &c. The reason of the major-general's sudden acuteness of observation was this :—he was about to give a ball at his own house, and for some inexplicable cause had not invited any of the officers of her Majesty's — Regiment of Foot. But on the morning of the night on which the ball was to take place, he requested his aide-de-camp to write the following note :—

"The Major-General commanding the Division desires that the band of H.M.'s — Foot may be in attendance at the Major-General's house at half-past nine precisely."

And the band went at half-past nine, for the General had a perfect right to order the men to attend at his house whenever he pleased ; but the band went without their musical instruments, for they (as I believe is the case in all regiments) were the private property of the officers for the time being, and, like the regimental plate, the loan thereof for any particular occasion must be regarded as a matter of favour, and not as a matter of right. So the General had no music out of the band : and the officers in the station had no comfort in their dress, until the General left the station for his command at Bombay.

It may possibly be imagined that the General had, in his earlier days, done the State great service as a military commander, and for that his appointment was the reward. Nothing of the kind. When he left the army, and became unattached, he was only a regimental colonel, and had only been once mentioned by the Duke of Wellington in his despatches, as having gallantly led his regiment into action; for this single mention he was made a brevet major-general and a C.B., while other colonels who had performed precisely the same service, remained unpromoted and undecorated. Sometimes, during his Indian career—not that he was intoxicated by wine, for the General in his dotage was rather abstemious—he would be utterly oblivious to the fact that he *was* in India, and would hold a conversation with some young ensign, (who had been one of his dinner party, and who, in haste to get away early to billiards, came up to say good night) after the following fashion:—

"Look here, my pretty boy, as you will be passing Fribourg and Pontet's, just look in and tell them—O, how like you are to your dear mother! I can remember her when she was thought, and truly, to be one of the prettiest women in all Europe! Charming eyes—lovely complexion! Well, look in at Fribourg and Pontet's."

"Yes, General."

"And tell them to send me a canister of the Duke of Kent's mixture. O! how very like you are to your dear mother, my pretty boy! The last they sent me had scent in it. Tell them I hate scent in snuff."

"Yes, General."

"O! how VERY like you are to your dear mother!"

(The General had never seen the boy's mother in the course of his long and useless life.)

"Yes, General."

"Well, do not forget the snuff."

"O, no, General! Good night."

"God bless thee, my pretty boy! O! how like you are to your dear mother!"

I do not mean to say that General Sir Doodle Dudley was an average specimen of the General officers sent out by the Horse Guards to command divisions in India. That would be untrue: for some, though very old and inefficient, could see, hear, and understand. But within the past ten years, some others that I know of have been sent out, to Bengal alone, who were not one whit more efficient than General Sir Doodle Dudley.

The nights being more enjoyable, comparatively, than the days, no wonder that they are rarely given up for sleep by the majority of military men or younger civilians in India. Of course, married men with families must, and do, for the most part, lead regular lives, or, at all events, conform to some fixed domestic rules. But it is not so with the unmarried, who take their rest (sleep) much in the same way that inveterate drunkards take their drink—"little and often." You will see a young officer playing at billiards at half-past two or three in the morning, and at five you will see him on the parade-ground with his company. He has had his sleep and his bath, and, to use his own words, he "feels as fresh as a three-year-old." Between seven and twelve he will also have an hour or so of "the balmy," and then, after tiffin, he will perhaps get a few winks while reading the newspaper or a book, or while sitting on the bench in the billiard-room, "watching the game." Have these young men, it may be asked, nothing to do? Have they no occupation? Yes. They have to keep themselves alive and in good spirits, and that is no easy task either, in the hot weather of the Upper Provinces. Some of them (a few) in the East India Company's Service will take to studying the languages, in the hope that proficiency therein will lead to staff employ. Those, however, who do not happen to have good interest to back their claims soon find out that the order of the Governor-General in Council touching a knowledge of the Native languages is a mere sham; and that ignorance clothed with interest is—so far as advancement in life is concerned—far preferable to a well-stored head and a steady character.

MILITARY MATTERS.

"A COURT MARTIAL! Is it possible?" exclaimed my friend, on looking into the general order book, which was put before him on the breakfast-table. "Well, I did not think it would come to that."

"I did," said the Major of the regiment, who was sitting opposite to him. "For it strikes me that the chief is never so happy as when he is squabbling with the members of the courts, and publicly reprimanding them for their inconsistency, or whatever else may occur to him. This is the seventh court martial held in this station within the past two months, and with the exception of one case, the whole of them were unnecessary."

I was tempted to ask who was to be tried.

"Two boys," replied the Major, "who thought proper to quarrel at the mess-table, and to make use of a certain little word, not altogether becoming gentlemen, if applied to one another. The Senior Captain, who was the senior officer present, very properly put them under arrest, and sent them to their quarters. Our Colonel, who is, I am very happy to say, extremely particular on this as well as on every other point that tends to preserve the tone and character of the regiment, wished these lads to receive from a higher authority than himself a severe reprimand. That authority was the General of the Division; and if the General of the Division had been Sir Joseph Thackwell, an officer of sound judgment, or any commander of Sir Joseph's stamp, all would have been well. But the Colonel, who has since found out the mistake that he made in not weighing the individual character of Sir Doodle, forwarded the case on to him through the Brigadier in the regular way, the young gentlemen meanwhile remaining under arrest. The Colonel also saw Sir Doodle privately, and pointed out to him, so far as he could make himself understood, that a severe reprimand was all that was required. Sir Doodle, however, did not view the matter in this light, and forwarded the proceedings to the Commander-in-Chief, at Simlah. After a fortnight's delay, during which time those two boys have been confined to their respective bungalows, the order has come down for a general court martial, to assemble and try them. This will involve a further imprisonment of some three or four weeks; for the chief is sure to find fault with the court's finding, and send back the proceedings for revision and reconsideration previous to confirming and approving of them."

"And what do you suppose will be the upshot?" I asked.

"That the lads will be released, or ordered to return to their duty," said the Major. "Have you ever witnessed a military court martial?"

"No."

"Then I would advise you to witness this."

On the following day, a frightfully hot day, the thermometer being at ninety-two, I accompanied my friend in his buggy to the mess-room of the regiment, where I beheld some five-and-twenty officers in full dress. All these officers were in some way or other connected with the trial; besides these there were present some five-and-thirty officers in red or blue jackets, but without their swords; these were spectators. It was altogether a very imposing scene; especially when the thirteen members took their seats around the table, the President in the centre, and the Deputy-Judge-Advocate of the Division opposite to him; the prisoners standing behind the chair of the Deputy-Judge-Advocate-General. The lads were now perfectly reconciled to each other, and as good friends as ever. Indeed, on the morning that followed their use of the one very objectionable little word, mutual apologies and expressions of regret passed between them; and, in so far as the settling of the quarrel between themselves was concerned, it was most judiciously and satisfactorily arranged by their respective friends.

The court having been duly sworn, and the charges read aloud by the Deputy-Judge-Advocate-General, the prisoners were called upon to plead. Both of them wished to plead guilty, and said so in a low tone to the Deputy-Judge-Advocate-General, who in an equally low tone of voice, said—

"No, don't do that; say 'Not guilty.'"

"But look here, my dear fellow," said one of the prisoners to that functionary, who was the prosecutor on the occasion; "what's the use of denying it? We did make two fools of ourselves."

"Yes; what's the use of wasting time?" said the other prisoner.

"If we plead guilty, there's an end of it, and the court can sentence us at once, and send the papers up to Simlah by to-night's post. I am sick of that cursed bungalow of mine, and want to have a change of air."

"Well, do as you like," said the Deputy-Judge-Advocate. "But my advice is that you plead *Not* guilty, and then in your defence you can put forth whatever you please in extenuation, and mitigation of the punishment."

"But here we are brought up for calling each other liars in a moment of passion, and if we say we did not call each other liars, we *are* liars."

"And what is more, we are liars in cold blood," urged one of the prisoners.

"Will you admit that you were drunk?" said the Deputy-Judge-Advocate-General.

"No," they both called out. "We were not strictly

sober, perhaps. But where is it about being drunk? We didn't see that in the charge."

"Yes, here it is, in the second instance of the second charge, 'having while in a state of intoxication at the mess-table of her Majesty's — Regiment of Foot, on the night,'" &c., &c.

"Oh! that's an infamous falsehood, you know. Who said that? Not Captain Stansfield, who put us under arrest? If he swears that he shall answer for it. Intoxicated! not a bit of it! Screwed, nothing more!" cried the young officer in a sort of stage whisper. "On my honour, as an officer and a gentleman, nothing more."

"These charges have come down from head-quarters, having been prepared in the office of the Judge-Advocate-General."

"Who is he? What's his name?" asked the prisoners.

"Colonel Birch," was the reply.

"Then he shall give up his authority."

"Well, plead Not guilty, and you will have it."

"Very well, then, off she goes: 'Not guilty!' Fifty not guilties, if you like, on that point."

While this little, but interesting, debate was pending between the prosecutor and the prisoners, the various members of the court were holding with each other a miscellaneous conversation, or otherwise amusing themselves.

"Colonel Jackstone, of the Native Infantry (who

was the president of the court martial, in virtue of the seniority of his rank), was talking to Colonel Colverly of the Dragoons, about some extraordinary ailment of his wife which required the constant administration of brandy and soda-water, in order to keep her alive. It was a low sinking fever, he said, from which she had suffered for the last six or seven years at intervals of three months; and it was always worse in the hot weather than at any other season of the year. Captain Bulstrade, of the Artillery, was talking to Major Wallchaffe, of the Light (Bengal) Cavalry, concerning a fly-trap which he had that morning invented; a ginger-beer or soda-water bottle half filled with soapsuds and the opening besmeared with honey or moistened sugar. Captain Dundriffe was recommending Captain Nolens to buy some beer which a native merchant had recently imported into the station. Lieutenant Blade, of the Dragoons, was playing at odd and even with his fingers, on honour, with Lieutenant Theston, of the same regiment; and, with a pretence of being ready to take notes of the proceedings of the court martial, each, pen in right hand, was keeping an account of the score. Blade used to boast of being the inventor of this simple game, but there were officers in India who declared that it owed its existence to a late Commander-in-Chief of the Forces, and who invented it at school when he had been shut up in a dark room (with another boy as fond of gambling as himself), as a punishment for card playing and other games of chance requiring light to see what was going on. Nothing could possibly be simpler than the game, and played as it was, on honour, nothing could be fairer. Blade lost thirty pounds on the first day of the court martial, but won the greater part of it back on the day following. Of course it would not do to play at this game with strangers or promiscuous acquaintances. Lieutenant Belterton of the regiment was making use of the pens, ink, and paper, by sketching the President and several others who had somewhat prominent noses; and young Lofter was trying to rival him in this amusement. My own friend was very busy writing; and, from the serious expression on his countenance, you might have fancied he was composing a sermon, or writing a letter of advice to a refractory son; he folded up the paper, and passed it round till at last it reached me. I opened it, and read as follows:—"We shall be here till four. Take the buggy and drive up to the bungalow, and tell the khitmutghur to bring down the ice-basket, also Mr. Belterton's ice-basket, with a plentiful supply of soda-water from our mess; for they are rather short here, and can't stand a heavy run upon them. Tell him also to bring several bottles of our Madeira, for theirs I do not like, and wont drink. It has not age, and has not travelled sufficiently. Cigars also. I am literally bathed in perspiration, and so I fancy are most of us at this end of the table, for the punkah is too far distant to admit of our receiving any benefit therefrom. This is an awful business."

In compliance with the request contained in the above note, I left the Court, drove off as rapidly as possible, and communicated my friend's wishes to his servant, who immediately hastened to fulfil them. By the time I returned to the Court the first witness was under examination. Such a waste of time! Such a trial to the temper of all present! Instead of allowing the Senior Captain to state the facts—and he would have done so in less than three minutes—and then take them down on paper, each question was written on a slip of paper, and submitted to the President, by the Deputy-Judge-Advocate, who showed it to the officers sitting on either side of him, who nodded assent. The question was then read aloud to the witness:—

"Were you present on the night of the 10th of April, at the mess-table of her Majesty's — Regiment of Foot?"

The Captain replied, "I was."

The question and answer were then copied into "the book," and the slip of paper on which the question was originally written was torn up. This occupied (for the Deputy-Judge-Advocate was not a rapid writer, and was apparently in no particular hurry, being a man of very equable temperament) eight minutes. The second question was put in precisely the same way, the same ceremonies having been gone through. The second question was:—

"Were the prisoners present on that occasion?"

"They were," replied the Captain.

Again the copying process went on, slowly and methodically, and Blade, who was still playing odd and even, called out in a loud voice, to make it appear that he was giving up his mind entirely to the investigation:—

"What was the answer? I did not hear it distinctly; be so good as to request the witness to speak up."

"He said, 'They were,'" returned the Deputy-Judge-Advocate-General.

"Oh! 'They were,'" repeated Blade; writing down a mark, signifying that he had just lost four rupees.

Twenty minutes had now elapsed, and the above was all that had been elicited from the first witness, who was seemingly as impatient as most of the members of the Court. The Deputy-Judge-Advocate-General, however, had patience enough for all present, and so had Blade, and his adversary at odd and even. My friend having scowled at Blade for putting his question, and thus prolonging the inquiry, that aggravating officer now periodically spoke to the Deputy-Judge-Advocate-General, who invariably put down his pen to answer him; just as if he could not possibly speak with that instrument in his hand. It was a quarter-past two when the examination in chief was concluded. It began at twelve precisely; so that two hours and fifteen minutes had been consumed in taking down the following, and no more:—

"I was present on the night in question, and placed the prisoners under an arrest, for giving each other the lie in an offensive and ungentlemanlike manner. They were excited seemingly by the wine they had taken; but I cannot say that they were drunk."

The Court then adjourned for half-an-hour to the mess-room, to take some refreshment—every one dripping, drenched. Then came the opening the fronts of the thick red cloth coats, and the imbibing of brandy and soda-water, iced beer, and other fluids, and sundry violent exclamations, that it was worse than the battle of Sobraon—more trying to the constitution. Every one then sat down to tiffin; and, having hastily devoured a few morsels, smoked cheroots.

"I say, Blade," said the Senior Captain, "what did you mean by wishing me to speak up? Surely you heard my answer?"

"Mean, my dear fellow? I meant nothing—or if I did, it was only to take a mild rise out of you However, don't interrupt me just now, for I am thinking over a lot of questions I intend to put to you, when we get back into Court."

"Questions? About what?"

"About drink! That's all I will tell you now. You don't suppose that I was born the son of a judge of the Queen's Bench for nothing, do you? If so, you are vastly mistaken. Is that your Madeira, or ours?"

"Ours."

"Then just spill some into this glass. Ours is not good, certainly, but it would not do to say so before the Colonel. Ah!" sighed the lieutenant, after taking a draught: "that is excellent! Yes. Drink is the topic on which I intend to walk into you, practically. And be very careful how you answer, or you will have the Commander-in-Chief down upon you with five-and-twenty notes of admiration at the end of every sentence of his general order; thirty-five notes of interrogation in the same; and every other word in italics, or capitals, in order to impress the matter of his decision firmly on our minds. 'Was the Court raving mad? Witness ought to be tried!!! folly! imbecility! childishness! The veriest schoolboy ought to know better! Deputy-Judge-Advocate ignorant of his duty!!! The President insane!!!! Confirmed, but not approved!!!'"

"What are you making such a noise about, Blade?" inquired the Colonel of his regiment, good-naturedly.

"Nothing, Colonel," said Blade. "No noise. But here is a man who has the audacity, in our own mess-house, to asperse the character of our Madeira." And, taking up the Senior Captain's own bottle, and holding it before the Senior Captain's face, he exclaimed,—looking at the Colonel, "he positively refuses to taste it, even."

"Nonsense," said the cavalry Colonel, approaching them with a serious air, and with an empty glass in his hand. "Nonsense! Do you really mean to say that our Madeira is not good—excellent?"

"No, Colonel," said the Senior Captain of the Royal Infantry regiment.

"Taste it, and say what you think of it, Colonel," said Blade, filling the Colonel's glass, which was held up to receive the liquid, with a willingness which imparted some mirth to the beholders. "Taste it. There."

"I have tasted it," said the Colonel, "and pronounce it to be the best I ever drank in my life, and, in my judgment, infinitely superior to that of any other mess."

"So I say," said Blade, filling his glass; "but the misfortune is, he won't believe me."

"Order a fresh bottle of our wine for him, Blade," said the Colonel, "and let him taste the top of it."

"No, thank you, Colonel," said the Senior Captain; "I would rather not. Remember, I have to conclude my examination."

"Ah, so you have," said the Colonel, moving away. "But take my word for it, that better Madeira than ours was never grown or bottled."

When the Court resumed its sitting, I observed that some of the members of the Court became drowsy, and dropped off to sleep, opening one eye occasionally, for a second or two; others became fidgety, impetuous, and argumentative. The President inquired if the members of the Court would like to ask the witness any questions. Several responded in the affirmative, and began to write their questions on slips of paper. Blade, however, was the first to throw his slip across the table to the Deputy-Judge-Advocate-General, who, having read it, handed it across to the President, who showed it to the officers on either side of him, who nodded assent. The question was then handed back to the Deputy-Judge-Advocate-General, who proceeded to read it aloud.

"You have stated that the prisoners were under the influence of wine, but that they were not drunk. What do you mean?"

"I mean," said the Senior Captain, "that they—"

"Not so quick, please," said the Deputy-Judge-Advocate-General. "You mean that?—Yes—I am quite ready."

"I mean," said the witness, "that though they had both been partaking freely of wine, they were not—"

"Freely of wine—don't be in a hurry," said the Deputy-Judge-Advocate-General, repeating each word that he took down.

"Mind, he says 'Freely,'" said Blade. "'Freely of wine.' The word 'freely' is important—very important. Have you got down the word freely?"

"Yes," said the Deputy-Judge-Advocate-General,

having put down his pen to ascertain the fact, and make it known to his interrogator.

"Very well," said Blade. "Then put the rest of the answer down, at your earliest convenience. I am in no particular hurry."

"Well?" said the Deputy-Judge-Advocate-General to the witness—"they were not—not what?"

"Not drunk," said the witness.

"There is nothing about drunkenness in the charges," said the President; "where are the charges?"

"Here, sir," said the Deputy-Judge-Advocate-General. "But, please let me write down your remark before we go any further."

"What remark?" inquired the President.

"That there is nothing about drunkenness in the charges. According to the last general order by his Excellency the Commander-in Chief, on the last court martial held in this station, everything that transpires should be recorded." And the Deputy-Judge-Advocate-General then resumed his writing in the slowest and most provoking manner imaginable. Several of the audience walked out of the Court, and went into the room where the refreshments were. I followed them. We remained absent for more than ten minutes; but, when we came back, the Deputy-Judge-Advocate-General had not yet written up to the desired point, previous to going on with Blade's question. This at length accomplished, he looked at the President and said, "Yes, sir?"

"There is nothing about drunkenness, and the prisoners are not charged with it," said the President. "The words, 'while in a state of intoxication,' are to all intents and purposes surplusage."

"There I differ with you, sir," said the Deputy-Judge-Advocate-General.

"So do I," said Blade.

"Clear the Court!" cried the President; whereupon the audience, the prisoners, the witnesses—in fact, all save the members of the Court and the Deputy-Judge-Advocate-General, withdrew, whilst a discussion, which lasted for three-quarters of an hour was carried on, every member giving his opinion, and most of them speaking at the same time.

When we returned to the Court, after three-quarters of an hour's absence, the Senior Captain resumed his seat near the Deputy-Judge-Advocate-General. We were not informed of what had taken place. A pause of several minutes ensued, when Blade threw across the table another little slip on which was written a long sentence. The Deputy-Judge-Advocate-General handed it to the President, who, on reading it, looked a good deal astonished, and shook his head, whereupon Blade, who was evidently bent on mischief, called out, "We are all of that opinion at this end of the table."

The President then handed Blade's written question to the officer who sat next to him on his right, and that officer passed it on to the next, the next to the next, and so on till it had been seen by every member of the Court. Some signified by a nod, some by a shake of the head, others by a shrug of the shoulders, what they thought about it; and as there seemed to be a difference of opinion, the Court was again cleared in order that the vote for or against might be taken. So once more we were driven into the mess-room to refresh ourselves and laugh over the absurdity of the whole proceeding. After waiting there for about five-and-thirty minutes, the Adjutant announced, in a loud voice, "The Court is open!" and we returned to hear the President say that, as it was now nearly four o'clock, the Court must be adjourned—another absurdity in connexion with courts martial. After four o'clock, the Court must not sit, even if twenty minutes in excess of that hour would end the proceedings, and render another meeting unnecessary.

The Deputy-Judge-Advocate-General then locked up his papers in a box, placed it under his arm, bowed to the Court, walked off, called for his buggy, and drove home. The members of the Court, the prisoners, and the audience then dispersed, and retired to their respective bungalows; all very tired, and very glad of some repose. My friend, on taking off his coat, asked me to feel the weight of it, out of curiosity. Saturated as it was, it must, including the epaulettes, have weighed some five-and-twenty pounds.

The next day at eleven the Court again met. The

first thing that was done was to read the proceedings of the previous day. This duty was performed by the Deputy-Judge-Advocate-General, and, slowly as he read, it was over in twelve minutes, for I timed him. That is to say, it had taken four hours and a half to get through the real business of twelve minutes, or, giving a very liberal margin, the business of half-an-hour.

And now another very curious feature of an Indian court martial presented itself. The President asked the Deputy-Judge-Advocate-General if he had furnished the prisoners with a copy of the past day's proceedings. The Deputy-Judge-Advocate-General said :—

"No ; the prisoners had not asked for a copy."

The President said :—

"That does not signify. Did you tender them a copy?"

"No, sir."

"Then you ought to have done so."

The prisoners here said that they did not want a copy.

The President's answer to this innocent remark was, that whatever they had to say they must reserve till they were called upon for their defence.

Desirous of not provoking the animosity of the President, they bowed, and very respectfully thanked him for the suggestion. Whereupon the President, who was a terrible talker, and passionately fond of allusions to his own career in the army, mentioned a case within his own personal knowledge. It was a case that happened in Canada, and he had reason, he said, to remember it, because he was at the time on the staff of that distinguished officer, Sir James Kemp, and heard Sir James remark upon it. The Honourable Ernest Augustus Fitzblossom, a younger son of the Earl of Millflower, was tried for cheating at cards, was found guilty, and sentenced to be cashiered. This sentence was confirmed and approved by the General Commanding-in-Chief, and the Honourable Lieutenant went home. An appeal was made to the Horse Guards, and it came out that no copy of each day's proceedings had been tendered to the prisoner, and upon that ground the whole of the proceedings were declared by his Royal Highness the Duke of York to be null and void. He (the President) did not mean to offer any opinion on that case, but he merely quoted it, and being on Sir James's staff at the time, he had reason to remember, in order to show that such was the rule.

A Captain in the Bengal Cavalry said he knew of a case which occurred in this country (India) where the very reverse was held. The prisoner—a Lieutenant Burkett, of the Bengal Native Infantry—was tried for being drunk whilst on outpost duty. The trial lasted for seventeen days, for no less than thirty-eight witnesses—principally natives—were examined. The Lieutenant, at the close of the case for the prosecution, demanded a copy of the proceedings, in order to assist him in drawing up his defence. His demand was not complied with. He was convicted and dismissed the service. He appealed to the Commander-in-Chief, who ruled that a prisoner had no right whatever to a copy of the proceedings until after his conviction, and therefore he confirmed and approved the sentence, or rather, as he had done that already, he rejected the appeal.

"Did he appeal to the Horse Guards?" asked the President.

"No; he belonged to the Company's service."

"Well, did he appeal to the Directors? They might have restored him. They have just restored a man, Bagin, who was cashiered two years ago for gross fraud and falsehood in several instances."

"Yes, I know. Bagin was in my regiment. But Bagin has an uncle in the direction, besides a step-father who would have had to support him and his family if his commission had not been restored to him. Burkett had no friends, and very lucky for him."

"How do you mean?"

"He entered the service of a native prince, and, being a steady fellow and a clever fellow, he made a fortune in the course of nine years, and is now living at home on his fifteen hundred a year."

"I know of another case," said another member of the court, and he proceeded to detail the particulars. When he had finished, another member told of another case; and so this desultory narration of individual experiences went on for one hour and a half—the Deputy-Judge-Advocate, with his tongue protruding, writing away as methodically as possible. What he was writing I do not know; but I fancy he was taking down the "heads" of the various cases that were quoted, in order that his Excellency the Commander-in-Chief might have the satisfaction of examining them. I was told afterwards that we, the audience, and the prisoners, ought not to have been allowed to remain in court during this narration of cases, and the anecdotes which the narrators wove into them; but I need scarcely say I was very glad that our presence had been overlooked; for if I had not seen and heard what took place, I should not certainly have believed, and therefore should not have dreamt of describing, it. It was during this conversation that Blade won back from his adversary, at odd and even, the greater portion of the money he had lost on the previous day; nor that either Blade or his adversary failed to take a part in the conversation, for both of them would now and then ejaculate, "What an extraordinary case!" "Did you ever!" "No, never!" "It seems impossible!" "Cashiered him?" "Shameful!" "Who could have been the chairman of the Court of Directors?" "A Dissenter, I'll be bound!"

"Well, sir," said the Deputy-Judge-Advocate-General to the President, when he had finished his writing, "what shall we do? Shall we adjourn the

Court until a copy of yesterday's proceedings is made, and given to the prisoners?"

"No doubt," said the President; "that is the only way in which the error can be repaired. But a copy must be delivered to each of them."

"But had we better not take the opinion of the Court on the subject?" suggested the Deputy-Judge-Advocate-General.

"By all means," conceded the President; "but in that case, the Court must be cleared, while the votes are taken."

"Clear the Court!" cried the Adjutant; and out we all marched again, into the mess-room, where more cheroots were smoked, and more weak brandy-and-water imbibed.

The third day came, and the Court re-assembled. The Deputy-Judge-Advocate-General read over the entire proceedings, beginning from the very beginning, the swearing of the members, up to the adjournment of the Court, and the reasons for such adjournment. Here another discussion or conversation ensued, as to whether it was necessary to read more than the last day's proceedings. The Deputy-Judge-Advocate-General said he was quite right. The President thought otherwise. All the other members of the Court spoke on the subject, many of them at the same time. Blade and his adversary also gave their opinions, the former for, and the latter opposed to the view taken by the President. As this was a point that must be cleared up, insomuch as the decision that might be come to would regulate the future proceedings in this respect, the Court was again "cleared," and we again marched into the room where the refreshments were to be had. In half-an-hour's time we were re-admitted. But it was not until the following day (for members are not allowed, in short, they are bound by oath not to divulge what may be decided when the doors are closed), that we learnt the Deputy-Judge-Advocate-General had carried his point, and that a sort of parody of that old nursery story, about "the fire began to burn the stick, the stick began to beat the dog, the dog began to bite the pig," was the proper way to open the proceedings of each day during a protracted trial by general court-martial!

So curiously is human nature constituted, that I, in common with the rest of the audience, began, after the fifth day, to like the business, and to watch its various twistings and turnings with great interest. The mess-house, at which the Court was held, became a favourite lounge for almost everybody in the station; and it was curious to hear the bets that were made with reference to the probable "finding," and the sentence. The trial lasted over thirteen days, inclusive of two Sundays which intervened; and the proceedings were then forwarded to Simlah, where they remained for a fortnight awaiting the decision of the Commander-in-Chief, who, in fulfilment of Blade's prophecy, certainly did put forth "a snorter of a General Order," and as full as it could be of italics, capitals, and notes of exclamation and interrogation. His Excellency "walked into" the President, and recommended him to study some catechism of the Law of Courts Martial, such a book as children might understand. His Excellency further remarked that the Senior Captain (the principal witness), or any man wearing a sword, ought to be ashamed of admitting that he was unable to define the various stages of intoxication; and that he was astounded to find that the Court in general should have paid so little attention to the admirable reasoning, on this point, of a junior member whose intelligence appeared to have enlisted no sympathy. (This had reference to Blade.) His Excellency went on to say, that he had never himself been drunk in the whole course of his long life, and to that fact he attributed his position; that if the Court had done its duty it would have cashiered the prisoners; that a "severe reprimand which the Court awarded was a mockery which stunk in the nostrils," and that the prisoners were to be released from arrest and return to their duty without receiving it. But the Chief did not end here. He went on to say, that he would maintain the discipline of the British army in the East, in all ranks, or else he would know the reason why. And being, I fancy, in some difficulty as to what to use, in the case (whether marks of admiration or interrogation), he emphasized the last word of this culminating and very relevant sentence thus:—

"WHY?!!!"

It was a matter of grave doubt whether the determination, thus expressed, to uphold discipline in the army, was in any way assisted by such general orders as those fired off from the pen of the ardent Commander-in-Chief; the more especially as such general orders were copied into the newspapers, and were read by (or listened to while others were reading aloud,) every non-commissioned officer and private in Upper India, Native and European. Three weeks after the promulgation of the general order just alluded to, a trooper in the dragoons having been talked to seriously by the captain of the troop, for some irregular conduct, thus unburthened himself:—

"You! What do I care for what YOU say? You are one of those infernal fools whom the Commander-in-Chief pitched into the other day for BEING a fool." And as the peroration of this speech consisted of the dashing off of the speaker's cap, and hurling it into the captain's face, the man was tried, convicted, and sentenced to be transported for life.

If it be inquired by the reader whether the above description of a Court Martial in India is a fair specimen of what usually transpires at these tribunals, I reply, emphatically, "Yes;" and I make the assertion after having watched the proceedings of no fewer than eighteen Courts Martial during my sojourn in the East Indies.

* * * *

Four officers who had obtained six months' leave of absence, and who had rented between them a furnished house at Simlah, were about to proceed there. I was tempted to accompany them. We left Umballah at sunset in palkees, and at seven o'clock on the following morning arrived at the foot of the hills, at a place called Kalka, where there is an hotel. Having breakfasted, we commenced the ascent on ponyback, and in the course of an hour and a half arrived at Kussowlie, where a regiment of her Majesty's Foot was quartered. Here we rested for a brief while, and then pursued our journey. Strange to say, although the climate is superb, and the scenery grand beyond description, the men (so I was told) preferred the plains, regarding them—to use their own words—"less like a prison than the hills." From Kussowlie we pushed on to Sirée, which is about half way between Simlah and Kalka. Here there is a bungalow, at which we dined on the everlasting "grilled fowl," hard-boiled eggs, and unleavened bread. Some friends at Simlah, who had been written to previously, had sent five horses to meet us; so that, when we resumed our journey, we were mounted on fresh cattle. All along the road the scenery is extremely picturesque and beautiful; but, in point of grandeur, it does not, in my opinion, equal that of the Alps.

It was nearly dark when we arrived at our destination and entered the house, where we found everything ready for our reception; the servants had been sent on a day or two in advance of us.

It is a long and fatiguing ride, forty miles in the sun, albeit there is generally a light breeze to modify the heat; and we were all disposed to retire to rest. But we were unable to do so. The gentlemen who had sent the horses to meet us, as soon as they were informed of our arrival, came to see us, and, what was more, to take us to a subscription ball, which was to take place that night at the Assembly Rooms. It was useless to plead weariness. We were compelled to go.

The society of Simlah, though composed of the same elements, differs very much from the society of Mussoorie. The presence of the Commander-in-Chief, or the Governor-General, and sometimes both (as was the case when I was at Simlah), imposes a restraint on the visitors to this sanitarium. The younger men are less disposed to run riot, and incur the risk of having their leave cancelled, and themselves sent down to the plains. A ball, therefore, at Simlah differs from a ball at Mussoorie. It is so much more sedate. More than one half of those who prefer Simlah to Mussoorie, do so in the hope of prepossessing one or other of the Great Authorities, by being brought into contact with them, and thus obtain staff employ or promotion; and very amusing is it to look on at a public entertainment and witness the feelings of jealousy and of envy that swell the breasts of the various candidates for notice and favour. Nor are the little artifices that are resorted to unworthy of observation and a smile. At this ball there was a lady, the wife of a civilian (a sad fool), who had a great facility in taking likenesses, and she had drawn the Governor-General in every possible attitude, both on foot and on horseback. These clever and admirably-executed sketches were laid upon a table in the ball-room, and excited very general admiration; and it was very soon "buzzed about" who was the artist. The wife of another civilian, however, maliciously neutralized the effect these sketches would probably have had, by falsely saying, loud enough for his Lordship to hear, "Ah! she said she would do the trick with her pencil!" The consequence was, that when the lady's husband begged his Lordship would accept this collection of portraits, as well as a few sketches of the house inhabited by the Great Man, his Lordship,—as delicately and as gracefully as the circumstances would admit of,—"declined them with many thanks;" just as though they had been so many unsuitable contributions to some popular periodical. The wife of a military officer, however, was rather more fortunate. She, too, had a great talent for drawing, and had taken an excellent likeness in water colours of the Commander-in-Chief's favourite charger—the charger that had carried the old Chief through his battles; and as the lady begged that the Chief would accept the picture, he did so, and the next *Gazette* made known that Captain Cloughcough was a Major of Brigade. By the way, this was an excellent appointment, for the office required no sort of ability, and Cloughcough had none; he was, moreover, a most disagreeable person in his regiment, and constantly quarrelling with his brother officers, who were delighted to get rid of him. To chronicle *all* the seductive little arts which were resorted to on that night, to effect a desired end, would half fill a volume. But I cannot omit the following: it struck me as so *extremely* ingenious. There was a lady, the wife of a young civilian, who had two very pretty little children—a boy and a girl. Of these children, the Governor-General took great notice, and, whenever he saw their mother, made inquiries touching "the little pets," as he was wont to speak of them. On the night of that ball, his Lordship did so. The lady replied that they were quite well; but that the doctor had said their return to the plains would be fatal to them, and that they must be sent to England.

"Then you had better take the doctor's advice," said the Governor-General.

"But, alas! my Lord," said the lady, "we have not the means. My husband's pay is only 700 rupees a month, and we are, unfortunately, very much in debt."

"That's a bad job," said my Lord.

"Yes," sighed the lady; "it is a very painful reflection—the idea of losing one's little dears. But what is to be done? I dread the coming of the 15th of October, when my husband's leave will expire, more than I dread my own death."

"Could you not remain up here with them through the winter?"

"And be absent from my husband, my Lord? Besides, two establishments on 700 rupees a month!"

"That is true."

"If we could *send* them to England under the care of some friend, we would do so, before the hot weather sets in. But we cannot afford it. Or if my husband had an appointment in some healthy station, out of the plains, then they might be spared to us. The thought of the beautiful roses on their cheeks just now leaving them, and their dear little faces becoming pale and sallow, and their little limbs shrinking till they are almost skeletons—it makes my very heart bleed!" (And the pretty and ingenious little lady took her kerchief, raised it to her eyes, and suppressed something like one of Mrs. Alfred Mellon's stage sobs, which went, straight as an arrow, to the Governor-General's sensitive heart.) "If," she continued, "my husband were a favourite with the Secretary; but he is not—for he is too independent to crave—then the case would be very different."

"The Secretary!" exclaimed the Governor-General, "what has he to do with it?"

(The lady had aroused his Lordship's sympathy, and now she had touched his pride, and inflamed his vanity.)

"I thought he had all to do with it, my Lord."

"You shall see that he has *not*," said the Governor-General. "Be comforted, my dear madam, and come to the refreshment room." His Lordship gave her his arm, and led her away from the couch on which they had been conversing.

This "children's dodge," as it was called, was eminently successful. The lady's husband was appointed superintendent of one of the most delightful hill stations in India, on a salary of 1200 rupees (120*l.*) per mensem.

The ball over, at half-past two in the morning we returned to our house, where I was disgusted to hear that a leopard had carried off out of the verandah a favourite dog of mine. It is no easy matter to keep a dog in Simlah, except in the house. The leopards are always on the look-out for them, and will often carry them off in your very sight, while you are riding or walking along the road.

The great business at Simlah, as at Mussoorie, is devising the means of amusement, or rather of varying the amusements so as to render them less irksome than they would otherwise become. Cards and billiards are the principal pastimes; and, now and then, pic-nic and excursion parties are got up; and, once or twice a month, private theatricals are resorted to.

Invitations to dinner-parties and evening-parties are plentiful enough; but to men who go to Simlah without wives and families, and who don't intend to marry in the East, these reunions are a bore rather, after a brief while, and such men prefer dining under their own roofs. There was an hotel at Simlah, kept by a Frenchman, who provided a *table d'hôte* every day at seven o'clock. This used to be very well attended; for, generally speaking, better fare was to be got there than anywhere else. By the way, the host had once been an officer in the French army, and was rather a touchy man. On one occasion an officer complained of the character of some dish on the table, and was challenged to "fight with either sword or pistol." This challenge was declined; but the officer said he would have no objection to an encounter, provided the weapons were cold legs of mutton.

There is an enormous mountain at Simlah, and around its base there is a good macadamized road, some fifteen feet wide. This is the favourite ride of the visitors, and every fine afternoon some sixty gentlemen, and nearly as many ladies, may be seen upon it taking the fresh air.

Simlah is a much more expensive place to spend the summer at than Mussoorie, in consequence of its great distance from the plains, whence almost every article of food and all descriptions of "stores" are carried on men's shoulders. The mutton of the hill sheep is not equal to Welsh mutton; but when properly kept and dressed, it is very good eating. The hill cattle also afford tolerable beef; but the joints are very small. House-rent at Simlah is also much dearer. The furnished abode, for which we paid 100*l.* for the season, we could have got at Mussoorie for 60*l.* The same may be said of articles of clothing and of merchandize. The majority of the European shopkeepers (there were only five or six) appeared to be doing a good business; but I question whether they made money. They have to give, in most cases, very long credit, pay high rates of interest to the banks for money, and high rents for the extensive premises they are obliged to occupy, to say nothing of having to live as all English people must live in India. The hotel did not pay the proprietor, notwithstanding his house was generally full of people, and his charges were seemingly exorbitant.

There was no club at Simlah when I was there; but, since then, one was established. Its existence, however, was very brief. The fact is, people in India very soon grow tired of a thing; and, what is even worse, you will find that when a large number of persons, who have really nothing to do but amuse themselves, very frequently meet, they wrangle, quarrel, split into small coteries, and become on very bad terms with each other. How the old Himalaya Club at Mussoorie has existed so long, is miraculous. A club in India is not like a club in England, where scores of the members are unknown to each other, even by name, and possibly do not meet more than once in a month.

Some of the views at Simlah are magnificent; and from several points may be seen, in the far distance, the river Sutlej, stealing its way through the mountains. The water has the appearance, when the sun is shining upon it, of a narrow stream of quicksilver. Some of the hills are literally covered with rhododendron trees, fifty or sixty feet high, and when they are all in full bloom the effect may be easily imagined.

To Jutsy, some five or six miles from Simlah, and where one of the Ghoorka battalions was always stationed, I have already alluded. There are but two or three bungalows there, and they are occupied by the officers of the battalion.

The season that I spent at Simlah was a very pleasant one, and notwithstanding it was enlivened by several exciting incidents—to wit, a duel, a police affair, a court martial, and an elopement,—I was very glad when it was over, and we could return to the plains.

TANTIA TOPEE.

When I visited the Nena Sahib, I saw this miscreant, who has since so distinguished himself as a soldier and a general, and has recently been captured and hanged. He was not called Tantia Topee at Bhithoor, but "Bennie," simply. He was not a servant exactly—at all events not a menial servant; but one of those numerous "hangers-on" of Nena Sahib who repaid by flattery the favours they received in the shape of board, lodging, and presents. The name of "Tantia Topee," so a native gentleman in India informs me, was an assumed one; and I will, therefore, speak of the hero as "Bennie," whom I remember sufficiently well to describe him. I had not the least idea when I gave him a general letter of recommendation, that he would fill so many pages of Indian history, and give brigades and divisions of British troops such trouble and vexation before they succeeded in catching him.

Bennie was not more than thirty, and at the time of his execution his age could not have exceeded forty years. I question even if he were so old as that, though he may have looked older. He was a man of about the middle height—say five feet eight—rather slightly made, but very erect. He was far from good-looking. The forehead was low, the nose rather broad at the nostrils, and his teeth irregular and discoloured. His eyes were expressive and full of cunning, like those of most Asiatics; but he did not strike me as a man of eminent ability. There were a few men amongst Nena Sahib's flatterers who were really clever men, but they were not Mahrattas; and my impression is that Bennie was not a Mahratta, but a member of some obscure family in the Upper Provinces of India, under British rule. Like the rest of the tribe of flatterers who surrounded Nena Sahib, Bennie was obsequious and cringing to every European who visited Bhithoor. This demeanour, of course, was not the offspring of respect, but prompted rather by the impression that it might tend to some advantage.

There are many persons in India, natives especially, who are of opinion that Nena Sahib did not dictate the atrocities that were committed at Cawnpore; but that they were committed by order of the various adventurers, such as Bennie, who became powerful the moment that Nena Sahib consented to rebel and raise his standard. Asiatics are frequently placed in the awkward position of being responsible for the acts of their retainers—acts that they not only do not sanction, but forbid. This was the case with Moolraj, the Governor of Mooltan. From the first, and to the day of his death, he declared (and his declaration was supported by the very strongest circumstantial evidence) that so far from giving an order to his turbulent soldiery to kill or attack Messrs. Vans Agnew and Anderson, he did all in his power to shield them from harm. Indeed the verdict of the camp which condemned him, rather inconsistently, brought in a verdict of "Guilty; but a victim of circumstances."

That Nena Sahib well deserves the fate that is in store for him, whenever he is captured, there can be no species of doubt; but, in the absence of some proof, I should be sorry—especially after the letters I have read on the subject—to attribute to the man that fiendish treachery and horrible massacre which took place at Cawnpore in July, 1857. Nena Sahib had seen so much of English gentlemen and ladies was personally (if not intimately) acquainted with so many of the sufferers, that it is only fair to suppose, when he ordered boats to be got ready, he was sincere in his desire that the Christians should find their way to Calcutta, and that what ensued was in violation of his orders, and the act of those who wished to place for ever between Nena Sahib and the British Government an impassable barrier, so far as peace and reconciliation were concerned. No one knew better than Nena Sahib that, in the event of the British becoming again the conquerors of India, the very fact of his having spared the lives of those who surrendered, would have led to the sparing of his own life, and hence the promise he made to Sir Hugh

Wheeler. One friend (a gentleman of great experience) writing from India on this subject, says :—

"In my opinion it was the Mahommedan soldiery who insisted on that awful measure. Having so many helpless Christians in their absolute power, they could not resist the temptation of sacrificing them, for their *faith's sake.*"

It is to be regretted that previous to hanging "Tantia Topee," some statement was not extracted from him touching what took place at Cawnpore. Of course, it could not have been relied upon *per se*, but, as evidence, confirmatory or contradictory, of other statements made by other miscreants, who may yet fall into our power, it would not have been *entirely* valueless. I do not mean to say that the culprit should have been allured to confess by any promise, or insinuation, that his life would be spared if he spoke the truth. That is, I would not have breathed the word of promise to his ear, and then have broken it to the hope; nor would I have subjected him to any *corporeal* torture. Nevertheless, I would have had "out of him" something like "the truth"—if not "the whole truth, and nothing but the truth," and so would Sir John Lawrence, or Mr. Wingfield, now at Lucknow, or Mr. Dampier, or Major Elwall, and a score of ex-Thuggee officers now living. It is a sad mistake to hang this sort of people in a hurry; or, for the matter of that, to hang them at all. They have not that dread of death that Europeans have, but almost invariably meet their fate without exhibiting the faintest fear. There are punishments which, to their minds, are far more terrible. They are not as "cowards who die a thousand deaths in dreading one which must come at last." They are rather cowards who die a thousand deaths in dreading one *life* which they long to end. I was never more impressed with the truth of this than when, with the permission of Lord Dalhousie, I had an interview with Moolraj in his cell at Lahore; he was then under the charge of Dr. (now Sir John) Logie, who is "in attendance" on the Maharajah Dulleep Singh. The constant cry of the wretched captive was, "Ah, let them take my life by one blow; but not draw it out of me by slow degrees!" As far as I can recollect, it was not then decided whether his life should be spared or not.

I would treat culprits like Tantia Topee, Nena Sahib, Bahadoor Khan, the Nawab of Bandah, &c., much in the same way as the convicts of Norfolk Island were treated in former days—make death the first favour for which they should crave, and the last which should be granted unto them; but with this difference, that if they murdered each other, the hope of ending their days for the deed should be a vain one. To hang such men is to frustrate the end and real object of all punishment, which is to deter others from the commission of the same offence. When such men are exterminated they are speedily forgotten, and their end is not regarded as an example for the prevention of evil; but so long as they are living, and suffering what to them is far worse than death, the case is otherwise. Be it known, however, that I am not an advocate for the abolition of capital punishment in *this* country for the crime of murder. The gallows, judiciously used, is, in my humble judgment, a very wholesome terror.

THE END.